Joseph Woodfall Ebsworth

Merry Drollery Compleat, Being Jovial Poems, Merry Songs

Joseph Woodfall Ebsworth

Merry Drollery Compleat, Being Jovial Poems, Merry Songs

ISBN/EAN: 9783744771719

Printed in Europe, USA, Canada, Australia, Japan

Cover: Foto ©Thomas Meinert / pixelio.de

More available books at **www.hansebooks.com**

Merry DROLLERY COMPLEAT

BEING

JOVIAL POEMS, MERRY SONGS,
&c.,
COLLECTED BY W.N., C.B., R.S., & J.G.,

Lovers of Wit,

Both Parts; 1661, 1670, 1691.

Now First Reprinted from the Final Edition, 1691.

EDITED,

With a Special Introduction,

AN APPENDIX OF

Notes, Illustrations, and Emendations of Text;
And Frontispiece;

By J. WOODFALL EBSWORTH, M.A., CANTAB.

BOSTON, LINCOLNSHIRE:
Printed by *Robert Roberts*, Strait Bar-Gate.
M,DCCCLXXV.

TO THOSE

STUDENTS OF HISTORY

WHO DESIRE TO LEARN

𝔈𝔥𝔢 𝔗𝔯𝔲𝔢 𝔖𝔱𝔞𝔱𝔢 𝔬𝔣 𝔈𝔫𝔤𝔩𝔞𝔫𝔡,

AT THE CLOSE OF THE CIVIL WARS;

THIS EXACT REPRINT

OF THE

MERRY DROLLERY, COMPLETE,

(FIRST COLLECTED IN 1661,)

IS

DEDICATED.

May, 1875.

CONTENTS.

DEDICATION

PRELUDE

INTRODUCTION TO "MERRY DROLLERY:"—   i.

    § 1. MERRY DROLLERY, 1661,—2. THE BALLADS AND THE COMMONWEALTH,—3. THE WRITERS OF THE SONGS.

ORIGINAL ADDRESS TO THE READER .   3

MERRY DROLLERY, COMPLETE, PART I.   5

     ,,   ,,   ,,   ,, II.   209

ORIGINAL TABLE OF CONTENTS .   351

ORIGINAL LIST OF BOOKS .   358

APPENDIX OF NOTES TO MERRY D. C. .   363

     ,,   ,,   WESTM. D. .   405

FINALE .   403

PRELUDE

To the Reprint of

"MERRY DROLLERY, COMPLETE."

" Merry and Wise" the proverb bade us be :
" Wise," ruled the Saintly, "but by no means Merry ! "
And straightway sought all joy to kill and bury.
 Marvel not, then, if Cavaliers we see
 (By ample proof within this *Drollerie,*)
Chose Mirth alone, quaffing too much of Sherry.

 Merry and Wise ! Welcome be smiles of youth,
On lips not yet in anguish blenched or bitten ;
Be sportive gambols of each lamb and kitten !
 He who would banish Mirth is scant of ruth :
 Why should grim visages repel from Truth ?
Soon shall the joyous heart be cold, or smitten.

 Merry and Wise ! True text for books like ours,
Which tell of troubled times, and men half frantic,
Drunk with a short-lived glee, playing their antic.
 Seek for more innocent mirth, and fragrant bowers
 That show no reptile-slime upon the flowers :
Shun Mirth that stains, and Wisdom grown pedantic.

J. W. E.

MAY, 1875.

EDITORIAL
INTRODUCTION
TO THE
MERRY DROLLERY, COMPLETE:
1661, 1691.

Malvolio.—"My Masters, are you mad? or what are you? Have you no wit, manners, nor honesty, but to gabble like tinkers at this time of night? Do ye make an alehouse of my Lady's house, that ye squeak out your Coziers' Catches without any mitigation or remorse of voice? Is there no respect of place, persons, nor time, in you?

Sir Toby.—We did keep time, Sir, in our Catches. Sneck up!

. . . . . .

Maria.——Sometimes he is a kind of Puritan.

Sir Andrew.—O, if I thought that, I'd beat him like a dog.

Sir Toby.—What, for being a Puritan? thy exquisite reason, dear Knight?

Sir Andrew.—I have no exquisite reason for 't, but I have reason good enough."—(*Twelfth Night.* Act ii. sc. 3.)

§ 1. MERRY DROLLERY, 1661.

WHEN the four "Lovers of Wit" collected these Jovial Poems, Merry Songs, and Witty Drolleries, not forgetting what are rightly called pleasant Catches, and produced them as "MERRY DROLLERY" in 1661, they gave us no more of preface or advertisement than the few lines following the original title-page, and addressed To the Reader. They told us that many of the pieces " were obtained with much difficulty, and at a chargeable rate," and we see no reason to doubt the truth of the assertion. At that time, doubtless, one or other of the compilers must have known particulars of authorship and date concerning a much larger number of the songs and poems than is now attainable by learned students. But W.N., C.B., R.S., and even the mysterious J.G., have given us no help by a single note, and we must do as well as we are able without them. Therefore, it seems not unreasonable, (at the risk of some exceptional Subscriber grumbling because the meat is getting cold, while his host fumbles with the carving knife), that we ourselves should try to give an Introduction; as we attempted to do—not without pleasant meed of thanks thereafter, from men the world holds high in honour—when lately editing the choice *Westminster Drolleries.*

But we are like the Scottish wight who gained wealth and fame, to a certain extent, by displaying to view for a small charge a veritable Golden Guinea at the Falkirk Tryst. Each beholder was delighted at the time; and the fortunate possessor was elated to observe their pleasure, and to pocket the penny siller that rewarded the exhibition. Alas! a season of dearth and penury soon followed in his experience, and under

pressure

INTRODUCTION.   iii.

pressure of some flinty-hearted landlord, or other creditor, who, like a Polypus, maintained a mockery of existence without any bowels, Tugalt parted with the golden goose that had laid so many copper eggs. The story runs, that he determinately offered himself again at Trysting-time, and was hailed by many of the drovers and stock-buyers with a request to show the guinea, while they gladly proffered the hire-penny as reward. Having no longer any guinea to display, he let them know that he, instead, would show the bag or "pock" which used to hold the coin, and only charge "ae bawbee for it;" expatiating on its beauty and completeness, more than he had needed to declare about the precious metal.

Such may be deemed our present situation. Of the *Westminster Drollery* we deliberately proclaimed— "There is no collection of songs surpassing it in the language, and as representing the lyrics of the first twelve years after the Restoration it is unequalled." We do not recall this statement, but are inclined to affirm it anew. What then can we say in favour of the "*Merry Drollery*," or of the final volume with "*Choice Drollery*" and other rarities that is next to follow? Have we nothing but an empty bag to offer?

Our *Merry Drollery* of 1661 is quite distinct in character from the *Westminster Drolleries* of 1671, 1672, but forms an almost indispensible companion to
that

that ten years later volume. It is not only amusing in itself, but as an historical document it is of great value. Of the more than two hundred pieces contained in *Merry Drollery, Complete,* (the edition of 1691, here re-printed page for page, line for line, and letter for letter,) fully a third are elsewhere unattainable, and nearly all the rest are scarce. In its entierty it was a favourite for at least thirty years, until its political attractions were superseded by fresh embroilments calling forth new satires, lampoons, and parodies, when the Restored Stuarts were once again a banished family, never more to recover the English throne and crown. Some few of its social and mirthful portraitures still lingered in the memory of the people, but new comicalities displaced the old, no whit more decent or refined for a century at least, but simply tempting by their novelty. And now, when most of the old merriment has gained an archæologic rust, and things antiquated have risen in value by becoming ancient (to borrow a contrast from the late Lord Lytton), we believe that acceptance may be found among students of old literature for this our scrupulously-accurate re-print of *Merry Drollery, Complete.* It should be observed that the few rectifications of a corrupt text are invariably shown, by being held within square brackets, when not reserved for the Appendix of Notes, Illustrations, and Emendations.

The

INTRODUCTION.   v.

The only alterations made, additional, are in a few cases of departure from the mere accident of *broken* words in the original, caused by an insufficient length of line. In almost all cases, even this typographical peculiarity, when extended to words displaced, has been retained. The Editor is responsible for them.

As mentioned on the title-page, we follow the enlarged edition of 1691. Twenty-five songs and poems, that had not appeared in the 1661 edition, were added to the subsequent editions; but they effected no material change in the character of the work. Displaced to make room for them, as for other reasons not declared, thirty-four songs after appearing in the edition of 1661 were now omitted. These we shall give separately in a companion volume; most of them are rare, and only known to us in this most scarce early edition. The intermediate edition of 1670 also deserves notice, but agrees virtually with that of 1691.

Among the numerous attractions of our present work, we may mention the rare song of "Love lies bleeding" (found on p. 191): an earnest protest against the evils of the days when Parliament and Army were struggling for the mastery, and the country suffered from the exactions of both. It is only here that we know of it complete. "Lay by your pleading, Law lies a bleeding," its companion song and model, to the same tune, is also given (p. 125), entitled " The
Power

Power of the Sword." Such contemporary records as these, with many others in the same volume, enable us to realise the situation. Let us mention some, as being closely connected: "Pym's Anarchy" (70); "The Scotch War" (93); "Mardyke" (12); "The New Medley of the Country-man, the Citizen, and the Soldier" (182); "The Rebel Red Coat" (190); and "Cromwell's Coronation" (254); with the masterly description of Oliver's Routing the Rump (52). Nor must be forgotten the burlesque extravagance, by worthy Bishop Richard Corbet, of a zealous Puritan, utterly crazed in fanaticism and conceit (234). This was written in earlier days (Corbet died about 1638), when Cavalier and Churchman laughed at the extravagance of the Puritan; scarcely foreseeing how grim in power would be those stalwart Ironsides of Cromwell, who afterwards exultingly stabled their horses in Cathedrals, hacking wood-carvings of Prebendal stalls with their sabres, burning organs and muniment chests for fire-wood, and discharging muskets at stained glass windows or sculptured saints; savagely haling men and women to prison or to execution: and — believing themselves specially inspired and chosen to bind kings in chains and nobles with links of iron — praying fiercely before battles, in which they bore down irresistibly upon the foe that had first in ignorance despised them.

Nor

Nor without solid value to us are the few humourous accounts of Puritans in their New England settlements or infant colony beyond the Atlantic. Though it is framed in mockery, something of an earnest and impressive fervour speaks in the Zealous Puritan (p. 95), who gathers his family and friends together, about to voyage across seas to seek "freedom to worship God." This was recorded nearly two hundred years later in the hymn by Felicia Hemans, which has for ever become associated with the Pilgrim Fathers of the Mayflower, 1620. Unfortunately, their Puritan followers failed to learn the lesson of Toleration. Unlike Sterne's negro girl, they had suffered persecution, but not learned mercy, or even justice. They ruthlessly murdered Quakers, and others who claimed right of private judgment in religion, and shewed more cruelty to Anne Hutchinson, Mary Dyer, Robinson, Stevenson, and many more, than they had ever borne themselves from their enemies. As the Rev. J. B. Marsden says, of the time when they savagely silenced with drums, and then butchered, the Quakeress Mrs. Mary Dyer on the first of June, 1660, at Boston Common :—" The brand of that day's infamy will never disappear from the annals of Massachusetts, nor from the story of the Pilgrim Fathers." (*History of the Early Puritans*, p. 324.)

We may smile at the quaint directness of the narrative

narrative, in reading " The West-Countryman's Voyage to New England " (p. 275); but while we smile, we can see the incidents clearly, as they might have been beheld by more friendly eyes. No wonder he was willing to quit the land after he had " staid there among them till he was weary at heart," even independently of the crowning grievance that he " had threescore shillings for swearing to pay." If personal luxuries are to be so heavily taxed it is distressing. We may be sure that he was in earnest when he declared " Itch do think they shall catch me go thither no more."

Even the Captain of the Mayflower himself, if we may credit that impartial witness Professsor H. W. Longfellow, had become heartily tired of his pious companions :—

" Meanwhile the Master alert, but with dignified air and important,
Scanning with watchful eye the tide and the wind and the weather,
Walked about on the sands; and the people crowded around him,
Saying a few last words, and enforcing his careful remembrance.
Then, taking each by the hand, as if he were grasping a tiller,
Into the boat he sprang, and in haste shoved off to his vessel,
Glad in his heart to get rid of all this worry and flurry,
Glad

Glad to be gone from a land of sand and sickness and sorrow,
Short allowance of victual, and plenty of nothing but Gospel."

Again, when yielding to the sly humour of "The Way to Woo a Zealous Lady" (77), we must be hard to impress if no conviction is formed that even thus dangerous to silly women were many who assumed for their own purposes the Puritan disguise, and were ready to wear whatever mask might be in fashion. Some hidden joke against the Citizens, known to contemporaries, but now almost beyond discovery, enhanced the mirthfulness of even such absurdity as "The Bow Goose" (153). The account of a Fire on London Bridge (87), gains all its grotesqueness from being in the manner of pious balladmongers, such as framed some of those doleful ditties of Providential Warning and Goodly Counsels that were dispersed on broadsheets to the delectation of the faithful. To us it gains some interest when seen to be the original of the still-familiar and condensed Nursery rhyme :

"Three Children sliding on the Ice,
    All on a summer's day ;
It so fell out they all fell in,
    The rest they ran away.

But had these children *been at Church*,
    Or sliding on dry ground,
I durst to wage a hundred mark
    They had not then been drown'd.

You

>   You parents that have children dear,
>   And eke you that have none,
>   If you would have them safe abroad,
>   Pray keep them safe at home."
>
>   (M. Cooper's *Philomel*, 1744, p. 209.)

Stories of Countrymen astonished at the rarities of London Town have always been a source of glee, and one is here (323), as well as a description of the New Exchange with all its curious wares, not forgetting the Buttoned Smock (134). The changes in Old England, almost turned to New (266), and the censure of the Apostate World (79), as well as the contrast afforded by an Old Soldier of the Queen's (31) and the still earlier description of the defeat of Spain and her Armada in eighty-eight (82), lend zest to the Cromwellian contrast. A few whimsical stories in verse are of the ruder humour which has always been popular; A Merry Song of a Husbandman, whose wife cleverly gets him released from a bad bargain, cheating the Devil (p. 17), or the still coarser tale on a similar theme (110): a tale that, with frequent variations, meets us often elsewhere. Both are narrated with a homely directness, not unlike the free handling which worthy Mat. Prior delighted in; and which, we are assured by Dr. Johnson, did not hinder the Poems of Hans Carvel, the Dove, and Paulo Purganti from being, even until close on the end of last century, "a Lady's Book." Well then, by right of way established

by

by Dr. Richard Corbet, Bishop successively of Oxford and Norwich (p. 234, and see his "Journey into France," edit. 1661, p. 64), and probably by Archbishop Usher likewise (p. 110), the *Merry Drollery* may, perhaps, be regarded as a Bishop's Book; if that be any compliment and recommendation. Even the Puritans and Sectaries would not have objected to it being so esteemed. But they held none of the Drolleries in favour; *Choice Drollery* being treated by them with the utmost rigour, so that its rare occurrence now is not anyway marvellous.

§ 2.—THE BALLADS AND THE COMMONWEALTH.

No good end can be served by exaggerating the importance of political ballads. We may leave the continually misquoted words of Fletcher of Saltoun quietly in a corner, for once, regarding the popular songs of a nation; inasmuch as, if the phrase he employed means anything at all, it makes quite as much for falsehood, and the misleading of public opinion, as it does for inducing sound judgment. The facts of the case are not hard to discover. Who among us would be willing to accept as final the verdict of some street rhymester or Mug-house politician, even although it found acceptance with a multitude of the gross vulgar? Your ballad-monger, your inventor of "Cocks," your penny-a-liner for the prints that circulate amidst what

we

we irreverently term the Masses or the Million, have so little personal respect for Truth, that they not only are unwilling to misemploy their time in a wild-goose chase after her, but they actually yield a determined preference to falsehood, on account of it leaving them such unrestricted play of fancy as may satisfy their self-conceit. No need to specify offenders. So long as such catch-pennies circulate, and attract attention, the originators heed not what amount of adulteration may have become mingled with a semblance of truth. As the manufacture of a fraudulent account is easier than investigating conflicting evidence, let us not wonder that these caterers for the public give preference to what is untrue.

A remembrance of this tendency to falsify ought to accompany our examination of such historical ballads or political songs and satires as may be proffered, assuming to be important contributions to a knowledge of history. Lord Macaulay, it is well known, was the most skilful employer of the varied hints and details, gathered by combined industry and intelligence, from amid those dusty archives of the mob, broadsides, garlands, penny merriments, and song-books, manuscript or printed. But, it is fair to the memory of that sound-hearted man and captivating historian to remember, that in most cases he attached no more importance to those fugitive records of the past than was

was their due. They enriched his pages, and gave them colour, but he sought elsewhere for his groundwork and outline. His chief, and almost his only, fault was an obstinate retention of any expressed opinion of his own, despite the weight of opposing evidence that might be afterwards brought to bear against it. He knew, as well as anybody, that a person who by some accident or other becomes a favourite or object of aversion to "the many-headed," can either be painted brightly or bespattered foully by the Balladist who seeks for praise and pence, with total independence of all facts or even probabilities. And the prejudice extends much higher in the social scale than we are at all times ready to admit. We greedily accept whatever seems to favour our particular choice, and as willingly acknowledge the sufficiency of anything that tells against the persons or the practices honoured by our hatred.

We do not, therefore, attach extraordinary weight to the historical evidence afforded by the songs against the Rump Parliament in *Merry Drollery*. Partizan spirit has been busy, and where such is the case there is always a likelihood that the features of the individual portraiture may be more than a little distorted. But, after making this concession, we think it will be admitted that such materials as we have in this volume, combine fairly with what is told elsewhere by State enactments,

enactments, proclamations, digests, and private diaries or biographies. They reveal a most uncomfortable state of affairs, political and social, in the closing days of the Long Parliament. Not even so large a collection of avowedly "malignant" writings, as the celebrated "Rump" Ballads of 1660 and 1662, could show us, so well as our own more varied *Drolleries*, how men thought and acted, murmured under oppression, paltered with the truth, sotted and rotted in foul corners, slinking out of danger, and cherishing a hope of revenge or licentious revelry, while the iron hand of Despotism tried to fetter the nation, and sanctimonious schismatics warred with one another for supremacy.

Of late days, thanks in great part to the labours of Thomas Carlyle, we have learned to understand what true greatness there was in one man, who alone was able to keep the troubled realm in order; who both by his own right arm and by his skilful management of others, each the right worker in the fitting place and at the proper time, secured more of success for this our Commonwealth than could reasonably have been expected, when remembering what mutually-antagonistic natures composed the government. As one of our songs declared of that day (p. 167), "We are fourscore Religions strong!" And it is noteworthy that, while contempt and abhorence are lavished on a

host

host of selfish, arrogant, or hypocritical time-servers, there is a very different treatment accorded to OLIVER CROMWELL. Jests are frequent on his copper nose, it is true, and on his supposed early connection with brewing vats; the steps of his advancement are satirically chronicled, and his assumption of almost regal power. Nevertheless, it is evident that personally he is regarded with more favour than the hated Harrison, the contemptible Lambert, Hewson the one-eyed Cobbler, the gloomy Bradshaw, or Hugh Peters the fanatical Tub-preacher; than the licentious buffoon (as he was held to be) Henry Marten, or the prosy and intolerable Sir Harry Vane, from whom Cromwell himself solemnly prayed to be delivered. Even as, in earlier days, the bloodthirstiness, rapacity, and unbridled lust of the huge Henry VIII. did not destroy the popularity he enjoyed as "bluff King Hal;" so, it is evident, the harsh discipline and oppressive exactions of Oliver Cromwell, with all the manifestations of his selfish ambition and indulgence in regal pomp and splendour, did not altogether hinder him from being regarded with affection among the Cavaliers themselves, who learnt to talk of him familiarly as "Old Noll." Had it not been for the remembrance of one black deed,—the written consent he had given in 1649 to the useless slaughter of their King, Charles I.,—there can be no doubt that Oliver had grown to
be

be understood and liked sufficiently, even by those who had wagered their lives against him, to have been accepted as their lawful sovereign, if he had obeyed the satirical command (p. 254) "Oliver, Oliver, take up the Crown!"

It has been the fashion of later years to try and deify many of the inferior actors of that tragic drama, and with prolix exactitude we have been treated to the details of thoughts, words, and deeds of several other Regicides, leaders in parliament if not in the army. But the simple fact remains, that, in these days of the Civil War and Protectorate, no figure stands out as the embodiment of a stalwart Englishman, so entirely commanding the sympathies of after-times, as Oliver Cromwell himself. He was far from faultless, but his rugged nature, his commanding abilities, and a certain large-hearted honesty, even amid the perplexing intrigues and pious fraudulence of his companions, lift him high above the crowd of usurpers. His rude humour was, like that of the first Napoleon, not unalloyed with horse-play and coarse jests: as witness his unseemly inking Henry Marten's face when signing the Royal death-warrant; and his unsavoury rejoinder when Magna Charta was mentioned to him, as an impediment to some of his proceedings. The extremely rigid formalists were incapable of seeing anything agreeable in merriment; even as other invalids

invalids are afflicted with colour-blindness, or inability to distinguish betwixt the fragrance of flowers and those rank odours whereof Coleridge at Cologne counted two-and-seventy distinct varieties, as indeed he might have done in his own country. But the reputation of Cromwell suffered not through indulgence of his pleasantries. On the contrary, such unbendings from austerity drew many towards him. His army loved him, like his own family; and the contrast between true grandeur and pestilent incompetence was beheld whenever he had passed away, in 1658, and left The Gang of rival claimants, who were all proved incapable to bend the bow of the dead Ulysses.

The Restoration became a necessity, not so much from a survival of enthusiastic love to the Stuarts as from the intense disgust excited by the Parliament, the Independents, and the disorganised soldiery. These fell, chiefly owing to their own inherent rottenness. How little was done to reward the hopes of those who looked for establishment of a pure exalted monarchy, avails not now to tell.

Of the conflict between Oliver and the men who were endeavouring to dispossess him of the power he held, few records surpass in value one contemporary ballad (found here on page 62), filled with exultation over the downfall of the Rump. What masterly satire,

satire, cutting both ways, we find in the verse telling of "brave Oliver's" rebuke to his old companion :—

> "It went to the heart of Sir Henry Vane
>   To think what a terrible fall he should have:
> For he who did once in the Parliament reign
>   Was call'd, as I hear, a dissembling knave.
> *Who gave him that name* you may easily know,
>   *'Twas one that studied the art full well;*
> *You may swear it was true, if he call'd him so,*
>   *And how to dissemble I'm sure he can tell."*

There is no mistaking it, despite this irresistible gibe against Noll himself, he is the better loved for crushing the horde of public enemies thus summarily. The Commonwealth is divided against itself, and its fall is known to be inevitable. There had been nothing (scarcely excepting his incurable duplicity and continual breaches of faith) which had been charged against the murdered King, during the Civil War—and for which he was brought to trial in a dangerously illegal manner, and slaughtered ruthlessly,—but what was afterwards perpetrated against the constitutional liberties of England by the men who had arrogated to themselves the right to judge and execute their Sovereign.

As helping us materially to understand those times, which can never be without the gravest interest to us while we remain a nation, the *Merry Drollery, Complete*, is truly valuable, and now re-printed. *Ridentem dicere verum quid vetat?*

§ 3.

§ 3. THE WRITERS OF THE SONGS.

We need not go to Joseph Addison to learn that " a reader seldom peruses a book till he knows whether the writer of it be a black or a fair man, of a mild or choleric disposition, married or a bachelor, with other particulars of the like nature, that conduce very much to the right understanding of an author." "Who wrote it?" is a question most of us are in the habit of asking, when any book or song gives us pleasure. Let us mention the writers of some songs and ballads in *Merry Drollery, Complete.*

Ten of the Songs are by Alexander Brome, whose gay spirit made him a favourite among the Cavaliers; his numerous Epistles in verse, preserved among his Poems, prove the intimacy of his friendship with many leading men,—Charles Cotton, Colonel Lovelace, Thomas Stanley, &c. Though given to writing Bacchanalian ditties, he does not seem to have been of dissolute habits, and his Muse is singularly decorous in morals, like himself preferring Wine to Women. A word here or there of plain language may exceed our present forms of speech; but he never wantonly indulges in foulness of thought or expression, and we love him well for his own sake, as also for the friendly labours he encountered to print and publish his namesake Richard Brome's choice Comedies. Few of these might have come down to us, but for such editorial care.

care. He himself was reproached by a friend (J. B.) for wasting his poetic gifts in mere Song-writing:—

> "Why *pedler'st* thus thy muse? Why dost set ope
> A shop of wit to set the *fidlers* up?
> Fie, prodigal! canst statuated shine,
> By the abuse of *Women*, praise of *Wine?*
> Or such like toyes, which every hour are
> By every pen spu'd forth int' every ear?
>   Thy comely Muse dress up in robes, and raise
> Majestic splendour to thy wreath of bayes:
> Don't prostitute her thus, her Majesty
> (Like that of Princes) when the vulgar see
> Too frequently, respect and awe are fled,
> Contempt and scorn remaineth in their stead."

But we believe that Alexander Brome received quite as much fame, and more instant popularity, for this light work in his Lyrics, as he could have won by sustained labours at such disturbed times. He answers J. B. (who wrote a Tragedy, not traced, in 1652):—

> "If making Sonnets were so great a sin,
> Repent; 'twas you at first did draw me in:
> And if the making one Song be not any,
> I can't believe I sin in making many.
>   But oh! the Themes displease you, you repine,
> Because I throw down *Women*, set up *Wine:*
> Why that offends you, I can see no reason,
> Unless, 'cause I, not you, commit the treason.
> Our judgments jump in both, we both do love
> Good Wine and Women; if I disapprove
> The sleights of some, the matter's understood,
> I'm ne'er the less belov'd by th' truly good."

And

And he plainly declares that, already, for having written on some of those high themes, "of State-matters, and affairs of Kings," his teeth had been nearly beaten out by the Parliamentarians. He died in 1665, within a lustre after the Restoration.

We feel less certain as to the authorship of Thomas Jordan; some of the flowers of his "Royal Arbor of Loyal Poesie," 1664, being apparently of foreign growth, and transplanted. But, probably we have to thank him for the clever parody on Thomas Carew, which describes "Pym's Anarchy" of 1642, beginning,

"Aske me no more why there appears
Dayly such troops of Dragooneers," &c. (p. 70).

We know not to whose pen we are indebted for the delightful companion-songs, "The Cavalier's Complaint," beginning "Come, Jack, let's drink a pot of Ale" (p. 52), with Answer to it, "I marvel, Dick, that having been," &c. They lift our thoughts to consideration of a nobler type of gentlemen than the roysterers who brought discredit on the King's party. Printed, and widely popular as a broadside, within a few months after Charles the Second arrived in London, they give trustworthy evidence of what was felt and spoken by those gallant Royalists who had so often imperilled life and liberty in his cause. For him their cash and plate had been cheerfully given, their estates had been seized and confiscated

by

by the rebel Parliament, and their sufferings had been borne patiently, until the last lingering hopes were dispelled on beholding the personal unworthiness of the monarch whom they had welcomed back to the throne of his murdered father. We mark them retreating, disappointed and disgusted, from the Court, where gilded popinjays, sleekest time-servers, and handsome wantons alone are cherished. We remember an event of evil augury was recorded, that, even on the night of that memorable twenty-ninth of May, 1660; the royal birthday, moreover; when all his Capital was a-blaze with bonfires, and filled with loyal enthusiasm, and when many an earnest thanksgiving to heaven was uttered by devoted Cavaliers who had prayed for him and for his cause during more than ten years of exile—the King himself was so lost to a sense of common decency, as well as of honour and religion, that he allowed it to become publicly notorious he was then toying with Barbara Palmer, afterwards the Duchess of Cleveland, at Sir Samuel Morland's house in Lambeth. Thenceforward, all was in accordance with the bad beginning. Female influence enslaved him, and the most easy and good-natured of all monarchs, whose abilities as well as disposition had offered much for praise, lent himself to such counsellors as not only degraded him personally, but also impoverished, humiliated and in

great

great part corrupted the nation. How gross was the mismanagement, how foul were the orgies, we can best understand by one fact, that those English Cavaliers whose hearts were sound came speedily to regret the triumph of their cause, and almost to lament the passing away of the Commonwealth, which, although intolerant, covetous, arrogant and cruel, had yet been respected abroad for courage and high principle. So much more unwilling are we, generally, despite Hamlet's experience, to

> "bear the ills we have,
> than fly to others that we know not of."

Historically of deep significance is the dialogue (on p. 131), "a Quarrel betwixt Tower-Hill and Tyburn," referring to the expected execution of the Regicides. There is no mirth here, scarcely any humour even of a sardonic kind ; all is stern, bitter hatred and scorn. It is not a ravening for blood, as though revengefully afraid of the criminals escaping punishment, but rather a contemptuous and cruel impatience to cleanse the land from the presence of those who in their day of power had shown themselves devoid of mercy. Nothing but abhorrence salutes the miserable and cowardly Hugh Peters, whose blood, it was felt, would defile the scaffold on which braver men had laid down their lives. The fanatical enthusiast Harrison, a ruthless tool of tyranny, and probably a mad man,

man, had three days earlier died gallantly at the same place, Charing Cross, (on 13th October, 1660,) as became one who believed he saw the coming Millenium of the elect saints. On his way to execution, some unfeeling spectator called out mockingly, "Where is your good Old Cause?" With a cheerful smile, the dying man clapt his hand on his breast, and answered, "Here it is! I am going to seal it with my blood." As he drew nearer to the gallows, beholding it, he seemed transported with joy, and when asked how he did, replied ". Never better in my life," declaring that he saw the crown of glory prepared for him. Sir Henry Vane, we must admit, approved himself to be no unworthy follower of the ancient stoics and republicans he admired, by the dignity wherewith he made his place of butchery on Tower Hill become an altar of self-sacrifice. After a long imprisonment, he suffered in June, 1662. His address to the people had been forbidden, and as he himself declared, "It is a bad cause which cannot bear the words of a dying man." Samuel Pepys had witnessed the execution of Harrison: quaintly recording how at being hanged, drawn, and quartered, he was "looking as cheerful as any man could do in that condition;" and how it was reported that Harrison said "he was sure to come shortly at the right hand of Christ to judge them that now had judged him;" and that "his wife do expect his coming again."

again." Pepys seems to have enjoyed the view of several other such scenes of slaughter, and indeed all sight-seeing was pleasant to him; but he yields steady testimony to the gallant bearing of Vane, who "in all things appeared the most resolved man that ever died in that manner, and showed more of heate than cowardize, but yet with all humility and gravity." Later, he mentions that "the courage of Sir H. Vane at his death is talked on every where as a miracle." And Will Swan declared to him that "Sir H. Vane must be gone to Heaven, for he died as much a martyr and saint as ever man did; and that the King hath lost more by that man's death than he will get again a great while." There can be no question of the fact that a reaction began to set in after beholding such courage, and contrasting it with the misconduct of those in power, whose loyalty could only manifest itself in servility and persecutions. Let us confess, however, that if there was not to be entire amnesty or indemnity, such men as Hugh Peters were more fitted for Tyburn tree than the block on Tower Hill: the rabble rout of rebellion was not worthy of mingling blood with those royalist soldiers who had died valiantly, imploring a blessing on King Charles.

A score of songs were added, indeed several of them had been written after the publication of *Merry Drollery*, the first edition, in 1661. Among them are two,

two, from his comedies, by "Glorious John," whose hey-day of popularity belongs properly to the date of our *Westminster Drolleries*. As we pass onward from our earlier choice in poetry,—such time as Keats and Tennyson allured us chiefly, with sensuous imagery and artificial trickeries of pleasant sound—some of us, whose love of verse is strong enough to have survived the *sturm und drang Zeit* of youthful passion, and our entrance on the practical business of middle age, feel an ever-deepening sense of Dryden's grandeur. Other men have surpassed him in the ability to harmonize their powers,—powers immeasurably weaker than his, and have secured a position in their country's literature by single poems complete in themselves, and thus satisfying a fastidious taste. But of all the great, capricious, blundering giants and heroic demi-gods in the poetic Walhalla, none is more absolutely a crownless king of the *Infanti Perduti* than our almost-forgotten John Dryden. The robust manliness, the sound-heartedness of this sturdy Englishman, against whom faction clamoured loudly, is so imperishable that his most grievous faults cannot efface his grandeur. His worst utterances we are willing to forget, his errors of judgment and of conduct are at once condoned, by all who have learnt to know him thoroughly. His genius was irregular, it is true, but it was genius such as few have equalled. His grasp of power once laid

on

on us, the sustained strength and beauty of his verse,

"The long majestic march, and energy divine,"

once fairly recognised, he is mighty enough to hold us bound to him for ever. He was alike the sociable and homely-attired Citizen, who gave delight to a circle of admiring Wits at coffee-houses ; and yet, when a dress-suit was donned and actors were obsequious, the Playwright whom a clamourous public set to task-work, loving somewhat to excess bombastic rant and courtly gallantry: whose tragedy queens bespoke their sorrows in rhymed couplets, and whose impassioned heroines threw overboard their modesty, with less compunction than measly pork is cast into the deep within the Tropics. Glorious John ! He could captivate men with his flowing talk at Wills', and no less bind attention to his pages by vivacious criticism in sparkling Prefaces, that half disguised the soundness of their common-sense by seeming to have been written without more premeditation than his daily gossip. What scores of lesser men are talked about, and commented on by learned Pundits, to the world's admiration, simply because they are the lesser and more easily measured; while Dryden in unwieldy folios remains comparatively unread, unpraised. Yet was he the creator of the loftiest satires in the English language, the writer of a manly, masterly prose style, distinct from all preceding, the voluminous author of translations,

translations, panegyrics, fables, and odes, beside tragedies and comedies that enwrap two score of songs delightfully musical, and not so naughty as to sin beyond forgiveness. Even such trifles as we have here from him (on pp. 171, 292) are pleasant gifts that we can thankfully receive.

His friend and fellow-workman, Sir William D'Avenant, yields us two other songs: One of which helped Mistress Mary Davis, the lady who first sang it, to a reversion of the heart of our inflammable "Old Rowley." " My lodging is on the cold ground," is here, and also another half-phrensied but pathetic ditty, a sort of dirge, " Wake all you dead, what ho ! " (pp. 290, 151). The Anacreontic, beginning " The thirsty earth drinks up the rain," meets us (on p. 22) from one of the three friends who feasted D'Avenant with praise for his poem of " Gondibert " (concerning which unfinished Epic, see the lampoons from mocking wits, on pp. 100, 118): that "melancholy Cowley," whose " Essays in Prose and Verse," left as a legacy, and published by Bishop Sprat, 1668, are among the most delicious that were ever penned; and whose choice " Chronicle" of imaginary Mistresses,

> " Margarita first possest,
> If I remember well, my breast," &c.,

we prize more highly than his ambitious " Davideis," or the " Davideidos."

Some

INTRODUCTION.   xxix.

Some doubt exists as to whether we owe to William Cavendish, first Duke of Newcastle, the lively Song (p. 237) "I doat, I doat, but am a sot to show it." It is partly quoted in his "Triumphant Widow," written during exile, but not printed until 1677. We have it complete in the 1661 edition of *Merry Drollery*. It is certainly in his spirit, and until the claim of another author to it has been proved by demonstration we may hold it to be his.

Fortunately, no doubt afflicts us concerning whom we have to thank for that gay "Ballad on a Wedding," and that mirthful record of "Apollo's Session of the Poets," which adorn our volume (pp. 101, 72). To Sir John Suckling be the praise for verses that never lose their charm. Men jested upon him for his gaudily-attired hundred horsemen, whose tailoring surpassed their prowess and their service in the field:

> "Sir John got him on an ambling Nag,
>   To Scotland for to ride a,
> With a hundred horse more, all his own he swore,
>   To guard him on every side a," &c.
>   —(*Musarum Deliciæ*.)

And again—

> "I tell thee, Jack, thou gav'st the King
> So rare a present, that no thing
>   Could welcomer have been;
> A hundred horse! beshrew my heart,
> It was a brave heroick part,
>   The like will scarce be seen," &c.
>   —(*Le Prince d'Amour.*)

This

This was answered by "I tell thee, fool, who e're thou be," &c. (*Ibid.* 1660, p. 148.) Some lack of moral or physical courage to repel and punish the ferocious ruffianism of a Court-bully exposed Suckling to a graver censure; and a degenerate namesake, so lately as 1836, had the vile mendacity to insinuate without proof a charge of suicide. But always by us must Sir John Suckling be lovingly remembered for some of the daintiest bewitching poems of love and merriment. One who assailed him ridiculously in the verses to the tune of "John Dory," referred to above, viz., Dr. James Smith (unless the mockery came from his friend Sir John Mennis) gave us "The Song of the Blacksmith (p. 225), having the burden of "Which no body can deny." For fully sixty years men seemed never weary of repeating it. We have another, and much more rare, Blacksmith Song (p. 319); as well as two songs in ironical praise of "The Brewer," in reference to stout old Oliver Cromwell, whose family connection with the maltster's trade was no more forgotten than Hewson's with cobbling, and Harrison's with that of a butcher: which trades seemed congenial to them.

Two other gallant Cavalier Poets, William Cartwright and Robert Herrick, are represented here, although only by a brief song from each, charming lyrists as they were (pp. 289, 199). Cartwright had given brilliant promise as a dramatist before he gained
fresh

fresh fame as a preacher, and like Thomas Randolph died young. Still earlier voices are heard echoing through our pages. A few lingering strains from the survivor of that literary brotherhood Beaumont and Fletcher (himself, alas! prematurely snatched away in all the ripeness of his manhood), greet us here (on pp. 92, 109, 196). There is an exuberance of mirth and poetry in John Fletcher that has rarely if ever been equalled. In this he takes after the man whom he loved to follow, and sometimes playfully to parody, William Shakespeare; even as John Phillips mocked the Miltonic style in his "Splendid Shilling," yet all the while loved the bard of Paradise Lost, and took him as exemplar in most things that he wrote. Ben Jonson, Thomas Middleton, Richard Brome, and Thomas Heywood, dramatic brethren all dead before the date of *Merry Drollery*, were not forgotten in it, or left without a verse from each to keep their memory green.

To "rare Ben Jonson" is another tribute, however, oddly expressed by Dr. Henry Edwards in the high-flown praise of Sack, with all its embodied transformations, beginning "Fetch me Ben Jonson's scull, and fill 't with Sack" (p. 293). Like many another bard of those wild days, he cannot resist defaming Ale, while yielding a laudation to the Vine. How he finds heresie in hops, and condemns beer to be given
to

to Calvin and his disciples, is not quite clear. It was Luther who, if not misrepresented, told a grievously self-tormented casuist, beseeching ghostly counsel as a medicine, to "Drink beer, and dance with the girls!" advice which, if the brew were good and lasses young and pretty, was by no means to be sniffed at, except by the degenerate Barebones sectaries or Agnewites. By many a roystering Cavalier (see p. 121) excuse was made that he abhorred malt liquor, from its connection with Noll Cromwell and his brewery. A reveller, overcome by potations, mentions the *Brewer's Dog* as having bitten him (p. 255); and another (p. 348) acting anticipatively on homœopathic theories, *similia similibus curantur*, recommends a hair of the said dog to be taken medicinally:—

> "If any so wise is, that Sack he despises,
> Let him drink small beer, and be sober,
> Whilst we drink Sack and sing, as if it were Spring,
> He shall droop like the trees in *October*.
> But be sure if over-night this dog do you bite,
> You take it henceforth for a warning,
> Soon as out of your bed, to settle your head,
> Take a hair of his tail in the morning," &c.

In one of our songs we find a Lover so addicted to his cups that he prefers Sack to his mistress, and his mistress gives him the sack accordingly (pp. 304, 306); she yet shews sign of a relenting, if he will but quit his bottle and be constant to herself. In much later days, we we should remember, one jovial swain defended himself from a charge of fickleness, by pleading the unfailing smiles of the goblet he loved better :—

"The Women all tell me I'm false to my Lass,
That I quit my poor *Chloe*, and stick to my glass;
But to you, Men of Reason, my reasons I'll own,
And if you don't like them, why let them alone,

"Altho' I have left her, the Truth I'll declare,
I believe she was good, and I'm sure she was fair;
But goodness and charms in a Bumper I see,
That makes it as good and as charming as she.

"My *Chloe* had dimples and smiles, I must own,
But though she could smile, yet in truth she could frown,
But tell me, ye Lovers of Liquor divine,
Did you e'er see a frown in a Bumper of Wine?

"Her Lillies and Roses were just in their prime,
Yet Lillies and Roses are conquer'd by Time;
But in Wine from its age such a Benefit flows,
That we like it the better, the older it grows."
                                        (5 verses more.)

"Then let my dear *Chloe* no longer complain;
She's rid of her Lover and I of my pain;
For in Wine, mighty wine, many comforts I spy;
Should you doubt what I say—take a Bumper and try."

This, sung by Beard, before 1754, or when remodelled in our own days, "They tell me I've proved unkind to my Lass," is as complete a statement of the superior advantages of the flask as could be desired. In *Merry Drollery* there is somewhat too much about Sack. But it is not unimportant, as indicating the besetting dangers of the Cavaliers. Their enemies' cannon balls had not damaged them so much as their friends' grape. Nowadays, to our young men, Bitter Beer is the peril. Cassandra gives warnings, but their rock-ahead is the Bass. As Tom Hood used to say of his Lieutenant, "The rock he split upon was quarts."

Although, for reason such as the above, Wine gained more praise than Ale, we find that "A Cup of Old Stingo" was recognized as being potent, and "Ale in a Saxon Rumkin" had its Laureate, even in those days of vinous revelry (pp. 140, 164, 259). Chocolate, also, then coming into vogue for public drinking, as soon as the Restoration gave license for more sociality, has a special song in its honour, that we have not found elsewhere (p. 48). And the best known song of moralizing on Tobacco is seen adorning our volume (p. 26).

Although drinking and love-making were favourite themes among the Cavaliers, our English fondness for field-sports shows itself in the brisk song of the Angler's Recreations (p. 146), such as Izaak Walton and his friend Charles Cotton delighted to troll merrily. A Fox hunt (pp. 38, 300, 30), Coursing the Hare (p. 296), Cock-fighting (242), and Sir Eglamore's encounter with a stupendous dragon, which carries off his trusty sword for an internal decoration (257), as also the mirthful account of rare Arthur O'Bradley's wedding festivities (312), help to vary the diversions.

Mirthful

Mirthful rogues chant lustily their own praises, and tell how they impose upon the sober citizens (204): "The Vagabond" sings of his numerous disguises, as lame, blind, naked, maimed, disbanded, or shipwrecked, nay, even resorting in extremity to the likeness of an honest hawker, "Oftimes to 'scape the Beadles." Pedlers and Gipsies were always musical in their wanderings from before the days of that incorrigible pilferer Autolycus, whose lay contains so much of sound philosophy :—

> "Jog on, jog on the foot-path way,
>   And merrily hent the stile-a;
> Your merry heart goes all the day;
>   Your sad tires in a mile-a.
>
> "Your paltry money-bags of gold,
>   What need have we to stare for?
> When little or nothing soon is told,
>   And we have the less to care for.
>
> "Cast care away, let sorrow cease,
>   A fig for melancholy!
> Let's laugh and sing, or, if you please,
>   We'll frolick with sweet Dolly."
>   —*(Antidote against Melancholy.)*

We are glad to find Autolycus, even at so late a date as 1661, far enough advanced on the path of Reformation to confine his frollics to the companionship of a Dolly, whether sweet or otherwise. His earlier choice of his "aunts," when inclined to enjoy the hay field (according to the unquestionable authority of Shakespeare,

Shakespeare, at the beginning of the century, if not earlier) was scarcely to be commended. Our excellent friend Andrew Wilson could offer nothing of plea in extenuation, beyond the admission that Autolycus "his tastes were peculiar." In another gay "Song of the Pedlers" (p. 291), beginning

> "From the fair *Lavinian* shore
> I your markets come to store,"

we are brought to what has been guessed at as a possibly Shakesperian relic, certainly set to music by that Dr. John Wilson who loved to be associated with the lyrics of "Sweet Willy." For the Tinker of Turvey (see p. 27); for Gipsies and Beggars (92, 197, 196, 230), and for praise of Sailors, Soldiers, and Country ploughmen (162, 182, 338) these pages need not be searched in vain.

Less of railing against Matrimony meets us at this date than a few years later, when the Comedies in favour were crammed full of jests against hood-winked or hen-pecked citizens, and all the estimable gallants seemed to take their motto from Rochester, "Never Marry!" We have, it may be conceded, a satirical praise of the Bull's Feather (p. 264), or, in other words, of that matrimonial horn which was not absent from the prognostics of Benedict, who sagely remembered that no staff was so reverend as one tipped with it. The lamentations of an ill-used husband (p. 85), who finds his family newly increased after he has been

seventeen

INTRODUCTION. xxxvii.

seventeen months beyond seas, may be read with varying emotions. As Mephistopheles mildly observes, "She is not the first." One determined wife-hater (p. 342), gives an almost exhaustive list of female candidates whom "persons about to marry" are carefully to avoid. He leaves few to choose from. The expenses of matrimony are summed up alarmingly to warn Bachelors (23). Another singer (p. 302) admits, with an affectation of candour sitting easily on him, that "Some wives are good, and some are bad." The manner in which the chorus take up any reference to their individual help-mates is suggestive of a very closely-tiled Lodge indeed, and no clock-case admitted for fear of accident.

It would be intolerable if we found no love songs here to relieve the atmosphere. Gladly we turn to Nicholas Breton's song of 1580 (p. 99), telling of Phillida and Coridon's wooing "in the merry month of May." James Shirley's " Come, my Daphne," and " A Rhapsody," may also be mentioned (91, 7); and the lively ditty, "Come, my delicate bonny sweet Betty" (34). No one but the most rigid formalist need censure the sly fun of the whimsical confession beginning, "I came unto a Puritan to wooe" (p. 77); which is perfection in its own way: so dainty and "pawky" in humour that we must go to the North, beyond the Border, to find its equal. As Robert Browning's dying but only half-penitent old sinner admits, in *his* confessions :— "Alas,

> " Alas,
> We lov'd, Sir—used to meet:
> How sad and bad and mad it was—
> But then, how it was sweet!"

It is not expected that this volume will ever be seen by any one belonging to the gentler sex (would that they were indeed all gentle! but we have heard whispers to the contrary; let us say, in other lands). Two or three pages, here or there, that need not be specified, are sufficiently objectionable to cause it to be "banned and barred, forbidden fare." We may as well honestly declare our intense disgust at such things, coarse, ribald, and degraded, utterly destitute of humour as of excuse. Like King Lear, we need an ounce of civet after compulsorily fingering them "to sweeten our imagination!" Students of old literature, we are not so ferociously proper as to utter a war-whoop against every mild impropriety. We do not go out of our way, like some folks of pseud-anonymity whom we could mention, to hunt for naughty words or double meanings. If people will let us go on blindly, deafly, unregardingly, and not poke us in the ribs with their clumsy fingers (as S. T. Coleridge's neighbour at Drury Lane did, quite unnecessarily, regarding Maturin's "Bertram"), we shall remain none the worse, and they will be all the better. But our honest acknowledgment is, concerning some few things in the Drollery, that if the four original editorial "Lovers of Wit" had exercised a

more

more rigid censorship, keeping out Sir John Denham's and half-a-dozen other objectionable pieces, the book would have been doubly welcome to nearly everybody two hundred years ago, *and now*. An expurgated edition is wholly valueless for antiquaries and historical students: If an editor tampers with his original by excision, few persons know where he may stop, or can rely upon his discretion. Scissors are dangerous in the hands of infants or pedants. Worse still, if he leave out six bad things, and in mere ignorance or slovenliness retain a seventh, readers are more shocked and disquieted than when he tells them plainly that he is not answerable for such selection, but preserves the text with all its manifest corruptions. He marks up *Cave Canem*, with a hint of spring-guns and Upas trees. If anybody wander into quagmires after this, it must be intentionally.

One word more: disagreeable as such flaws may be, they are not without historical value, as showing precisely the plague spot and the canker-worm which account for mortality. Here, in whatever is foul, we see the cause of the decay among the Cavaliers. This book was essentially an offspring of the Restoration year, 1660-61, and it thus gives us a genuine record of the triumphant party of the Royalists in their festivity. Whatever is offensive, therefore, is still of historical importance. The bitterness of sarcasm against the Rump Parliament, under whose rule so many families had

had long groaned; the personal invective, the unsparing ridicule of leading Republicans and Puritans; were such as not unnaturally had found favour during the recent Civil Wars and usurpation. The preponderance of songs in praise of Sack and loose revelry is not without significance. A few pieces of coarse humour, *double entendre*, and breaches of decorum, attest the fact that already among the Cavaliers were spreading immorality and licentiousness. The fault of an impaired discipline had borne evil fruit, beyond defeat in the field and banishment from positions of power. Mockery and impurity had been welcomed as allies, during the warfare against bigotry, hypocrisy, and selfish ambition. We find, it is true, few of the sweeter graces of poetry in *Choice Drollery*, 1656, and in *Merry Drollery*, of 1661; less than in the *Westminster Drollery* of 1671, '72; but, instead, even amid the very faults and deficiencies, much that helps us to a sounder understanding of the social, military, and political life of those disturbed times immediately preceding and following the Restoration.

J. W. E.

29TH MAY, 1875.

Merry Drollery,
Compleat.

MERRY DROLLERY COMPLEAT.

OR, A COLLECTION

Of { Jovial Poems,
    Merry Songs,
    Witty Drolleries,

Intermixed with Pleasant Catches.

The First Part.

Collected by *W.N. C.B. R.S. J.G.*
LOVERS OF WIT.

LONDON

Printed for *William Miller*, at the *Gilded Acorn*, in St. *Paul's* Church-yard, where Gentlemen and others may be furnished with most sorts of Acts of Parliament, Kings, Lord Chancellors, Lord Keepers, and Speakers Speeches, and other sorts of Speeches, and State Matters; as also Books of Divinity, Church-Government, Humanity, Sermons on most Occasions, &c. 1691.

TO THE

READER:

Courteous Reader,

E do here present thee with a Choice Collection of Wit and Ingenuity, many of which were obtained with much difficulty, and at a Chargeable Rate;

A 2

To the Reader.

Rate; It is Composed so as to please all Complexions, Ages, and Constitutions of either Sexes, and is now Completed.

Farewel.

Merry

Merry Drollerie.

A Rapsody.

NOW I confess I am in love,
  Though I did think I never could,
But 'tis with one dropt from above,
  Whose nature's made of better mould:
So fair, so good, so all divine,
I'd quit the world to make her mine.

Have you not seen the Stars retreat
When *Sol* salutes our Hemisphear,
So shrink the Beauties, called great,
When sweet *Rosela* doth appear;
Were she as other women are,
I should not love, nor yet despair.

But I could never wear a mind
Willing to stoop to common Faces,
Nor confidence enough can find
To aim at one so full of Graces;
Fortune and Nature did agree,
No woman should be wed by me.

Mirth in Sorrow.

BE merry with Sorrow: why are you so sad?
　　Let some mirth be found to make your heart
If troubles afflict thee, lament not therefore;　(glad:
For all men are subject to sorrows full sore.
　　Though grief be to night, yet joy comes to morrow,
　　And therefore, I pray you, be merry with sorrow.

With what grief soever a man be afflicted,
Unto over-much sorrow be not thou addicted,
For a sorrowful heart, the wise-man doth say,
Doth dry up the bones, and the body decay;
　　And therefore I say, both evening and morrow,
　　In all thy afflictions be merry with sorrow.

Hast thou been a rich man, and now art thou poor?
Be merry with sorrow, and pass not therefore;
For riches have wings to fly when they lust,
Both to thee, and from thee, as God hath discust;
　　And therefore I say, &c.

Art thou pinched with poverty, sickness, or need?
Be merry with sorrow, the better to speed:
For God is the God of the poor and oppressed,
Commit thy cause to him, and it shall be redressed;
　　And therefore I say, &c.

Art thou close in Prison, and locked up fast?
Whatsoever thy faults be, a God still thou hast:
Believe, serve, and fear him, thou shalt never lack,
If thou wilt cast thy cares on his back;
   And therefore I say, *&c.*

Art thou a Minister the people to teach,
And dost thou study good words for to Preach,
And for thy labour dost thou sustain blame?
Be merry with sorrow, and shrink not for shame;
   Such persons, I say, both evening and morrow,
   Ought still to rejoyce, and be merry with sorrow.

Hast thou enemies abroad, that seek for thy life,
Or hast thou at home, a shrew to thy wife?
Such sorrows, indeed, doth a number molest,
Those that be cumbred can tell their tale best,
   For they do sustain many a sowre good-morrow,
   But yet I could wish them to be merry with sorrow.

God make us all merry in Christ our Redeemer;
God save merry *England* & our Good King for ever,
God grant him long years, and many to raign
His word and his Gospel now still to maintain:
   And those that do seek to procure his sorrow, (row,
   God send them short lives, not to live till to mor-

A Catch.

Amarillis told her swain,
Amarillis told her swain,
That in love he should be plain,
And not think to deceive her,
    Still he protested on his truth,
    That he would never leave her.

If thou dost keep thy vow quoth shee,
If thou dost keep thy vow quoth shee,
And that now ne'er dost leave me,
There's never a swain in all this Plain,
That ever shall come near thee,
    For Garlands and Embroidered Scrips,
    For I do love thee dearly.

But *Colin* if thou change thy love,
But *Colin* if thou change thy love,
A Tigris then I'le to the[e] prove,
If ere thou dost come near me;
    Amarillis fear not that,
    For I do love thee dearly.

The Hectors *and the* Vintner.

CAll for the Master, O! this is fine, (wine
    For you that have *London's* brave Liquors of
For us the Cocks of the Hectors [:]
Wine wherein Flies were drown'd the last Summer;
  Hang't let it pass, here's a Glass in a Rummer,
  Hang't let it, &c.

Bold Hectors we are of *London, New Troy*,
Fill us more wine: Hark here, Sirrah Boy,
Speak in the *Dolphin*, speak in the *Swan*,
Drawer Anon Sir, Anon.
Ralph, George, speak in the *Star*,
  The Reckoning's unpaid; we'l pay at the Bar,
  The Reckoning's unpaid, &c.

A Quart of Clarret in the *Mytre* score:
The Hectors are Ranting, *Tom*, shut the door;
A Skirmish begins, beware pates and shins,
The Piss-pots are down, the candles are out,
The Glasses are broken and the pots flies about.
Ralph, Ralph, speak in the *Chequer*. By and by,
Robin is wounded, and the Hectors do flie,
Call for the Constable, let in the Watch, (match,
  The Hectors of *Holborn* shall meet with their
  The Hectors, &c.

At

At Midnight you bring your justice among us,
But all the day long you do us the wrong;
When for Verrinus you bring us Mundungus:
Your reckonings are large, your Bottles are small,
Still changing our wine, as fast as wee call;
Your Canary has Lime in't, your Clarret has Stum,
  Tell the Constable this, and then let him come,
  Tell the Constable, &c.

The Jovial Lover.

1.

ONce was I sad, till I grew to be mad,
    But I'll never be sad again boys;
I courted a riddle, she fancied a fiddle,
The tune does run still in my brain boys.

2.

The Gittarn and the Lute, the Pipe and the Flute
Are the new Alamode for the nan-boys;
With Pistol and Dagger the women out-swagger
The blades with the Muff and the Fan boys.

3

All the Town is run mad, and the Hectors do pad,
Besides their false Dice and slur boys:
The new-formed Cheats with their acts and debates
Have brought the old to a demur boys.

4.

Men stand upon thorns to pull out their horns,
And to cuckold themselves in grain boys;
                                 When

When to wear 'um before, does make their heads
But behind they do suffer no pain boys. (sore,

5
The Protestant, Presbyter, Papist, and *Prester John*,
Are much discontented wee see boys:
For all their Religion no *Mahomets* Pidgeon
Can make 'um be madder then we boys.

6.
There is a mad fellow clad alwaies in yellow;
And somewhat his nose is blew boys;
He cheated the divel, which was very evil
To him, and to all of his crew boys.

7.
But now he intends to make even amends
By wearing a crown of thorns boys;
For him that is gone, but before it be one
We shall his humility scorn boys.

8.
For all our new Peers are turn'd out with jeers,
The new Gentlemen Lords are trapan'd boyes;
Since the King, & no King, would pretend to a thing,
Which the Commons won't understand boyes.

9
And whilst we are thus mad, my Princess is glad
To laugh at the World, and at me boyes,
'Cause I can't apprehend what her colour command,
But it is not my self you see boyes.

Mardike.

Mardike.

When first *Mardike* was made a Prey,
'Twas *Canrea* carried the Fort away,
And do not lose your Valorous Prize
By staring in your Mistris eyes,
But put off your Petticoat-Parley,
Fame and Honour are covered early;
    Potting and sotting,
        And laughing, and quaffing of Canary
Will make good souldiers miscarry,
And ne'er travel for a true renown;
And turn to your marshall Mistris,
Fair *Minerva* the souldiers sister is;
    Calling, and falling, and cutting,
        And slashing of wounds Sir,
With turning, and burning, of Towns, are
High steps unto a Statesmans throne.

Let bold *Bellona's* Brewer frown,
And his Tun shall o'er flow the Town;
Or give a Cobler sword and State,
And a Tinker shall trapan the State,
Such fortunate Foes as these be
Turned the Crown to a Cross at *Naseby*;
    Father and Mother, and Sister
    And Brother confounded,
                                With

With many good families wounded
By a terrible turn of State ;
Such plentiful power the sword has,
And so little of late the word has ;
   He that can kill a man,
   Thunder, and plunder precisely ;
It's he is the man that does wisely,
And may climbe to a Chair of State.

It is the sword that doth order all,
Makes Peasants rise, and Princes fall ;
All Syllogisms in vain are spilt [,]
No Logick like a basket hilt :
It handles 'um joint by joint Sir,
And doth nimbly come to the point Sir,
   Thrilling, and drilling,
   And killing, and spilling profoundly,
Untill the despiter on ground lye,
And hath ne'er a word to say,
Unless it be Quarter, Quarter ;
Truth confuted by a Carter,
   Whipping, and stripping,
   And ripping, and stripping Evasions
Doth conquer the power of perswasions,
Aristotle has lost the day.

The Gown and Chain cannot compare
With Red-coat and his Bandeliers
The Musquets gave Saint *Pauls* the lurch,
        And

And beat the canons from the Church,
The pious Episcopal Gown too ;
   Taro, Tantaro, Tantaro,
   Tantaro, the trumpet
Hath blown away *Babylons* strumpet,
And Cathedrals begin to truck,
Your Councellors are struck dumb too ;
   Dub a dub, dub a dub,
   Dub a dub dub, an alarum,
Each Corporal now can out-dare 'um,
Learned *Littleton* now goes to rack.

Then since the Sword so bright doth shine
Let's leave our Wenches and our Wine ;
We'll follow Fate where ere she runs,
And turn our pots and pipes to guns :
The bottles shall be Grenadoes,
We will march about like bravadoes,
   Huffing, and Puffing,
   And snuffing and calling the Spaniard,
Whose brows have been dyed in a tann-yard :
Well-got fame is a Warriors wife,
The Drawer shall be a Drummer,
We'll be Generals all next summer,
   Pointing, and jointing,
   And hilting and tilting like brave boys ;
We shall have gold or a grave boys,
There's an end of a Souldiers life.

        A

A merry Song.

OF all the Crafts that I do know,
    That in the Earth may be,
Threshing is one of the weariest trades
That belong to husbandry.

Upon a time there was a poor man,
I swear by sweet Saint *Ann*,
And he had a wife and seven children,
And other goods had he none.

As he was a walking on the way,
Hard by a Forrest side,
There met him the divel, that Grisly Ghost,
This poor man to abide.

All hail, all hail, then quoth the divel,
I am glad to have met with thee;
What is thy business in this Country
Thou goest so hastily?

I have a wife, and seven children, quoth the poor (man,
And other goods have I none,
And I am to the Market going
To fetch them something home.

Wilt thou be my servant, quoth the divel,
And serve me for seven year,
And thou shalt have cattel and corn enough,
And all things at thy desire.

What shall be my office, quoth the poor man?
I am loth to bear any blame;
Thou shalt bring a beast unto this Forrest,
That I cannot tell his name.

If thou dost not bring me such a beast,
The name that I cannot tell,
Then both thy body and thy soul
Shall go with me to hell.

Indentures and Covenants were made anon,
And sealed by and by;
The poor man he to the market went
So fast as he could high.

And when that he came home again,
Corn and Cattel he had anon:
O this was some Lord, then quoth the Poor man,
For to believe upon.

His neighbours dwelling round about,
They marvelled very much:
They thought he had either robb'd or stole,
He was become so rich.

But

But when the seven years was near expir'd,
And almost at an end,
He made his moan unto his wife
Which was his own dear freind.

What aile you, what aile you, husband, quoth she,
What ailes you so sad to be?
You had wont to be one of the merriest men
In all the whole Country.

I have made a bargain, quoth the poor man,
I am loth to bear the blame:
I must carry the divel a beast to the Forrest
.That he cannot tell his name.

If I don't carry him such a beast,
The name that he cannot tell,
Then both my body and my soul
Must go with him to hell.

Lie still, lie still then, quoth the good Wife,
Lie still and sleep a while,
And I will bethink me of a thing,
We will the devil beguil.

Buy Feathers and Lime, then quoth the good wife,
Such as men catch birds in,
And I will put off all my cloaths,
And roul them over my skin   [.]

He wrapt his wife in Feathers and Lime,
Till no place of her was bare,
He tied a string about her hams,
And led her for chapmens ware.

He led her backwards of all four,
Till he came to the Forrest side,
There met he the divel, that grisly Ghost,
This poor man to abide,

I have brought thee the beast, then quoth the poor man
Thy bargain thou canst not forsake :
The devil stood as still as any stone,
And his heart began to quake.

What beast hast thou brought me, quoth the divel,
His cheeks they are so round?
I thought there had not been any such beast
Brought up in all this ground.

I have looked East, I have looked West,
I have looked over *Lincoln* and *Lyn*,
But of all the beasts that ever I saw
I never saw one so grim.

Where is the mouth of this same beast?
His breath is wondrous strong.
A little below, quoth the poor man,
His mouth stands all along.

That

That is a mad mouth, then quoth the divel,
It has neither cheeks nor chin,
Nay has but one eye in his head,
And his sight is wondrous dim.

If his mouth had stood but overthwart,
As it stands all a-length,
I would have thought it some Whale fish
Was taken by some mans strength.

How many more hast thou, quoth the divel,
How many more of this kind?
I have seven more, then quoth the poor man,
But I left them all behind.

If thou hast seven more of these beasts,
The truth to thee I tell,
Thou hast beasts enough to scare both me,
And all the devils in hell.

Here take thy Indentures and Covenants too,
I'll have nothing to do with thee,
The poor man he went home with his wife,
And they lived full merrily.

On Drinking, *out of* Anacrion.

THe thirsty Earth drinks up the Rain,
    And drinks, and gapes for drink again;
The Plants suck in the Earth, and are
With constant drinking fresh and fair.
The sea it self, (which one would think
Should have but little need to drink,)
Drinks ten thousand Rivers up,
So fill'd that they o'reflow the cup.
The busie Sun, as one would guess
By's drunken fiery face, no less
Drinks up the sea, and when that's done,
The Moon and Stars drinks up the Sun.
They drink, and dance by their own light,
They drink and Revel all the night;
Nothing in Nature's sober found
But an eternall health goes round:
Fill up the boale, and fill it high,
Fill all the glasses here : for why
Should every creature drink but I?
Thou man of moralls, tell me why.

*The Married Estate, or Advice to
    Batchelors and Maids.*

TO freind and to foe
    To all that I know
That to marriage estate do prepare;
    Remember your days
    In severall ways
Are troubled with sorrow and care:
    For he that doth look
    In the married mans book,
And read but his *Items* all over,
    Shall find them to come
    At length to a sum
Shall empty Purse, Pocket, and Coffer:
    In the pastimes of love,
    When their labours do prove,
And the Fruit beginneth to kick,
    For this, and for that,
    And I know not for what,
The woman must have, or be sick.
    There's *Item* set down,
    For a loose-bodied Gown,
In her longing, you must not deceive her;
    For a Bodkin, a Ring,
    Or the other fine thing,

For a Whisk, a scarf, or a Beaver,   [.]
    Deliver'd and well,
    Who is't cannot tell,
Thus while the Childe lies at the Nipple,
    There's *Item* for wine,
    And Gossips so fine,
And Sugar to sweeten their Tipple:
    There's *Item* I hope,
    For water and sope,
There's *Item* for Fire and Candle,
    For better for worse,
    There's *Item* for Nurse,
The Babe to dress and to dandle.
    When swadled in lap,
    There's *Item* for Pap,
And *Item* for Pot, Pan, and Ladle;
    A Corral with Bells,
    Which custom compells,
And *Item* ten Groats for a Cradle;
    With twenty odd knacks,
    Which the little one lacks,
And thus doth thy pleasure bewray thee:
    But this is the sport,
    In Country and Court,
Then let not these pastimes betray thee.

The Fashions.

The Turk in Linnen wraps his head,
    The Persian he's in Lawn too;
The Rush with sable furs his Cap,
And change will not be drawn to;
The Spaniard constant to his block,
The French inconstant ever,
But of all the Felts that may be felt
Give me the English Beaver.

The German loves the Cony-Wool,
The Irish man his shag too;
<small>Some love the rough, and some the smooth;   [delete.]</small>
The Welsh his Monmouth use to Wear
And of the same will brag too;
Some loves the rough, and some the smooth,
Some great and others small things:
But O the liquorish English man
He loves to deal in all things.

The Rush drinks quass, Dutch Rubrick beer,
And that is strong and mighty;
The Brittain he *Metheglin* quaffs,
The Irish *Aqua Vitæ;*
The French affects the *Orlian* Grape,
The Spaniard takes his Sherry,
                              The

The English none of these can shape, ['scape]
But with them all make merry.

The Italian in his High Chippin,   [her]
Scotch Lass, and comely Fro too;
The Spanish Don a French Maddam [Donna,]
He will not fear to go to;
Nothing so full of hazard, dread,
Nought lives above the Center:
No health, no fashion, wine, nor wench
Your English dare not venter.

On Tobacco.

TObacco that is withered quite
    Grown in the morning, cut down at night,
        Shews thy decay,
        All flesh is hay;
Thus think, then drink Tobacco.

And when the smoak ascends on high,
Think all thou seest is Vanity
        Of earthly stuff,
        Blown with a puff;
Thus think, then drink Tobacco.

And when the Pipes be foul'd within,
Behold the soul defil'd with sin,

> To Purge with fire
> He doth require;
> Thus think, then drink Tobacco.
>
> As for the ashes left behind,
> They fitly serve to put 's in mind,
> That unto dust
> Return we must;
> Thus think, then drink Tobacco.

The *Tinker* of Turvey.

There was a Jovial Tinker
    Dwelt in the Town of *Turvey*,
And he could patch a Kettle well,
Though his humours were but scurvy;
    Still would he sing, tarra ring, tarra ring Tinke,
    Room for a Jovial Tinker,
    He'll stop one hole and make two,
    Is not this a Jovial Tinker?

He was as good a fellow
As Smug, which mov'd much laughter;
You'd hardly think how in his drink,
He would beat his wife and daughter;
    Still would he sing, &c,

He walks about the Country,
With Pike-staff, and with Butchet,
Drunk as a Rat, you'd hardly wot
That drinking so he could trudge it;
    Still would he sing, &c.

There's none of his profession,
That hath such skill in mettle,
For he could mend the frying-pan,
The Skillet or the Kettle;
    Still would he sing, &c.

To toss the Jolly tankard,
The black pot and the pitcher,
No Ale or beer to him was dear,
To make his nose the richer,
    Still would he, &c.

He'd tink betime i' th' morning
Before the break of day,
For drinking dry he was willing,
To the Ale-house he went his way;
    Still would he, &c.

He knockt so roundly at the door,
Which made them all to waken:
Who's there, quoth the maid? It's I, he said;
It's the Tinker foul, I'll take him;
    Still would he sing, tarra ring, tarra ring Tinke,
                                        Room

Room for a Jovial Tinker,
He'll stop one hole, and make two,
Is not this a Jovial Tinker?

Nonsence.

Ow Gentlemen, if you will hear
Strange news, as I shall tell you,
Where ere you go, both far and near,
You may boldly say 'tis true.

When *Charing*-Cross was a little boy,
He was sent to *Rumford* to buy swine;
His mother made cheese, he drank the whay,
He never lov'd strong beer, Ale, nor wine.

When all the things in *England* died,   [? Kings]
That very year fell such a chance,
That *Salisbury* plain would on horseback ride,
And Paris Garden carry the news to *France*.

When all the Laywers they did Plead   [Lawyers]
All for love, and nought for gain;
Then 'twas a Joyful world indeed;
The blew bore of *Dover* fetcht apples out of *Spain*.

When Landlords let their farms cheap,
Because their tenant paid so dear;

The

'The man in the Moon made *Christmas* Pyes
And bid the seven stars to eat good chear.

Without a Broker or Cony-catcher
Pauls Church-yard was never free;
Then was my Lord Mayor a house thatcher,
Which was a wondrous sight to see.

When *Basingstoke* did swim on the Thames,
And swore all thieves to be Just and true;
The Sumners and Bayliffs were honest men,
And Pease and Bacon that year it snew.

When every man had a quiet wife,
That never could once scold or chide;
Tom Tinker of *Turvy*, to end all strife,
Roasted a Pig in a blue Cows hide.

A Catch.

THe Hunt is up,
    The hunt is up,
And now it is almost day,
And he that's abed with another man's wife,
It's time to get him away.

An old Souldier of the Queens.

OF an old Souldier of the Queens,
    With an old motley coat, and a maumsie nose,
And an old Jerkin that's out at the elbows,
And an old pair of boots, drawn on without hose
Stuft with raggs instead of toes;
    And an old Souldier of the Queens,
    And the Queens old Souldier.

With an old rusty sword that's hackt with blows,
And an old dagger to scare away the crows,
And an old horse that reels as he goes,
And an old saddle that no man knows,
    And an old Souldier of the Queens,
    And the Queens old Souldier.

With his old wounds in Eighty Eight,
Which he recover'd, at *Tilbury* fight;
With an old Pasport that never was read,
That in his old travels stood him in great stead;
    And an old Souldier of the Queens,
    And the Queens old Souldier.

With his old Gun, and his Bandeliers,
And an old head-piece to keep warm his ears,
With an old shirt is grown to wrack,

With a huge Louse, With a great list on his back,
Is able to carry a Pedler and his Pack;
    And an old souldier of the Queens,
    And the Queens old souldier.

With an old Quean to lie by his side,
That in old time had been pockifi'd;
He's now rid to *Bohemia* to fight with his foes,
And he swears by his Valour he'll have better cloaths,
Or else he'll lose legs, arms, fingers, and toes,
And he'll come again, when no man knows,
    And an old souldier of the Queens,
    And the Queen's old souldier.

Advice to Bachelours

IF thou wilt know how to chuse a shrew,
    Come listen unto me,
I'll tell you the signs, and the very very lines
    Of Loves Physiognomy.

If her hair be brown, with a flaxen crown,
    And grac'd with a nutmeg hue,
Both day and night, she's best for delight,
    And her colour everlasting true.

If her forehead be high, with a rolling eye,
    And lips that will sweetly melt:

The thing below is better you know,
   Although it be oftner felt.

If her hair be red, she'll sport in the bed,
   But take heed of the danger though:
For if she carry fire in her upper attire,
   What a divel doth she carry below?

If her hair be yellow, she'll tempt each fellow;
   In the *Immanuel* Colledge:
For she that doth follow the colour of *Apollo*,
   May be like him in zeal and knowledge.

If she be pale, and a Virgin stale,
   Inclin'd to the sickness green:
Some raw fruit give her, to open her liver,
   Her stomack, and the thing between.

If her Nose be long, and sharp as her Tongue,
   Take heed of a desperate maid:
For she that will swagger with an incurable dagger
   With stab and a kissing betray'd.

If her face and her neck have here and there a speck,
   Ne'er stick, but straight you go stride her:
For it hath been try'd and never denied,
   Such flesh ne'er fails the Rider.

If none of these thy fancy will please,
   Go seek thy complexion store,
And take for thy saint a Lady that will paint,
   Such beauties thou maist adore.

If beauty do write in her face red and white,
   And *Cupid* his flowers there breed,
It Pleaseth the eye, but the rose will dye,
   As soon as it runs to seed.

Fond Love.

COme my delicate bonny sweet Betty,
   Let's dally a while in the shade,
Where the Sun by degrees shines through the trees,
And the wind blows through the Glade;
Where *Telons* her Lover is graced,   [Tellus ?]
And richly adorned with green,
And the amorous boy with her mother did toy,
And the Uncan never was seen;
There we may enjoy modest pleasure,
As kissing and merry discourse,
And never controul a modest sweet soul,
For love is a thing of great force.

The green grass shall be thy Pillow
To comfort thy spherical head,
And my arms shall enjoin my love so divine,
                      And

And the earth shall be thy bed;
Thy mantle of fairest flowers,
My coat shall thy coverlet be,
And the whistling wind shall sing to our mind,
O dainty sweet Lullaby.

Old *Eolus* shall be thy Rocker,
With his gentle murmuring noise,
And loves mirtle tree shall thy Canopy be;
And the birds harmonious voice
Shall bring us into a sweet slumber,
While I in thy bosome do rest,
And give thee such bliss by that, and by ——
As by poetry can't be exprest.

While thy cherry cheek pleaseth in touching,
And in smelling her oderous breath;
Her beauty in my sight, and her voice my delight,
Oh my sweets are cast beneath;
Thus ravished with the contentment
In more than a lover exprest,
And think when I am here, I am in a sphear,
And more than immortally blest.

And thus with my mutual coying
My love doth me sweetly embrace;
With my hands in her hair, and her fingers so rare,
And her playing with my face,
We reapt the most happy contentment

That ever two Lovers did find;
What women did see but my Love and me,
Would say, that we use to be kind.

Grinning Honour.

NAY prithee don't fly me, but sit thee down by me,
    For I cannot endure the man that's demure,
A pox on your Worships and Sirs;
    Your conjeys and trips,
    With your legs and your lips,
    Your Madams and Lords,
    With such finical words,
    With a complement you bring,
    Which concerneth no thing
You may keep for the Gown and the furs.
    For at the beginning, &c. ———

These titles of Honours were at first in the Donours,
And not to the thing unto which they do cling,
If the soul be too narrow that wears them,
    No delight can I see
    In the thing called degree:
    Honest Dick sounds as well
    As the name with an L.
    And that with titles doth swell,
    And sounds like a spell
To affright mortal ears when they hear them;

                                He

He that wears a brave soul and dares honestly do,
He's a Herald to himself and a God-father too.

Why then should we doat on one with a fools coat on,
Whose Coffers are cram'd, but yet he'll be dam'd
E'er he do a good Act, or a wise one ;
   What reason hath he
   To be ruler o'er me,
   Who's a Lord in a chest :
   But his head and his breast
   Are as empty and bare,
   And but puft up with aire,
And can neither assist nor advise one ;
 Honour's but Air, and proud flesh but dust is,
 It's we Commons make the Lords, as the Clarks
        (make the Justice.
But since we must be of a different degree,
Cause most do aspire to be greater and higher
Than the rest of our fellows and brothers :
   He that hath such a spirit,
   Let him gain 't by his merit,
   Spend his brain, wealth, and 's blood
   For his Countries good,
   And make himself fit
   By his Valour and his wit
For things above the reach of all others :
 Honour's a prize, and who wins it may wear it,
 If not, it's a Bag, and a burthen to bear it.

For my part let me be but quiet and free,
I'll drink sack and obey, and let great ones bear sway
Who spend their whole time but in thinking;
      I'll ne'er trouble my pate
      With the secrets of State;
      The news books I'll burn all:
      And with the diurnall
      Light Tobacco, and admit,
      That they are so far fit
As to serve good company in drinking:
  All the name I desire, is an honest good fellow,
  Lets drink good Canary untill we grow mellow.

The Hunting.

A Fox, a fox, up Gallants to the field,
    List to the merry cry that sweetnes yields;
Joves high-bred boy rides mounted on a Tun;
Selenia makes his lasie Ass to run   [*Silenus*]
In persuit of the chace,
With which may none compare,
Neither for four miles race,
Nor hunting of the hare.
  Joyn Musick to the Cry, that hollow rocks
  May eccho forth the hunting of the Fox.

The Fox hath lost the field and left the Town,
And up your barly hill showrs up and down, [scowrs]
                                With

With fear inforc'd, weak Reynold seems to daunt
The courage of the warlike Elephant;
But hark, the Horns do blow,
And all the huntsmen shout;
There goes the Game, I know,
But Tickler drives him out;
   Joyn Musick, *&c.*

Ride, ride, *St. George*, he's stole into the bush,
Old Swag-pot makes him straight from thence to rush;
Then creeps into the vine, and there doth earth;
O heavenly cry, exceeding earthly mirth!
Hark Youland, and Pottle,
Old Gusquin and Rainsbolt,
But hark how *Pim* doth Tattle
Now he's got to the hole;
   Joyn Musick, *&c.*

The Fox quite spent, about the Town he reels,
And now in view he's followed at the heels;
Then climbs the tree, that climbing was his fall,
And to that fall came in the Huntsmen all:
Then Sug, and soot, swilback,
Cavil, and speckled Dyer,
Toss, swagger, and Spendall
Tug him through dirt and mire;
   Now Joyn our horn and voices all, that hollow rocks
   May eccho forth the hunting of the Fox.

A Song.

AH, ah, come see what's here!
    Young *Rufus* drawing near,
With his thoughts, and his eyes,
And his elevated cries;
Take heed how you come near,
For in a rapture his weak stature
Mounts above the Moon;
And being there, doth stamp and stare,
And swear there is no room
To contain his old brain in the skies,
But he'll go down below,
And he'll know if it be so,
Whether all the wild boyes,   [? Whither]
Having spent their mad daies,
Goes when such men dies.

But he finds no comfort there,
Back again to the man in the air;
He catches at the Moon,
And pulls off the shepherds shoone,
And leaves his ten toes bare;
Now the Youth grows mad,
The Moon-man, that was sad,
Starts up as wild as he,
With frowning angry look,

                                        Stood

Stood kirdling with his hook,
And demands what he might be:
He did reply, I will fly round the Globe;
Then make way Earth and Sea,
He'll not stay for to Play,
Consent with him importune,
He fears an evil Fortune,
All his delight's abroad.

A Droll.

LEt dogs and divels die;
Let Wits and Money fly;
Let the slaves of the earth
Be abortive in their birth   [,]
Well or Ill come, what care I;
For I will roar, I will drink, I will whore,
I spend nought but my own:
Let slaves of the world be suddenly hurl'd,
Or with a whirlwind blown,
In and out, round about, hey boyes, hey:
Let us sing, let us laugh;
Let us drink, let us quaff;
See the world is sliding,
Here is no abiding,
Our life's but a Hollyday.

The Jealous Husband.

A Young man that's in love with one that's wed,
Which of his sweet heart hath a Jealous head;
Hath hatched a furious beast,
For Jealousie takes no rest.

It is a mad frenzy that broiles in the brain,
It fumes in the stomack, and filleth the vein:
The handmaids that upon it do wait,
Is fear, suspition, and hate.

The smoak of Tobacco it troubleth the brain,
It makes a man giddy, and quiet again:
If once he cry, stand away, puff,
He taketh all kindness in snuff.

He holds it a scorn the trueness of love,
But woe to the woman that's forced to prove,
At home, and in every place,
She lives in a pitiful case.

If he do but miss her out of his sight,
He rangeth about like a wandring spright:
And though she be within the house,
He hunts her as a Cat doth a Mouse.

If any be with her, O how his heart akes!
He sickles, he tickles, he trembles, he quakes;
But if she be all alone,
He sneaks away like a mome.

If she be abroad, and not to be found,
He hunts, and he scents, like a bloud-hound;
If he her consort doth distaste,
O how the poor fool is aghast!

At feasts, and at meetings, O how he will pry,
He'll wink and nod, and observe her eye;
His mops and mows he will shape,
Like an old Paris-Garden Ape.

If any do kiss her, or kindly her use,
O how it doth vex him, and make him to muse!
And plague him with such a smart,
As gripeth his very heart.

Perhaps he will flatter, and make excuse,
Dissembling his folly, which might her abuse;
And seemingly shews himself kind,
When Jealousie sticks in his mind.

I'll tell you his vertues, to hold on my Rime,
No fool is kinder for a fit or a time;
He flatters, he kisses, he swears,
It is out of love that he bears.

If this be true love, I would have no such;
I'll rather wish no love than thus over much;
For thus a fond jealous Elfe
Disquiets his wife and himself.

I wonder what pleasure he findeth thereby,
To find his own torment that hidden may lye,
And frets like a canker in heart,
And breeds his continual smart.

He pouts, he lowrs, he looks like a Cur,
He'll chide, he'll brawl, he'll keep a foul stir,
And swear he will slit her face,
Before he'll endure disgrace.

He ruffles, he shuffles, he frets and fumes,
He Puffs, and snuffs, and sets up his plumes;
And though the fool have no hurt
He'll call for a Constable blurt.

He fretteth, he swelleth, he spoyleth his diet;
He stormeth, he rageth, he is seldom quiet;
He wastes away like dross,
When none but himself is his Cross.

He mumbles, and grumbles, poor silly man,
He whineth, he pineth, he looks pale and wan;
And when he perceives he must die
He cries, out upon Jealousie, fie.

I'd

I'd rather be a Cuckold, than be so possest
With such a foul spirit that never gives rest,
That when the Coxcomb should sleep,
Like a boy, he will play at bopeep.

Besides the great scandal Jealousie bears,
All men will deride him even to his ears,
And boys in the street as he goes
Will point with finger at nose.

He that's a Wittal doth live at more ease,
He knows the worst; and doth himself please:
But he that's a Cuckold known,
May swear it's no fault of his own.

A wife that's abus'd, if she would not tell,
May work out a charm to fill his night spell,
Much better to please his mind
And serve a fool in his kind.

She is now his equal, his flesh and his mate,
And none but the devil would work their debate:
For being of two made one,
It is fit he should let her alone.

And yet to conclude, though this is a curse,
A woman that's Jealous is twenty times worse:
For she, like a cackling hen,
Will giggle it out to all men.

Womens

Womens delight.

There dwelt a maid in the Cunny-gate,
    And she was wondrous fair,
And she would have an old man
    Was overgrown with hair;
        And ever she cry'd, O turn,
        O turn thee unto me,
        Thou hast the thing I have not,
        A little above the knee.

He bought her a Gown of green,
    Became her wondrous well:
And she bought him a long sword
    To hang down by his heel;
        And ever she cry'd, &c.

He bought her a Pair of sheers
    To hang by her side:
And she bought him a winding-sheet
    Against the day he dy'd;
        And ever she cry'd, &c.

He bought her a Gown, a Gown,
    Imbroider'd all with gold:
And she gave him a night-cap
    To keep him from the cold,
        And ever she cry'd, &c.

He bought her a Gown, a Gown,
   Imbroider'd all with red:
And she gave him a pair of horns
   to wear upon his head;
      And ever she cry'd, [O] turn,
      O turn thee unto me,
      Thou hast the thing I have not
      A little above the knee.

The Drunkard.

THe Spring is coming on, and our spirits begin
   To return to their places merrily home,
And every man is bound to lay in a good
Brewing of bloud for the year to come.

They are Cowards that make it of clarified whay,
Or drink, with the swine, of the Juice of grains;
Let me have the rasie Canary to play,
And the sparkling Rhenish to dance in my veins,

Let Dotards go preach, that our lives are but short,
And tell us much wine doth quick death invite:
But we'll be reveng'd before hand, and for 't
We'll croud a lives mirth in the space of a night.

Then stand we about with our glasses full crown'd,
Till every thing else to our postures do grow,
                          Till

Till our cups, and our heads, and the house go round,
And the Sellar become where the Chamber is now.

Come fill us some wine, we'll a sacrifice bring,
This night full of sack to the health of our K——
Till we baffle the stars, and the Sun fetch about,
And tipple, and tipple, and tipple, a rout.

Whose first rising raies that is shown from his throne
Shall dash upon faces as red as his own,
And wonder that Mortals can fuddle away
As much wine in a night as he water i' th' day.

In Praise of Chocolate.

Doctors lay by your irkesome books :
 And all the petty-fogging Rooks
Leave quacking, and enucleate
The vertues of our Chocolate.

Let th' universall medicine
(Made up of dead-mens bones and skin)
Be henceforth illegitimate,
And yield to soveraign Chocolate.

Let bawdy-baths be us'd no more,
Nor smoaky-stoves, but by the whore

Of

Of *Babylon*, since happy fate
Hath blessed us with Chocolate.

Let old *Puncieus* greaze his shooes
With his mock-Balsome, and abuse
No more the world : but meditate
The excellence of Chocolate.

Let Doctor *Trig* (who so excells)
No longer trudge to westward wells;
For though that water expurgate,
It's but the dregs of Chocolate.

Let all the Paracelsian Crew,
Who can extract Christian from Jew,
Or out of Monarchy or state [,]
Break all their Stills for Chocolate. [;]

Tell us no more of weapon-salve,
But rather doom us to a grave,
For sure our wounds will ulcerate
Unless they're washt with Chocolate.

The thriving Saint, that will not come
Within a sack-shops bouzing Room,
(His spirits to exhilerate)
Drinks bowls (at home) of Chocolate.

His spouse, when she (brim-full of sence)
Doth want her due benevolence,
And babes of grace would propagate,
Is alwaies sipping Chocolate.

The roaring Crew of gallant ones,
Whose marrow rots within their bones,
Their bodies quickly regulate,
If once but sous'd in Chocolate.

Young heirs, that have more Land than wit,
When once they do but taste of it,
Will rather spend their whole Estate
Than weaned be from Chocolate.

The nut-brown Lasses of the Land,
Whom Nature vail'd in face and hand,
Are quickly beauties of high rate,
By one small draught of Chocolate.

Besides, it saves the moneys lost
Each day in patches, which did cost
Them dear, untill of late
They found this heavenly Chocolate.

Nor need the women longer grieve,
Who spend their Oyl, yet not conceive :
But its a help immediate
If such but lick of Chocolate [.]

Consumptions

Consumptions too (be well assur'd)
Are no less soon than soundly cur'd
(Excepting such as do relate
Unto the purse) by Chocolate.

Nay more: Its Virtue is so much,
That if a Lady get a touch,
Her grief it will extenuate,
If she but smell of Chocolate.

The feeble man, whom nature ties
To do his Mistris's drudgeries:
O how it will his mind elate,
If she allow him Chocolate.

'Twill make old women young and fresh,
Create new motions of the flesh,
And cause them long for you know what,
If they but taste of Chocolate.

There's ne'er a Common-Council man,
Whose life will reach unto a span,
Should he not well affect the state,
And first and last drink Chocolate.

Nor ne'er a Citizen's chaste wife
That ever shall prolong her life,
(Whilst open stands her postern gate)
Unless she drink of Chocolate.

Nor dos't the Levite any harm,
It keepeth his devotion warm;
And eke the hair upon his pate,
So long as he drinks Chocolate.

Both high and low, both rich and poor,
My Lord, my Lady, and his ⸺
With all the folks at *Billingsgate*,
Bow, bow your hams to Chocolate.

A Catch.

There was an old man had an acre of land,
    He sold it for five pound a,
He went to the Tavern and drank it all out,
    Excepting half a crown a:
And as he came home he met with a wench,
    And ask'd her whether she was willing
To go to the Tavern and spend eighteen pence,
    And ⸺ for the other odd shilling.

The Cavalier's Complaint.

Come, *Jack*, let's drink a Pot of Ale,
    And I shall tell thee such a Tale
Will make thine ears to ring:

My Coyn is spent, my time is lost,
And I this only Fruit can boast,
    That once I saw my King.

But this doth most afflict my mind,
I went to Court, in hope to find
Some of my friends in Place;
And walking there, I had a sight
Of all the Crew: But, by this light,
    I hardly knew one face!

S'life [!] of so many Noble Sparkes,
Who on their bodies bear the Markes
    Of their integrity,
And suffer'd Ruin of estate;
It was my damn'd unhappy Fate,
    That I not one could see!

Not one, upon my life, among
My old acquaintance, all along
    At *Truro*, and before;
And, I suppose the Place can shew
As few of those, whom thou didst know
    At *York*, or *Marston-moore*.

But, truly, There are swarms of Those,
Whose Chins are beardless, yet their Hose
    And Buttocks still wear muffs;

Whilst the old rusty Cavaleer
Retires, or dares not once appear
  For want of Coin, and Cuffs.

When none of these I could descry,
Who, better far deserv'd ; than I   [,]
  [I] Calmly did reflect ;
Old services, (by rule of state)
Like *Almanacks*, grow out of date,
  What then can I expect ?

Troth, in contempt of Fortunes frown,
I'll get me fairly out of town,
  And, in a Cloyster pray,
That, since the Stars are yet unkind
To Royallists, the King may find
  More faithfull friends than they.

An Eccho to the Cavaleers complaint.

I Marvel *Dick*, That having been
 So long abroad, and having seen
The world, as thou hast done,
Thou should'st acquaint Me with a tale
As old as *Nestor*, and as stale
  As that of Priest and Nun !

         Are

Are We to learn what is a Court?
A Pageant made for fortune's sport,
    Where Merits scarce appear:
For bashfull Merit only dwells
In Camps, in Villages and Cells;
    Alas! it dwells not there,

Desert is nice in its Address,
And Merit oftimes doth oppress
    Beyond what Guilt would do:
But they are sure of there Demands,   [their]
That come to Court with Golden-hands
    And Brazen-faces too.

The King, they say, doth still profess
To give His Party some redress,
    And cherish Honesty:
But his good wishes prove in vain,
Whose Service with His servants gain,
    Not alwaies doth agree.

All Princes (be they never so wise)
Are fain to see with others Eyes,
    But seldom hear at all:
And Courtiers find't their interest,
In Time to feather well their nest,
    Providing for their Fall.

Our Comfort doth on Time depend;
Things, When they are at worst, will mend:
    And let us but reflect
On our Condition th' other day,
When none but Tyrants bore the sway,
    What did we then expect?

Mean while a calm retreat is best:
But discontent (if not supprest)
    Will breed Disloyalty.
This is the constant note I sing,
I have been faithfull to the King,
    And so shall ever be.

The Colchester Quaker.

All in the Land of *Essex*
    Near *Cholchester* the zealous,
    On the side of a bank,
    Was play'd such a prank,
As would make a stone-horse Jealous.

Help *Woodcock*, *Fox*, and *Nailor*,
For brother *Green's* a stallion,
    Now alas what hope,
    Of converting the Pope,
When a quaker turns *Italian?*

                      Unto

Unto our whole profession,
A scandall 'twill be counted,
  When 'tis talk't with disdain,
  Amongst the profane,
How Brother *Green* was mounted.

And in the good time of Christmas,
Which though the Saints have damn'd all,
  Yet when did they hear
  That a damn'd Cavalier
E'er play'd such a Christmas gamball, [?]

Had thy flesh, O *Green*, been pamper'd
With any Cates unhallow'd,
  Hadst thou sweetned thy Gums
  With Pottage of Plums,
Or Profane minc'd-Pie hadst swallow'd.

Roll'd up in wanton Swines flesh,
The fiend might have crept into thee,
  Then fulness of gut
  Might have made thee rut,
And the Divel so have rid through thee.

But alas, he had been feasted
With a spiritual Collation,
  By our frugal Mayer
  Who can dine with a prayer,
And sup with an Exhortation.

'Twas meer impulse of spirit,
Though he us'd the weapon carnall,
   Filly-Foal, quoth he,
   My bride thou shalt be:
Now how this is lawfull, learn all.

For if no respect of persons
Be due 'mongst the sons of *Adam*,
   In a large extent
   Then may it be meant
That a *Mare's* as good as a *Madam*.

Then without more Ceremony,
Nor Bonnet vail'd, nor kist her,
   He took her by force
   For better for worse,
And he us'd her like a Sister.

Now when in such a Saddle
A Saint will needs be riding,
   Though I dare not say,
   'Tis a falling away,
May there not be some back-sliding?

No surely, quoth *James Naylor*,
'Twas but an insurrection
   Of the Carnal part,
   For a Quaker in heart
Can never lose perfection.

For so our *Masters teach us,   *Hist. of *Jesuitism.*
The intent being well directed ;
      Though the divel trapan
      The Adamical man,
The Saint stands uninfected.

But yet a Pagan Jury
Still Judges what's intended,
      Then say what we can,
      Brother *Green's* outward man,
I fear, will be suspended.

And our adopted Sister
Will find no better quarter,
      But when him we inroule
      For a Saint ; Filly Foal
Shall pass at least for a Martyr.

Now *Rome* that Spiritual *Sodom*
No longer is thy debter,
      O *Colchester* now
      Who's *Sodom*, but thou
Even according to the Letter?

Help *Woodcock*, *Fox* and *Naylor;*
For Brother *Green's* a Stallion.
      Now alas what hope
      Of converting the Pope,
When a Quaker turns *Italian.*

The Character of a Mistris.

MY Mistris is a shittle-cock,
    Compos'd of Cork and feather,
Each Battledore sets on her dock,
    And bumps her on the leather:
But cast her off which way you Will,
She will requoile to another still, Fa, la, la, la, la, la

My Mistris is a Tennis-ball,
    Compos'd of Cotten fine;
She is often struck against the wall,
    And banded under-line,
But if you will her mind fulfill,
You must pop her in the hazard still, Fa, la, la.

My Mistris is a Nightingale
    So sweetly she can sing,
She is as fair as Philomel,
    The daughter of a King;
And in the darksome nights so thick
She loves to lean against a prick, Fa, la, la.

My Mistris is a Ship of war,
    With shot discharged at her
The Poope hath inferred many a scar
    Even both by wind and water;

                                                  But

But as she grapples, at the last
She drowns the man, pulls downs her mast, Fa, la, la.

My Mistris is a Virginal,
    And little cost will string her:
She's often rear'd against the wall
    For every man to finger,
But to say truth, if you will her please
You must run division on her keys, Fa, la, la.

My Mistris is a Conny fine,
    She's of the softest skin,
And if you please to open her,
    The best part lies within,
And in her Conny-burrow may
Two Tumblers and a Ferrit play, Fa, la, la.

My Mistris is the Moon so bright:
    I wish that I could win her;
She never walks but in the night,
    And bears a man within her,
Which on his back bears pricks and thorns,
And once a month she brings him horns, Fa, la, la.

My Mistris is a Tinder-box,
    Would I had such a one;
Her Steel endureth many a knock
    Both by the flint and stone.

                                    And

And if you stir the Tinder much,
The match will fire at every touch, Fa, la, la.

My Mistris is a Puritan,
    She will not swear an oath,
But for to lye with any man,
    She is not very loath;
But pure to pure, and there's no sin,
There's nothing lost that enters in, Fa, la, la.

But why should I my Mistris call,
    A shittle-cock or bawble,
A ship of war or Tennis-ball,
    Which things be variable?
But to commend, I'll say no more,
My Mistris is an arrant ———, Fa, la, la, la, la, la.

Oliver routing the Rump.

                                        (before,

Will you hear a strange thing, ne'er heard of
    A Ballad of news without any lyes:
The Parliament men are turn'd out of door,
And so is the Council of State likewise.

Brave *Oliver* came into th' House like a spright,
His fiery looks made the Speaker dumbe:
You must be gone home, quoth he, by this light,
Do you mean to sit here untill dooms-day come?
                                          With

With that the Speaker lookt pale for fear,
As if he had been with the night mare rid,
Which made most men believe, that were there,
That he did even as the Alderman did.

For *Oliver* thought he were Doctor at law, [though 't]
It seems he plaid the Physitian there :
Whose Physick so wrought in the Speakers maw,
That it gave him a stool instead of a Chair.

Sir *Arthur* thought *Oliver* wondrous bold,
Hoping there to make some stir :
But in the mean time, take this from me,
Sir *Arthur* must yield to brave *Oliver*.

Harry Martin wondred to see such a thing
Done by a Saint of so high degree :
An Act he did not expect from a King,
Much less from such a dry-bone as he.

But *Oliver*, laying hands on his sword,
Upbraids him with adultery :
Then *Martin* gave him never a word,
But humbly thank'd his Majesty.

Much wit he had shewed if that he had dar'd,
But silent he was for fear of some knocks :
Quoth he, if I get you within my ward,
I may chance to send you out with a Pox.

Allen

Allen the Copper-smith was in great fear,
He had done as much hurt since the war began :
A broken Citizen many a year,
And now he's a broken Parliament-man :

But *Oliver* told him what he had been,
And him a cheating Knave did call,
Which put him into a fit of the spleen,
For now he must give an account of all.

It went to the heart of Sir *Henry Vane*,
To think what a terrible fall he should have :
For he who did once in the Parliament raign
Was call'd as I hear, a dissembling Knave.

Who gave him that name you may easily know,
'Twas one that studied the art full well,
You may swear it was true, if he call'd him so,
And how to dissemble I'm sure he can tell.

Bradshaw, the President, proud as the Pope,
Who lov'd upon Kings and Princes to trample,
Now the House is dissolved, who cannot but hope
To see such a President made an example.

If I were one of the Council of state,
I'll tell you what my vote should be :
Upon his new Turret at *Westminster*,
There to be hanged he should be.

          Then

Then room for the Speaker without his mace,
And room for the rest of the rabble-rout :
My Masters, is not this a pittifull case
Like the snuff of a candle thus to go out?

I cannot but wonder you should agree,
You that have been such brethren in evill :
A dissolution there needs must be,
When the Divel is divided against a Devil.

Some like this change, and some like it not ;
Some say it was not done in due season ;
Some say it was the Jesuites plot,
It so much resembles the Gunpowder treason.

Some think that *Cromwel* and *Charles* are agreed,
And sure it were good policy if it were so,
Lest the Hollander, French, the Dane and the Swede
Should bring him in whether he will or no.

And now I would gladly conclude my song
With a prayer as Ballads use to do,
But yet I'll forbear, for I hope er't be long
We shall have the King and a Parliament too.

A Song of Nothing.

I'Le Sing you a Sonnet that ne'er was in Print,
  'Tis truly and newly come out of the Mint,
I'le tell you before-hand, you'l find Nothing in't,
On Nothing I think, and on Nothing I write;
'Tis Nothing I court, yet Nothing I slight,
Nor care I a Pin, if I get Nothing by't.   (men,
Fire, Air, Earth, and water, Beasts, Birds, Fish and silly
Did start out of Nothing, a Chaos, a Den;
And all things shall turn into Nothing agen.
'Tis Nothing sometimes makes many things hit [,]
As when fools among wise men do silently sit [;]
A fool that says Nothing, may pass for a wit.
What one man loves is another mans loathing,
This blade loves a quick thing, that loves a slow
And both do in the conclusion love Nothing.   (thing;
Your Lad that makes love to a delicate smooth thing
And thinking with sighs to gain her & soothing,
Frequently makes much ado about Nothing,
At last when his pat'ence and purse is decay'd
He may to the bed of a Whore be betray'd;
But she that hath Nothing, must need be a maid.
Your slashing, and clashing, and flashing of wit
Doth start out of Nothing, but fancy and fit;
'Tis little or Nothing to what hath been writ,   [.]
When first by the ears we together did fall,
                         Then

Then something got Nothing, and Nothing got all;
From Nothing it came, and to Nothing it shall.
That party that seal'd to a cov'nant in haste,
Who made our 3 Kingdoms, and Churches lie waste;
Their project, and all came to Nothing at last.
They raised an Army of horse, and Foot,
To tumble down Monarchy, Branches and Root;
They thunder'd and plunder'd, but Nothing would do't
The Organ, the Altar, and Ministers cloathing
In Presbyter *Jack* begot such a loathing,
That he must needs raise a petty New-Nothing.
And when he had rob'd us in sanctifi'd cloathing,
Perjur'd the people by faithing and trothing;
At last he was catch't and all came to Nothing.
In several Factions we quarrel and brawl,
Dispute, and contend, and to fighting we fall;
I'le lay all to Nothing, that Nothing wins all.
When war, and rebellion, and plundering grows,
The Mendicant man is the freest from foes,
For he is most happy hath Nothing to lose.
Brave *Cæsar* and *Pompey*, and Great *Al'xander*,
Whom Armies follow'd as Goose follows Gander,
Nothing can sayt' tis an action of slander.
The wisest great Prince, were he never so stout
Though [he] conquer the world, and give mankind a rout,
Did bring Nothing in, nor shall bear Nothing out.
Old *Noll* that arose from High-thing to Low-thing,
By brewing rebellion, Nicking, and Frothing,
In sev'n years distance was all things, and Nothing.

Dick (Oliver's Heir) that pitiful slow-thing,
Who was once invested with purple-cloathing,
Stands for a Cypher, and that stands for Nothing.
If King-killers bold are excluded from bliss,
Old *Bradshaw* (that feels the reward on't by this)
Had better been Nothing, than what now he is.
Blind Collonel *Hewson*, that lately did crawl
To lofty degree, from a low Coblers stall,
Did bring Aul to Nothing, when Aul came to all.
Your Gallants that Rant it in dell'cate clothing,
Though lately he was but a pit'ful low-thing,
Pays Landlord, Draper, and Taylor, with Nothing.
The nimble-tongu'd Lawyer that pleads for his pay,
When death doth arrest him and bear him away,
At the Gen'ral Bar will have Nothing to say.
Whores that in Silk were by Gallants embrac't;
By a rabble of Prentices lately were chac't [:]   (last.
Thus Courting, and sporting, comes to Nothing at
If any man tax me with weakness of wit
And say that on Nothing, I nothing have writ,
I shall answer *ex nihilo nihil fit.*
Yet let his discreet one be never so tall,
This very word Nothing shall give it a fall,
For writing of Nothing I comprehend all.
Let every man give the Poet his due,
'Cause then it was with him as now it's with you,
He studi'd it when he had Nothing to doe.
This very word Nothing if it took the right way

May

May prove advantagious [;] for what would you say,
If the Vintner should cry there is Nothing to pay.

A Catch.

BAcchus, I am come from the sun-shine fell
 To you, mad wags, the force of wine to tell,
And from those Sack-butts, Prest from grapes of
There's none shall taste but I will taste again. (*Spain*
 Sack, Sack is the thing that makes the brain rumble,
 It fools the wise, and makes the Gallant stumble.
Sack hath the power the sense of man depriving,
 O take heed then;
Sack keeps the wealthy man from thriving,
 Fools then be wise.
He that in drink doth keep no mean
 It makes him lean;
And he that reels,
See what he feels:
 Now in foul dirt he prostrate falls,
 And picks mad quarrels with the walls;
Nor shall his drouzie sense, that lies asleep,
Be well recover'd in a night of sleep.

A Catch.

BE not thou so foolish nice
 As to be invited twice;
Why should we men more incite
Than their own sweet appetite?

Shall

Shall savage things more freedom have
Than nature unto women gave?
The Swan, the Turtle, and the Sparrow,
Bill a while, and then take marrow;
They bill, they kiss, what else they do,
Come bill and kiss, and I'll shew you.

Pim's *Anarchy*.

ASke me no more, why there appears
Dayly such troops of Dragooneers,
Since it was requisite, you know,
They rob *cum privilegio*.

Aske me no more, why the Gule confines
Our Hierarchy of best Divines,
Since some in Parliament agree
'Tis for the subjects liberty.

Aske me no more, why from *Blackwall*
Great tumults come into *Whitehall*,
Since it was allowed, by free consent,
The Priviledges of Parliament.

Aske me not, why to *London* comes
So many Musquets, Pikes and Drums,
So that we fear They'll never cease,
'Tis to Protect the Kingdoms peace.

Aske

Aske me no more, why little *Finch*
From Parliament began to winch,
Since such as dare to hawk at Kings
Can easie clip a Finches wings.

Aske me no more, why *Strafford's* dead,
And why they aim'd so at his head,
Faith, all the reason I can give,
'Tis thought he was too wise to live.

Aske me no more, where's all the plate,
Brought in at such an easie rate,
They it back to the Owners soon will bring
In case it fall not to the King.

Aske me not, why the house delights
Not in our two wise Kentish Knights:
Their Counsel never was thought good,
Because it was not understood.

Aske me no more, why *Lasey* goes
To seize all rich men as his foes,
Whilst Country Farmers sigh and sob,
Yeomen may beg when Kings do rob.

Aske me no more, by what strange sight
Londons Lord Maior was made a *Knight*,
Since there's a strength, not very far,
Hath as much power to make, as mar.

Aske me no more, why in this age
I sing so sharp without a cage:
My answer is, I need not fear,
Since *England* doth the burden bear.

Aske me no more, for I grow dull,
Why *Hotham* kept the town of *Hull*:
This answer I in brief do sing,
All things were thus when *Pim* was K———

A Sessions of wit.

A Session was held the other day,
And *Apollo* was at it (they say :)
The Laurel, hath been so long preserv'd,
Was now to be given to him best deserv'd.

Therefore the Wits of the Town came thither,
'Twas strange to see how they flock together;
Each, strongly confident of his own way,
That day thought to carry the Laurel away.

There was *Selden*, and he sate close to the Chair;
Wainman not far off, which was very fair;
Sands with *Townsend*, for they kept no order;
Digby and *Shillingworth* a little further.

There

There was *Lucans* Translator too, and he
That made God speak so big in's Poetry;
Selwin, and *Waller*, and *Bartlets* both the Brothers,
Jack Vaughan, and *Porter*, and divers others.

The first that broke silence was good old *Ben*,
Prepar'd before with Canary wine,
And he told them plainly, he deserv'd the Bayes,
For his were call'd Works when others were call'd
                                        (Plaies.

Bid them remember how he had purg'd the Stage
Of errours that had lasted many an Age;
And he hoped they did not think the *Silent woman*,
The *Fox*, and the *Alchymist* out-done by no man.

Apollo stopt him there, and bid him not go on,
'Twas merit, he said, and not presumption,
Must carry't; at which *Ben* turn'd about,
And in great choler offered to go out.

But those that were there thought it not fit
To discontent so ancient a wit,
And therefore *Apollo* call'd him back again,
And made him mine Host of his *own newe Inne*.

Tom Carew was next, but he had a fault
That would not well stand with a *Laureat;*
His Muse was hide-bound, and the Issue of's brain
Was seldom brought forth but with trouble and pain.
                                        And

And all that were present there did agree
A Laureat Muse should be easie and free ;   (Grace
Yet sure 'twas not that, but 'twas thought that his
Consider'd he was well he had a cup-bearers place.

Will Davenant ashamed of a foolish mischance,
That he had got lately traveling into *France*,
Modestly hoped the handsomness of 's Muse
Might any deformity about him excuse.

And surely the company would have been content
If they could have found any precedent,
But in all there Records, either in *Verse* or *Prose*,
There was not one Laureat without a *Nose*.

To *Will Bartlet* sure all the Wits meant well,
But first they would see how his Snow would sell :
Will smil'd, and swore in their Judgments they went
That concluded of merit upon success.   (less,

Suddenly taking his place agen,
He gave way to Selwin, who straight stept in ;
But, alas, he had been so lately a wit
That *Apollo* himself scarce knew him yet.

Toby Mathews, (pox on him) what made he there ?
Was whispering nothing in some bodies eare ;
When he had the honour to be nam'd in Court,
But, Sir, you may thank my Lady *Carlisle* for't.

           For

For had not her Character furnish'd you out
With something of handsome, without all doubt,
You and the sorry Lady-Muse had been
In the number of those that were not let in.

In from the Court two or three come in,
And they brought Letters (forsooth) from the Queen:
'Twas discreetly done; for if th' had come
Without them, th' had scarce been let into the room.

This made a dispute, for 'twas plain to be seen
Each man had a mind to gratifie the Queen:
But *Apollo* himself could not think it fit: (wit.
There was difference, he said, betwixt fooling and

Suckling was next call'd but durst not appear,
But straight one whisper'd *Apollo* in the ear,
That of all men living he car'd not for't,
He lov'd not the Muses so well as his sport.

And priz'd black eyes, or a lucky hit
At bowls, above all the Trophies of wit;
But *Apollo* was angry, and publickly said,
'Twere fit that a fine were set upon's head.

Wat Montague now stood forth to his trial,
And did not so much as suspect a denial:
But wise *Apollo* asked him first of all,
If he understood his own *Pastoral*.
                         For

For if he could do't, 'twould plainly appear
He understood more than any man there,
And did merit the *Bayes* above all the rest,
But the *Monsieur* was modest, and silence confest.

During these troubles, in the croud was hid
One that *Apollo* soon miss'd, little *Cid*:
And having spide him, call'd him out of the throng,
And advis'd him in his ear not to write so strong.
Then *Murre* was summon'd, but it was urg'd, that he
Was chief already of another company.

Hales sate by himself, most gravely did smile,
To see them about nothing keep such a coile;
Apollo had spide him, but knowing his mind,
Past by, and call'd *Faulkland*, that sate just behind.

But he was of late so grown with divinity,
That he had almost forgot his Poetry,
Though, to say the truth (and *Apollo* did know it)
He might have been both his Priest and his Poet.

At length, who but an *Alderman* did appear,
At which *Will Davenant* began to swear;
But wiser *Apollo* bade him draw nigher:
And when he had mounted a little higher,

He openly declared, that it was a good sign
Of good store of Wit, to have good store of Coyn:

An

And without a Syllable more or less said,
He put the Laurel on the *Aldermans* head.

At this the Wits were in such a maze,
That for a good while they did nothing but gaze
One upon another; not one in the Place
But had a discontent writ at large in his face.

Only the small ones cheared up again,
Out of hope, as 'twas thought, of borrowing;
But sure they were out, for he forfeits his crown
When he lends to any Poet about the Town.

The way to wooe a zealous Lady.

I Came unto a Puritan to wooe,
   And roughly did salute her with a kiss;
She shov'd me from her when I came unto;
Brother, by yea and nay I like not this:
And as I her with amorous talk saluted,
My Articles with scripture she confuted.

She told me that I was too much prophane,
And not devout neither in speech nor gesture:
And I could not one word answer again,
Nor had not so much grace to call her Sister;
For ever something did offend her there,
Either my broad beard, hat, or my long hair.

My Band was broad, my 'Parrel was not plain,
My Points and Girdle made the greatest show;
My Sword was odious, and my Belt was vain,
My Spanish shoee was cut too broad at toe;
My Stockings light, my Garters ty'd too long,
My Gloves perfum'd, and had a scent too strong.

I left my pure Mistris for a space,
And to a snip snap Barber straight went I;
I cut my hair, and did my corps uncase
Of 'Parrels pride that did offend the eye;
My high crown'd Hat, my little beard also,
My pecked Band, my Shooes were sharp at toe.

Gone was my Sword, my Belt was laid aside,
And I transform'd both in looks and speech;
My 'Parrel plain, my Cloak was void of pride,
My little Skirts, my metamorphos'd breech,
My Stockings black, my Garters were ty'd shorter,
My Gloves no scent; thus march'd I to her Porter.

The Porter spi'd me, and did lead me in,
Where his sweet Mistris reading was a chapter:
Peace to this house, and all that are therein,
Which holy words with admiration wrapt her;
And ever, as I came her something nigh,
She, being divine, turn'd up the white of th' eye.

            Quoth

Quoth I, dear sister, and that lik'd her well;
I kist her, and did Pass to some delight,
She, blushing, said, that long-tail'd men would tell;
Quoth I[,] I'll be as silent as the night;
And lest the wicked now should have a sight
Of what we do, faith, I'll put out the light.

O do not swear, quoth she, but put it out,
Because that I would have you save your oath,
In truth, you shall but kiss me without doubt;
In troth, quoth I, here will we rest us both;
Swear you[,] quoth she, in troth? Had you not sworn
I'd not have don't[,] but took it in foul scorn.

The Apostate World.

GOod Lord what a pass is this world brought to,
Most men have forgot to be honest and Just;
When shall one find a friend to be honest and true
That with his chief secret he only may trust;
If thou hadst abundance of money to spend,
Then every man will be accounted thy friend; (cay
Find one that will love you where wealth doth de-
    You'd as soon find a needle in a bottle of hay.

True friendship is now adaies cunning and waining,
And every one learns to shift for himselfe;
What man will not falsifie friendship for gaining,
                                And

And wrong his best friend for lucre of pelf?
There was once a time when a friend for a friend
Would ever be constant his life for to spend;
But he that will find such a friend at this day,
  Had as good seek, *&c.*

There's many will hang on you while you have coyn
And swear they will venture their lives for your
But to any task, if you them enjoyn,   (sake:
They'll swear and protest they'll it undertake,
But if by mishap you be brought to a Pinch, (inch,
Though they promise an ell, 'twill scarce prove an
But find out a friend that will do and not say,
  You'd as soon find, *&c.*

For in this age one dare not trust one another,
For love is not known, but extremity shews,
For one Brother dares hardly trust another
With any thing but what he cares not who knows;
If thou hast not money nor means of thine own,
In thine extremity true friendship is known;
If thou livest in debt, find one that will good say,
  You'd as soon find, *&c.*

There's many a Lawyer will promise his Client
To finish his business in the next Term;
To finger your money he'll shew himself plient,
And vows that nothing but truth he'll explain;
And thus he will feed you with hopes to do well,
         When

When he means as false as the divel of hell;
Find one that will finish your Suit in a day,
  You'd as soon find, &c.

And thus you may see what an intricate matter
It is to find truth in a World of deceit;
It is counted but complement to face and to flatter [,]
And politick wisdom to cozen and cheat;
Plain dealing is a Jewel, but he that doth use it,
They say, dies a beggar, therefore men refuse it;
Find one that will deal upright, nay, good Sir stay,
  And first find a needle in a bottle of hay.

Lust described.

Walking abroad in a morning,
  Where *Venus* her self was adorning;
I heard a bird sing to welcome the Spring,
Their musick so sweetly according.

I listened unto them,
Me thoughts a voice did summon;
I spide an old whore, and a lusty young rogue
Together as they sate a wooing.

She tickled him under the sides
To make their courage coming;
She hoysted her thighs, and she twinkled her eyes;
'Twas a dainty fine curious old woman.

If *Venus* and *Mars* so stout
Had joyned together in battle,
There could not have been more claps & more bangs,
For he made her old buttocks to rattle.

She gave him a lift for his thrust,
And catcht him as he was a coming;
And ever she cry'd, you lusty young rogue
Will you murder a poor old woman.

She found that his spirits were spent,
And that he was no more a coming,
She gave him five shillings to make a recruit,
   And was not this a fine lusty old woman?

Eighty Eight.

IN Eighty Eight, e'er I was born,
   As I can well remember,
In *August* was a Fleet of *Spain*,
A month before *September*.

Lisbona, civill *Portingal*,
Tolledo, and *Germado*,   [*Grenado*]
They all did meet, and made a Fleet,
And call'd it the *Armado*.

                                      They

They came with great provision,
As Muttons, Beef and Bacon;
Some said, some Ships were full of Whips,
But I think they were mistaken.

There was a little man in *Spain*,
He shot well in a Gun a,
Don Pedro hight, as black a Wight
As the Knight of the Sun a.

They had ten men to one of ours,
And yet to do more harm a,
They said they would not come alone,
But with the Prince of *Parma*.

King *Philip* made him General,
And bid him not to stay a,
But to destroy both man and boy,
And so to come away a.

When they had sail'd along the seas,
And anchor'd before *Dover*,
Our English men did boord them then,
And cast the Rascals over.

At *Tilbury* there lay the Queen,
What would you more desire?
For whose sweet sake Sir *Francis Drake*
Did set them all on fire.

They ran away about *England*,
About *Scotland* also a,
Till they came to the Irish coasts,
Where they had many a blow a.

The Irish man did ding them then
And one man slew threescore a,
And had they not then run away,
They surely had slain more a.

Then let them never brag nor boast,
For if they come again a
They had best take heed, lest that they speed
As they did they know when a.

Loves Follies.

Nay out upon this fooling for shame
    Nay Pish, nay fie, in faith you are to blame;
Nay come, this fooling must not be;
    Nay pish, nay fie, you tickle me.

Nay out upon't in faith I dare not do't;
I'll bite, I'll scratch, I'll squeak, I'll cry out;
Nay come, this fooling must not be;
    Nay pish, nay fie, you tickle me.

Your Buttons scratch me, you ruffle my band,
You hurt my thighs, Pray take away your hand;
The door stands ope that all may see,
    Nay pish, nay fie, you tickle me.

When you and I shall meet in a place
Both together face to face,
I'll not cry out, nay you shall see,
    Nay pish, nay fie, you tickle me.

But now I see my words are but vain,
For I have done, why should I complain?
Nay to't again, the way is free,
    Since it's no more, pray tickle me.

A Song.

IF every woman were serv'd in her kind,
    And every man had his due desert,
The rooms in Bridewel would be well lin'd,
And a Coach could not pass the streets for a Cart;
Yet I am a little vexed at the heart,
And fain I would have my grief to be known,
The Punck would have me to play a kind part,
And to father a child that is none of mine own:

Full seventeen months I crost the seas,
Mean time I was crost as much on the land,

For all this while she sate at her ease,
And had her companions at her command;
There was never a Gallant but gave her his hand,
And said, it was pitty she should lie alone,
And now they would have me subscribe to a bond,
    And to father a child, &c.

Let every Father take care For his Child,
And seek to provide for the Mother and that;
Although I am a Buck, I am not so wild
To naile up my horns for another mans hat;
I'll never grieve, but let it pass,
Since 'tis my fortune to be overthrown,
Although I am an Oxe, I'll ne'er be an Ass
    To father a child, &c.

A man may be made a Cuckold by chance,
And put out another mans child to nurse,
And hoodwinke his Barn with ignorance,   [? Horns]
But he that's a Wittall is ten times worse;
And he that knows his cross and his curse,
And still will be led by a Strumpet's moan,
May sit and sell horns at *Brittains* Burse;
    And father a child, &c.

And if you will be my Judge,
Is not that man wondrous base,
To be another mans slave and his drudge,
And sell all his credit for disgrace;

Nor was I ever sprung from that race,
To call that my seed another hath sown;
Nor I'll never look King *Charles* in the face,
    If I father a child that's none of my own.

The Fire on London *Bridge*, &c.

SOme Christian people all give ear,
    Unto the grief of us,
Caus'd by the death of three children dear,
    The which it hapned thus.

And eke there befell an accident,
    By fault of a Carpenters Son,
Who to Saw chips his sharp Axe lent,
    Woe worth the time may *Lon.*——

May *London* say, woe worth the Carpenter,
    And all such *block*-head fools,
Would he were hang'd up like a Serpent here,
    For jesting with edg-tools.

For into the chips there fell a spark,
    Which *put out* in such flames,
That it was known into *Southwark*,
    Which lives beyond the *Thames*.

For *Loe* the Bridge was wondrous *high*
   With water underneath,
O'er which as many *fishes* fly,
   As *birds* therein do breath.

And yet the fire consum'd the Bridg,
   Not far from place of landing,
And though the building was full big,
   It *fell down* not with *standing*.

And eke into the water fell,
   So many Pewter dishes,
That a man might have taken up very well,
   Both *boyld* and *roasted* Fishes.

And thus the Bridge of *London* Town,
   For building that was sumptuous,
Was *All* by fire *Half* burnt down,
   For being too contumptuous.

And thus you have *all*, but *half* my Song,
   Pray list to what comes after;
For now I have *cool'd* you with the *Fire*,
   I'll *warm* you with the *Water*.

I'll tell you what the Rivers name is,
   Where these children did slide-a,
It was fair *Londons* swiftest *Thames*,
   That keeps both time and *Tide-a*.

                                All

All on the tenth of *January*,
   To the wonder of much People,
'Twas frozen o'er that well 'twould bear,
   Almost a Country Steeple.

Three children sliding thereabouts
   Upon a place *too thin*,
That so at last it did fall *out*,
   That they did all *fall in*.

A great Lord there was that laid with the King,
   And with the King great wager makes:
But when he saw he could not win,
   He sigh't, and would have drawn stakes.

He said it would bear a man for to slide,
   And laid a hundred pound;
The King said it would break, and so it did,
   For three children there were drown'd.

Of which ones head was from his *Should*———
   Ers stricken, whose name was *John*,
Who then cry'd out as loud as he could,
   O *Lon-a, Lon-a, London*.

Oh! tut-tut turn from thy sinful race,
   Thus did his speech decay:
I wonder that in such a case,
   He had no more to say.

                               And

And thus being drown'd, *alack, alack,*
   The water ran down there throats,
And stopt their breaths three hours by the Clock,
   Before they could get any Boats.

Ye Parents all that *children have,*
   And ye that have none yet ;
Preserve your children from the grave,
   And teach them at home to sit.

For had these at a Sermon been,
   Or else upon dry ground,
Why then I would never have been seen,
   If that they had been *drown'd.*

Even as a Huntsman ties his dogs,
   For fear they should go from him,
So tye your children with severities clogs,
   Untye-'um and you'l *undo-'um.*

God bless our Noble Parliament,
   And rid them from all fears,
God bless *all* th' *Commons* of this Land,
   And God bless *some* o' th' *Peers.*

A Catch.

Come my *Daphne*, come away,
    We do waste the Christal day ;
'Tis *Strephon* calls : What would my Love ?
Come follow to the Mirtle Grove,
    Where *Venus* shall Prepare
    New Chaplets for thy hair.
Were I shut up within a tree,
I'd rent the bark to follow thee ;
    My shepheard make haste,
    The Minutes fly too fast.

In those cooler shades will I,
Blind as *Cupid*, kiss thine eye ;
On thy bosome there I'll stray,
In that warm snow who would not lose their way ;
We'll laugh, and leave the World behind ;
    The Gods themselves that see,
    Shall envie thee and me   [,]
And never find such joys
When they embrace a Deity.

The Beggar, a Catch.

Cast your Caps and cares away,
    This is the Beggars holliday;
At the crowning of our King
Thus we dance, and thus we sing;
    Be it peace, or be it war,
    Here at liberty we are,
    And enjoy our peace and rest,
    To the Field we are not prest,
Nor be raised in the Town
To be troubled with a Gown.

In this world behold and see,
Where's so happy a King as he?
Where's the Nation lives so free,
Or so merry as do we?
    Hang up the Officers we cry,
    And your Masters we defie;
    When the Subsidy daies encreas'd
    We are not a penny seased;
Nor will any go to law
With the Beggar for a straw:
    All which happiness, he brags
    He doth owe unto his rags.

The Scotch War.

When first the Scottish War began (& Pike,
The English man, we did trapan, with pellit
The bonny blythe and cunning Scot (like;
Had then a plot, which they did not well smell, it's
Although he could neither write nor read,
Yet our General *Lashly* cross'd the *Tweed*
With his gay gangh, of Blew-caps all,
Along we marcht with our General:
We took *New-Castle* in a trice,
But we thought it had been paradice,
They did look, all so bonny and gay,
Till we took all, their Pillage away.

Then did we streight to plundering fall (day;
Of great & small, for we were all most Valiant that
And *Jinny* in a Satten Gown, the best in the Town,
From heel to Crown was gallant and gay;
Our silks and sweets made such a smother,
Next day we knew not one another:
For *Iockie* did never so shine,
And *Iinny* was never so fine,
A geud faith a gat a ged Beaver then,
But it's beat into a blew-cap agen
By a Red-coat, that did still cry, Rag,
And a red snowt a the Deel aw the Crag.

The

The English raised an Army streight (well
With mickle state, and we did wait to face them as
Then every valiant musquet-man put fire in pan,
And we began to lace them as well;
But before the sparks were made a Cole
They did every man pay for his Pole;
Then their bought land we lent them agen,
Into *Scotland* we went with our men;
We were paid by all, both Peasant and Prince,
But I think we have soundly paid for it since,
For our Silver is wasted, Sir, all,
And our Silks hang in *Westminster* Hall.

The godly Presbyterian, that holy man,
The war began with Bishop and King,
Where we like waiters at a Feast, (thing
But not the least of all the guest, must dish up the
We did take a Covenant to pull down
The Cross, the Crosier, and the Crown,
With the Rochet the Bishop did bear,
And the Smock that his Chaplain did wear:
But now the Covenant's gone to wrack,
They say, it looks like an old Almanack,
For *Iockie* is grown out of date,
And *Ienny* is thrown out of late.

I must confess the holy firk did only work
Upon our Kirk for silver and meat,
Which made us come with aw our broods,
         Venter

Venter our bloods for aw your goods, to pilfer and
But we see what covetousness doth bring,   (cheat;
For we lost our selves when we sold our King;
And alack now and welly we cry,
Our backs mow and bellies must dye;
We fought for food, and not vain-glory,
And so there's an end of a Scottish mans story;
I curse all your Silver and Gold,
Aw the worst tale that ever was told.

The Zealous Puritan.

MY Bretheren all attend,
   And list to my relation:
This is the day[,] mark what I say,
Tends to your renovation;
Stay not among the Wicked,
Lest that with them you perish,
But let us to *New-England* go,
And the Pagan People cherish;
   Then for the truths sake come along, come along,
   Leave this place of Superstition:
   Were it not for we, that the Brethren be,
   You would sink into Perdition.

There you may teach our hymns
Without the Laws controulment:
We need not fear the Bishops there,

Nor Spiritual-Courts inroulment;
Nay, the Surplice shall not fright us,
Nor superstitious blindness;
Nor scandals rise when we disguise,
And our Sisters kiss in kindness;
    Then for the truths sake, *&c.*

For Company I fear not,
There goes my Cosin *Hannah;*
And *Ruben,* so perswades to go
My Cosin *Joyce, Susanna,*
With *Abigal* and *Faith,*
And *Ruth,* no doubt, comes after;
And *Sarah* kind, will not stay behind,
My Cosin *Constance* Daughter;
    Then for the truth, *&c*

Now *Tom Tyler* is prepared,
And the Smith as black as a coal;
Ralph Cobler too with us will go,
For he regards his soul;
And the Weaver, honest *Simon,*
With *Prudence, Iacobs* Daughter,
And *Sarah,* she, and *Barbary*
Professeth to come after;
    Then for the truth, *&c.*

When we, that are elected,
Arrive in that fair Country,

Even

Complete.

Even by our faith, as the Brethren saith,
We will not fear our entry;
The Psalms shall be our Musick,
And our time spent in expounding,
Which in our zeal we will reveal
To the brethrens joy abounding;
    Then for the truths sake, *&c.*

A Merry Song.

Come let us drink, the time invites,
    Winter and cold weather,
For to pass away long nights,
    And to keep good Wits together;
Better far than Cards or dice,
    Or *Isaacs* ball, that quaint device,
Made up of fan and feather.

Of great actions on the seas
    We will ne'er be Jealous;
Give us liquor that will please,
    And 'twill make us braver fellows
Than the bold Venetian Fleet
    When the Turks and they do meet
Within the Dardanellows.

Mahomet was no Divine,
   But a senseless Widgeon,
To forbid the use of wine
   Unto those of his religion :
Falling sickness was his shame,
   And his throne will have the same
For all his whispering pigeon.

Sack is the Princes only guard,
   If he dare but try it :
No designs were ever hard
   Where the Subjects use to ply it ;
And three Constables, at most,
   Are enough to quell an host
That so disturbs our quiet.

Vallenchyn, that famous Town,
   Stands the French mans wonder,
Water it inclos'd to drown,
   And to cut the Troops asunder;
Turain cast a helpless look,
   Whilst the crafty Spaniard took
La Ferte and his plunder.

Therefore water we disdain,
   Mankinds adversary,
Once it made the Worlds whole frame
   In the Deluge to miscarry :
Nay the enemy of joy,

Seeks

Seeks with envy to destroy,
And murder good Canary.

See the Squibs, and hear the Bells
   The fifth day of *November*,
The Preacher a sad story tells,
   And with horror doth remember,
How some dry-brain'd Traitor wrought
   Plots that might have ruine brought
On King and every member.

We that drink have no such thoughts,
   Black and void of reason,
We take care to fill our Vaults
   With good wine for every season:
And with many a chearfull cup
   We blow one another up,
And that's our only treason.

Philiday and Coridon.

IN the merry month of *May*,
   On a morn by break of day,
Forth I walk the wayes so wide,
When as *May* was in her pride.
   There I spide all alone
   Philiday and *Coridon*.

Much ado there was I wot,
He could love, but she could not,
His love he said was ever true,
Nor was mine e're false to you.
    He said he had lov'd her long,
    She said love should do no wrong.

Coridon would kiss her then,
She said maids must kiss no men ;
Till they kiss for good and all,
Then she made the shepherds call
    All the Gods to witness south,   [sooth,]
    Ne'er was lov'd a fairer youth.

Then with many a pretty Oath,
As yea, and nay, and faith and troath,
Such as silly shepherds use
When they will not love abuse.
Love that had been long deluded,
Was with Kisses sweet concluded.
    And *Philiday* with Garlands gay
    Was crown'd the Lady of the *May*.

On the Preface to Gondibert.

ROom for the best Poets heroick,
    If you'l believe two Wits and a Stoick ;
Down go the *Iliads*, down go the *Eneidos*,
All must give place to the *Gondibertiados*.

                          For

For to *Homer* and *Virgil* he has a just Pique,
Because one writ in Latin[,] the other in Greek;
Besides an old grudge (our Criticks they say so)
With *Ovid*, because his Sirname was *Naso*:
If Fiction the fame of a Poet thus raises,
What Poets are you that have writ his praises;
But we justly quarrel at this our defeat,
You give us a stomach, he gives us no meat.
A Preface to no Book, a Porch to no house:
Here is the Mountain, but where is the Mouse;
But, Oh, *America* must breed up the Brat
From whence 'twill return a *West-Indy* Rat.
For *Will* to *Virginia* is gone from among us
With thirty two slaves, to plant *Mundungus*.

The Wedding.

I'LL tell thee *Dick* where I have been,
   Where I the rarest things have seen,
     O things beyond compare!
Such sights as these cannot be found
   In any part of English ground,
     Be it at Wake or Faire.

At *Charing-Cross*, hard by the way
   Where we, thou know'st, did sell our hay,
     There is a house with staires;

Where I did see them coming down
Such folk as are not in the Town,
    Forty at least in paires.

One of them was pestilent fine,
His beard no bigger though than mine,
    Walk'd on before the rest:
Our Landlord look'd like nothing to him,
The King, God bless him, 'twould undo him
    Should he go still so drest.

At Course-a-park, without all doubt,
He should have there been taken out
    By all the maids of the Town;
Though lusty *Roger* there had been,
Or little *George* upon the Green,
    Or *Vincent* of the Crown.

But wot you what, the youth was going
To make an end of all his wooing,
    The Parson for him staid:
But by your leave, for all your haste
He did not wish so much all past,
    Perchance, as did the maid.

The maid, and thereby lies a tale,
For such a maid no Whitson-Ale
    Could ever yet produce;

                                No

No Grape, that's kindly ripe, can be
So round so plump, so soft as she,
    Nor half so full of juice.

Her fingers were so small, the ring
Would not stay on which they did bring,
    It was too wide a peck;
And to say truth, for out it must,
It lookt like a great Collar just
    About our young colts neck.

Her feet beneath her Petticoat,
Like little Mice, stole in and out,
    As If they fear'd the light:
But O she dances such a way,
No Sun upon an Easter day
    Is half so fine a sight.

He would have kist her once or twice,
But she would not, she was so nice
    She would not do't in sight;
And then she look't, as who would say,
I will do what I list to day,
    And you shall do't at night.

Her cheeks so fair a white was on,
As none darst make comparison,
    Who sees them is undon;

For streaks of red were mingled there,
Such as are on a Catharine Pear
    That side that's next the Sun.

Her mouth so small, when she doth speak,
Thou'dst swear her teeth her words do break
    That they might passage get:
But O she handles so the matter,
They come as good as ours, or better,
    And are not spoyl'd one whit.

Her lips so red, and one so thin,
Compar'd to that was next her chin.
    Some Bee had stung it newly;
But *Dick*, her eyes so grac'd her face [? guard]
I durst no more upon her Gaze
    Than on the sun in *July*.

If wishing had been any sin
The Parsons self had guilty been;
    She look'd that day so purely;
And did the Youth so oft the feat
At night, as some did in conceit,
    It would have spoyl'd him surely.

Passion, oh me how I run on,
There's that that would be thought upon,
    I trow beside the Bride:

The business of the Kitchin great,
For it is fit that men should eat,
    Nor was it there deny'd.

Just in the nick the Cook knockt thrice,
And all the Waiters in a trice
    His summons did obey;
Each serving-man with dish in hand
March't boldly up like our Train-band,
    Presented, and away.

Now hats fly off and Youths carrouse,
Healths first go round, and then the house,
    The Brides came thick and thick;
And when 'twas nam'd another health,
Perhaps he made it hers by stealth,
    And who could help it *Dick!*

O' th' sudden, up they rise and dance,
Then sit again, and sigh and glance,
    Then dance again and kiss:
Thus several waies the time did pass,
While every woman wish'd her Place,
    And every man wish'd his.

By this time all were stollen aside
To counsell and undress the Bride,
    But that he must not know;

                                      But

But it was thought he guess'd her mind,
And did not mean to stay behind
    Above an hour or so.

When in he came, *Dick*, there she lay,
Like new-faln snow, melting away,
    'Twas time, I trow, to part;
Kisses were now the only stay,
Which soon she gave, as who would say,
    God b'wy with all my heart.

But just as heavens would have, to Cross it,
In came the Bridemaids with the posset,
    The Bridegroome eat in spight:
Or had he left the women to 't,
It would have cost two hours to do 't,
    Which were too much that night.

At length the Candle's out, and now
All that they had not done they do,
    What that is, who can tell?
But I believe it was no more
Than thou and I have done before
    With *Bridget* and with *Nel*.

A Song.

How happy is the prisoner who conquers his fate
With silence, & ne'er on bad fortune complains,
But carelesly plaies with his keyes, on the grate,
And makes sweet consort with them & his chains;
He drowns care with Sack, when his heart is opprest,
And makes his heart float like a Cork in his brest.

Chor. Then since we are all slaves who Islanders be,
And our land is a large Prison enclos'd with the sea,
We'll drink off the Ocean, and set our selves free,
For man is the Worlds Epitomie.

Let tyrants wear Purple, deep dy'd in the blood
Of those they have slain, their Scepter to sway;
If our consciences be clear, and our titles be good
To the rags that hang on us, we are richer than they;
We drink up at night what we can beg or can borrow,
And sleep without plotting for more the next morrow.

Come Drawer, fill each man a pint of Canary,
This brimmer shall bid all our sences good night;
When old *Aristotle* was frolick and merry,
With the Juyce of the Grape he turn'd stagarite;
Copernicus once in a drunken fit found
By the course of his brains that the world went round.

'Tis

'Tis Sack makes our faces like Comets to shine,
And gives us a beauty beyond complexions masque ;
Diogenes fell so in love with his wine
That when 'twas all out he dwelt in the Cask :
He liv'd by the scent in that close wainscoat room,
And dying, requested the tub for his Tombe.

Though the Usurer watch o'er his bags and his house,
To keep that from robbers he rackt from his debtors ;
Each midnight cries thieves at the noise of a mouse,
Then looks if his bags are fast bound in their fetters ;
When once he's grown rich enough for a state-plot,
In one hour Buff plunders what threescore years got.

Let him never so privately muster his gold,
His Angels will there intelligence be
How close they are prest in their Canvas hold,
And long that state souldiers should set them all free ;
Let him pine and be hang'd we will merrily sing,
Who have nothing to lose, may cry, God bless the
(King.

Chor.   Then since we are all slaves who Islanders be,
And our land a large prison enclos'd with the sea ;
We'll drink off the Ocean, and set our selves free,
For man is the worlds Epitomie.

The

The Devil transformed.

I Met with the divel in the shape of a Ram,
I then over and over the sowgelders ran; [came]
I rose, and I haltred him fast by the horns,
I stabb'd him softly, as you would pick out corns,
Nay, [Baa] quoth the divel, with that out he slunk,
And left us the Carkass of a Mutton that stunk.

I chanc'd to ride forth some mile and a half,
Where I heard he did live in disguise of a Calf;
I bound him, and I gelt him ere he did any evill,
For he was at his best but a young sucking divel;
Meaw[!] yet he cry'd, and forth he did steal,
And this was sold after for excellent veal.

Some half a year after, in the shape of a Pig,
I met with the rogue, and he look'd very big,
I caught him by the leg, laid him down on a log,
Ere a man told forty twice I made him a hog;
[Owgh!] Oh, quoth the divel, and gave such a yerk,
That a Jew was converted and did eat of the Porke.

In womans attire I met him most fine,
At first sight I thought him some Angel divine:
But viewing his crab face I fell to my trade,
I made him forswear ever acting a maide;
                                        Meaw

Meaw, quoth the divel, and so ran away,
And hid him in a Fryers old weed, as they say.

I walked along, and it was my good chance
To meet with a Grey-coat that was in a trance,
I grip'd him then speedily, and I whipt off his Cods,
'Twixt his head and his breech I left little odds ;
O quoth the divil, the hurt thou hast done
Thou still wilt be curst for by many a [wo]man.

Miseries of humane Life.

THE World's a bubble, and the life of man
   Less than a span ;
In his conception wretched from his wombe,
   So to his tombe ;
Curst from the Cradle and brought up to years
   With care and fears ;
Who then to frail mortality shall trust,
Limns but in water, or but writes in dust.

Now since with sorrow man lives here opprest,
   What life is best ?
Courts are but only superficial Schools
   To dandle fools ;
The rural parts are turn'd into a den
   Of savage men ;
And where's a City from all vice so free,
But may be term'd the worst of all the three.

         Domestick

Domestic cares afflict the husbands bed,
   Or pains his head ;
Those that live single take it for a curse,
   Or do things worse ; (moan,
Some would have Children, those that have them
   Or wish them gone ;
What is it then to have, or have no wife,
But single thraldome, or a double strife.

Our own affection still at home to please
   Is a disease ;
To cross the seas to any forraign soyl
   Is dangerous toyl ;
Wars with their noise affright us, when they cease
   We are worse in peace ;
What then remains, but that we still should cry,
Not to be born, or being born to dye.

A Cambridge Droll.

THe Proctors are two and no more,
 Then hang them that makes them three :
The Taverns are but foure,
I wish they were more for me,
Chor. For three merry boyes, and three merry boyes,
And three merry boys are we.
        We'll

We'll make, if our numbers mix,
The Muses triple trine,
For two and four make six,
As all men do divine;
For two three and four makes nine.

The Myter no more shall sink,
Though *Pym* himself were there,
For that were Popery to think
That Puritans dare come there,
For catholic Sack is there.

The Dolphins were numbered never,
As all men plainly see   [;]
For I am sure for ever
The Dolphin shall swim free;
And that's enough for me.

The three tuns are forgot
When few do go to see;
But there's a tun behind
For him, for thee, and for me,
To make us frolick and free.

But if the Doctors droop
In whom our number dies,
As the Arches put us in hope
They are not like to rise,
And wine shall make us wise.

The

The wise men they were seven,
I wish they were more for me,
The Muses they were nine,
The Worthies three times three,
And three merry boyes, and three merry boyes,
And three merry boyes are we.

Resolved not to part.

Man. MY Mistris, whom in heart I loved long,
      Her unkind words, alas, have done me
Loe where she comes, I mean her love to try : (wrong,
Oh stay a While and hear her kind reply.

My faithful friend, whom I esteem'd so deer,
Rejected is, and gone I know not where;
Forlorn I live, away all joyes are fled,
I lost my Love, alas, my heart is dead.

I will go sail into some Forraign Land,
To *France* or *Flanders* I'll go out of hand :
When I come there, to strangers I'll complain,
And say, my Love hath me unkindly slain.

Wo. If into *France* or *Flanders* you do go,
I'll not stay here, but follow thee also ;
If false report abroad there thou dost tell,
I'll check thee for't, and say, thou didst not well.

Ma. Else to the Wilderness full fast I'll high,
Among wild beasts there I mean to dye;
Where Wolves, and Bears and other Creatures,
The Elephant and Unicorn with their odd features.

Wo. O stay at home, sweet heart, and go not there,
For those wild beasts will thee in pieces tear;
If that I should behold them suck thy blood   (good.
Thou shouldst have mine, sweet heart, to do thee

Ma. I would I were all in the raging seas,
Or in some Bark to go even where it please,
Where comfort none, alas, is to be found,
And every hour in danger to be drown'd.

Ma. I would I were all in the lofty skies,
So far from ground as any Eagle flies,
For to fall down to ease me of my pain,
That I might die, but die to live again.

Wo. If in the lofty sky thou should'st remain,
I'd soar so high, thy love for to obtain:
And like the Eagle keep thee from all harms,
That thou shouldst fall in no place but mine arms.

Ma. Thus many wishes have I wisht in vain,
But none of these can ease me of my pain;
This marshall ponyard that shall end all grief,
Shall ease my heart that findeth no relief.

                                        Wo.

Wo. O stay at home, good heart, let it not die,
Thy life I love, thy death I do defie:
Come live in love, and so thou'lt banish pain,
Take a good heart, and I will love again.

Ma. Go lusty lads, go you the Musick fetch,
Your nimble legs and joynts you shall out stretch;
While others dance and caper in the streets,
We'll dance at home the shaking of the sheets.

The Power of Money.

TIS not the silver nor Gold for it self,
   That makes men adore it, but 'tis for its power:
For no man does doat upon pelf because pelf,
But all Court the Lady in hope of her dower:
The wonders that now in our daies we behold;
Done by the irresistible power of gold,
Our Zeal, and our Love, and Allegiance do hold.

                                   (Crowns;
This purchaseth Kingdoms, Kings, Scepters, and
Wins battels, and conquers the Conquerors bold;
Takes Bulwarks, and Castles, and Cities, & Towns,
And our prime Laws are writ in letters of Gold;
Tis this that our Parliament calls and creates,
Turns Kings into keepers, and Kingdoms to States,
And peopledoms these into highdomes translates.

This made our black Synod to sit still so long,
To make themselves rich, by making us poor;
This made our bold Army, so daring and strong,
And made them turn them, like Geese out of door;
'Twas this made our Covenant-makers to make it,
And this made our Priests for to make us to take it,
And this made both Makers and Takers forsake it.
(tees and 'Strators,
'Twas this spawn'd the dunghil Crew of Commit-
Who live by picking the crockadile Parliaments gums[;]
This first made, & then prospered rebels & traitors,
And made gentry of those that were the nations scums[;]
This herald gives arms not for merit, but store [,]
And gives coats to those that did sell coats before,
If their pockets be but lin'd well with argent & ore.

This, plots can devise, and discover what they are;
This, makes the great Fellons the lesser condemn;
This, sets those on the Bench, that should stand at
(the Bar,
Who judge such, as by right ought to execute them;
Gives the boysterous Clown his insufferable pride,
Makes beggars, and fools, and Usurpers to ride,
Whiles ruin'd Propriators run by their side.

Stamp either the Arms of the ——— or the ———
St. *George* or the Breeches, ——— or *O. P.*
The Cross or the Fiddle, 'tis all the same thing;
This, this is the Queen whosoe'er the King be;
This

This, lines our Religion, builds Doctrine and Truth,
With zeale and the Spirit the factious endueth,
To club with Saint *Catharine*, or sweet sister *Ruth*.

          (plead
'Tis money makes Lawyers give judgment, or
On this side, or that side, on both sides or neither;
This makes young men Clerks that can scarce write
          (or read,
And spawns arbitrary orders as various as the
          (weather;
This makes your blew Lectures pray preach & prate,
Without reason or sence against Church, King, or
          (State,
To shrew the thin lining of his twice-covered pate.

          (Esquires
'Tis money makes Earls, Lords, Knights, and
Without breeding, descent, wit, learning or merit;
This makes ropers, & ale-drapers, Sheriffs of shires,
Whose trade is not so low, nor so base as their spirit;
This Justices makes, and no wise one we know,
Furr'd Aldermen too, and Maiors also; (go.
This makes the old wife trot, and makes the mare to

This makes your blew aprons right worshipfull;
And for this we stand bare, and before them do fall;
They leave their young heirs well fleec'd with wooll
Whom we must call Squires, and they pay all;
Who with beggarly souls, though their bodies be
          (gawdy,
          Court

Court the pale chamber-maid, and nick-name her a
(Lady,
And for want of good wit they do swear and talk
(bawdy.
This, marriage makes, 'tis the Center of love,
It draws on the man, and it pricks up the woman,
Birth, Virtue, and parts no affection can move,
Whilst this makes a Lord stoop to the Brat of a
(Broom man ;
This gives virtue and beauty to the Lasses that you
Makes women of all sorts and ages to do ;   (wooe,
'Tis the soul of the world, and the worldling too.

This procures us whores, hawks, hounds, and hares ;
'Tis this keeps your groom and your groom keeps
(your gelding ;
This built Citizens wives as well as their wares :
And this makes your coy Lady so coming & yielding;
This buys us good Sack, which revives like the
(spring ;
'Tis this your Poetical fancies do bring ;
And this makes you as merry as we that do sing.

On Gondibert.

I

After so many sad mishaps,
   Of drinking, riming, and of claps,
I pity most thy sad relaps.

That

2

That having past the souldiers pains,
The States-mens Arts, the sea-mens gains,
With *Gondibert*, to break thy brains.

3.

And so incessantly to ply it,
To sacrifice thy sleep, thy diet,
Thy business; and what's more our quiet.

4.

And all this stir to make a story,
Not much superior to *John Dory*,
Which thus in brief I lay before ye.

5

All in the land of *Lombardie*,
A Wight there was of Knights degree,
Sir *Gondibert* ycleap'd was he.

6

This *Gondibert* (as saies our Author)
Got the good will of the Kings daughter,
A shame, it seems, the divel ought her.

7.

So thus succeeded his Disaster,
Being sure of the Daughter of his Master,
He chang'd his Princes for a Playster.

8.

Of person he was not ungracious,
Grave in debate, in Fight audacious;
But in his Ale most pervicacious.

9
And this was cause of his sad Fate,
For in a Drunken-street Debate
One night he got a broken Pate.

10.
Then being cur'd, he would not tarry,
But needs this simpling girle would marry
Of *Astragon* the Apothecary.

11.
To make the thing yet more Romancie,
Both wise and rich you may him fancie;
Yet he in both came short of *Plancy*.

12.
And for the Damsel, he did wooe so,
To say the truth she was but so-so,
Not much unlike her of *Toboso*.

13
Her beauty, though 'twas not exceeding,
Yet what in Face and shape was needing,
She made it up in Parts and Breeding.

14.
Though all the Science she was rich in
Both of the Dairy and the Kitchin:
Yet she had knowledge more bewitching.

15.
For she had learn'd her Fathers skill,
Both of the Alimbick and the Still,
The Purge, the Potion, and the Pill.

But

16

But her Chief Talent was a Glister,
And such a hand to administer,
As on the Breech hath made no blister,

17.

So well she handled *Gondbert,*
That though she did not hurt that part,
She made a blister on his heart.

18

Into the Garden of her Father:
Garden, said I; or Back-side rather,
One night she went a Rose to gather.

19

The Knight he was not far behind,
Full soon he had her in the wind;
(For Love can smell, though he be blind.)

20.

Her business she had finish'd scarcely,
When on a gentle bed of parsly   { *Desunt*
Full fair and soft he made her Arse-ly. { *Cætera.*

Canary Crowned.   *Jordan?*

Come let's purge our brains from hops & grains
    That do smell of Anarchy;
Let's chuse a King from whose veins may spring
    A sparkling Progeny;

It

It ill befits true wine-bred wits,
    Whose flames are bright and clear,
To bind their hands in dray-mens bands,
    When they might be clear;
Why should we droop or basely stoop
    To popular Ale or Beer?

Who shall be King is now the thing
    For which we all are met:
Clarret is a Prince that hath been long since
    In the royal number set:
His face is spread with warlike red,
    And so he loves to see men;
If he bears sway, his Subjects they
    Shall be as good as freemen;
Yet here's the plot, almost forgot,
    He is too much burnt by women.

By the river Rhine is a valiant wine
    That can all our veins replenish,
Let us then consent to the government
    Of the royal rule of Rhennish?
This German wine will warm the Chine,
    And frisk in every vein;
'Twill make the bride forget to chide,
    And call him to't again:
Yet that's not all, he is much to small
    To be our Soveraign.

Why then let's think of another drink,
      And with votes advance it high:
Let's all proclaim good Canaries name,
      Heaven bless his Majesty;
He's a King in every thing,
      Whose nature doth renounce all ill:
He can make us skip, and nimbly trip
      From the sealing to the groundsil,
Especially, when Poets be
      Lords of the Privy Council.

But a Vintner he shall his Taster be,
      There's no man shall him let;
And a Drawer, that have a good pallat
      Shall be made Squire of the Gimlet;
The Bar-boyes shall be pages all,
      A Tavern well prepar'd,
In jovial sort shall be the Court
      Where nothing shall be spar'd;
Wine-Porters shall with shoulders tall
      Be Yeomen of the Guard.

If a Cooper we with a red-nose see
      In any part of the Town,
That Cooper shall, with Adds royal,
      Be Keeper of the Crown,
Young Wits that wash away their Cash
      In Wine and Recreation,

Who hate dull Beer are welcome here
    To give their approbation :
So are all you that will allow
    Canaries Coronation.

Contentment.

WHat though the ill times do run cross to our
    And fortune still frown upon us,   (will,
Our hearts are our own, and shall be so still,
A fig for the plagues they lay on us ;
Let us take t'other Cup to chear our hearts up,
And let it be Purest Canary ;
We'll ne'er shrink nor care at the Crosses we bear,
Let them plague us untill they be weary.

What though we are made both beggars & slaves ;
Let's endure it, and stoutly drink on't,
'Tis our comfort we suffer 'cause we won't be knaves,
Redemption will come ere we think on't ;
We must flatter and fear those that over us are,
And make them believe that we love them,
When their tyranny is past, we can serve them at last,
As they served those have been above them.

Let the Levite go preach for the Goose or the Pig,
To drink Wine at Christmas or Easter :
The doctor may labour our lives to new trig,
                                  And

And make Nature fast while we feast her;
The Lawyer may bawl out his Lungs and his Gall
For Plaintiff, and for the Defendant,
At his Book the Scholar lie, while with *Plato* he die
With an ugly hard word at the end on't.

Then here's to the man that delights in *sol fa*,
For Sack is his only Rozin,
A load of hey ho is not worth a ha ha,
He's a man for my money that draws in;
Then a pin for the muck, and a pin for ill luck,
'Tis better be blithe and frolick,
Than sigh out our breath, and invite our own death
By the Gout, or the Stone, or the Collick.

The Power of the Sword.

LAY by your pleading, Law lies a bleeding,
Burn all your Studies down, & throw away your
Small power the Word has, & can afford us (reading;
Not halfe so many Priviledges as the Sword has:
It fosters your masters, it plaisters disasters,
And makes your servants, quickly greater than their
It venters, it enters, it circles, it centers,   (Masters;
And makes a Prentice free in spight of his Indentures.

This takes off tall things, and sets up small things,
This masters Money, though Money masters all
                                        (things
                                        'Tis

'Tis not in season to talk of Reason,
Or call it legal, when the Sword will have it treason;
It conquers the Crown too, the Furs & the Gown too;
This set up a Presbyter, and this pull'd him down too;
This subtill Deceiver turn'd Bonnet to Beaver,
Down drops a Bishop, and up starts a Weaver.

This fits a lay-man to preach and to pray man,
'Tis this can make a Lord of him that was a dray-
Forth from the dull pit of Follies full pit; (man,
This brought an Hebrew Ironmonger to the Pulpit,
Such pittiful things be more happier then Kings be;
This got the Herauldry of Thimblebee & Slingsbee;
No Gospel can guide it, no Law can decide it,
In Church or State untill the Sword hath sanctifi'd
(it.
Down goes the Law-tricks, for from that Matrix
Sprung holy *Hewsons* power, and tumbled down St.
The sword prevails so highly in *Wales* too, (*Patricks*;
Shinkin ap Powel cries, and swears Cuts-plutter-nails;
In *Scotland* this Waster did make such disaster, (too;
They sent their money back for which they sold their
Master;
It batter'd so their *Dunkirk*, and did so the *Don* firke
That he is fled, and swears, the devil is in *Dunkirke*.

He that can tower him o'er him that is lower,
Would be but thought a fool to put away his power;
Take

Take books and rent 'um, who would invent 'um,
When as the Sword replies, *negatur argumentum?*
Your grand Colledge Butlers must stoop to your
There's not a Library living like the cutlers ; (sutlers,
The bloud that is spilt, sir, hath gaind all the guilt, sir,
Thus have you seen me run the Sword up to the
                                                    (hilts Sir.

A Medly of Nations.

The Scots.

I Am a bonny *Scot*, Sir, my name is *mickle John*,
  'Twas I was in the Plot, Sir, when first the war
                                                    (begun :
I left the Court one thousand six hundred forty one,
But since the flight at *Woster*-fight we all are undone ;
I serv'd my Lord & Master, when as he lig'd at home,
[But since by a sad disaster, he receiv'd his doom,]
Our Cause did shrink, God's bread, I think
        The Deel's got in his room :
He no man fears ; but stamps and stares
        Through all Christendom.
I have travell'd mickle ground,
Since I came from *Worcester* Pound,
I have gang'd a gallant round
        Through all our neighbouring Nations,
And what their opinions are
Unto you I shall declare,
                                                        Of

Of the Scotch and English War,
    And their approbations;
We were beaten Tag and Rag,
    Foot and Leg, Wem and Crag;
Hark, I hear the Dutchmen brag,
    And begin to bluster.

The Dutch.

GOds Sacrament, shall *Hogen mogen* States
    Strike down their Topsailes unto puny powers;
Ten hundred tun of divels damn the fates
  If all their ships and goods do not prove ours;
Since that bloudy wounds delight them,
Tantara rara let the Trumpet sound,
Let *Vantrump* go out and fight them,
    Eldest states should first be crown'd   [;]
    English *Schellums* fight not on Gods side.
But alas, they have given our Flemish Boats such a
That we shall be forced to retreat;   (broad-side,
    See the French-man cometh in compleat.

The French.

BEgar *Monsieur* 'Tis much in vain
    For *Dutchland, France,* or *Spain*
      To cross the *English* Nation;
They are now grown so strong,
The divel ere it be long
                      Must

Must learn the English Tongue;
   'Tis better that we should combine,
   And sell them wine,
   And learn of them to make a Lady fine;
We'll learn of them to trip and mince,
   To kick and wince.
For by the Sword we never shall convince,
Since every Brewer there can beat a Prince.

The Spaniard.

WHat are the English so quarrelsome grown,
   That they cannot of late let their Neigh-
And shall a great and a Catholick King (bours alone?
Let his Scepter be controul'd by a Sword or a Sling?
   Or, shall *Austria* endure
   Such affronts for to be?
   No, we'll tumble down their power,
   As you shall *Senior* see.

The Welch.

TAffie was once a Cod-a-mighty of *Wales*,
   But her Cosin *O. P.* was a Greature,
Come into her Country, Cods-splutter-anails,
  Her take her welch-hook and her beat her;
Her eat up her Sheese, Turkey and Geese,
  Her Pig and her Capon did die for't,

Ap *Robert*, ap *Evan*, ap *Morgan*, ap *Stephen*,
  But *Shinkin* and *Powel* did flie for't.

The Irish.

O Hone, O Hone, poor *Irish Shon*
    Must howl and cry :
Saint *Patrick* help thy Country-man,
  Or faith and troth we dye ;
The English still doth us pursue,
  And we are forc'd to flee :
Saint *Patrick*, help[!] we have no Saint but thee,
Let's cry no longer, *O hone, a Cram a Cree.*

The English.

A Crown, a Crown, make room.
    The English man doth come,
Whose Valour is taller than all *Christendom ;*
The *Spanish, French,* and *Dutch, Scots, Welch* and
                                    (*Irish* grutch,
We fear not, we care not, for we can deal with such ;
  When you did begin in a Civil War to waste,
    Ye thought that our Tillage your Pillage should be
                                        (at last ;
And when that we could not agree, you did think
                                        (to share our fall,
But ye do find it worse, ne'er stir : for we shall noose
                                        (ye all.

A quarrel betwixt Tower-Hill and Tyburne.

I 'LL tell you a Story that never was told,
   A tale that hath both head and heel,
And though by no Recorder inroll'd,
   I know you will find it as true as steel.

When General *Monck* was come to the Town,
   A little time after the Rump had the rout,
When Royalty rose, and Rebellion fell down,
   They say, that Tower-hill and Tyburn fell out.

Quoth terrible Tyburn to lofty tower-hill,
   Thy longed-for days are come at last,
And now thou wilt dayly thy belly fulfill
   With King-killers bloud whilst I must fast.

The High Court of Justice will come to the Bar,
   There to be cooked and dressed for thee,
Whilst I, that live out of Town so far,
   Must only be fed by Fellony.

If Treason be counted the foulest act,
   And a dying be a Traitors due,
Then why should you all the glory exact?
   You know, they are fitter for me than you.

To speak the plain truth, I have groan'd for them
   For when they had routed the Royal Root, (long,
And done the Kingdom so much wrong,
   I knew at last they would come to't.

When *Tychburne* sate upon the Bench,
   Twirling his Chain in high degree,
With a beardless Chin, like a Withered Wench,
   Thought I, the Bar is fitter for thee.

But then, with stately composed face,
   Tower-hill to Tyburne made reply
Do not complain, in such a case
   Thou shalt have thy share as well as I.

There are a sort of Mongrils, which
   My Lordly Scaffold will disgrace :
I know *Hugh Peters* his fingers itch
   To make a Pulpit of the place.

But take him Tyburne, he is thine own,
   Divide his quarters with thy knife,
Who did pollute with flesh and Bone
   The quarters of the Butchers wife.

The next among these Petticoat-Peers
   Is *Harry Martin*, take him thither,
But he hath been addle so many years,
   That I fear he will hardly hang together.

                                          There's

There's *Hacker*, zealous *Tom Harrison* too,
   That boldly defends the bloudy deed,
He practiseth what the Jesuites do,
   To murder his King, as a part of his Creed.

There's single-ey'd *Hewson* the Cobler of Fate,
   Translated into Buff and Feather,
But bootless are all his seams of State
   When the soul is ript from the upper-leather.

Is this prophane mechanical blood
   For me that have been dignifi'd
With Loyal *Laud* and *Straffords* blood,
   And holy *Hewet*, who lately dy'd.

Do thou contrive with deadly *Dun*
   To send them to the River of *Stix*,
Tis Pitty, since those Saints are gone ;
   That Martyrs and Murtherers bloud should mix.

Then do not fear me that I will
   Deprive thee of that fatall Day :
Tis fit those that their King did kill
   Should hang up in the Kings high-way.

My Priviledge, though I know it is large,
   Into thy hand I freely give it,
For there is *Cook*, that read the Kings charge,
   Is only fit for the divels tribute.

Then taunting Tyburn, in great scorn,
  Did make Tower-hill this rude reply:
So much ranke bloud my stomack will turn,
  And thou shalt be sick as well as I.

These Traytors made those Martyrs bleed
  Upon the Block, that thou dost bear,
And there it is fit they should dye for the deed;
  But Tower-hill cryed, they shall not come there.

With that grim Tyburn began to fret,
  And Tower-hill did look very grim:
And sure as a club they both would have met,
  But that the City did step between.

The New Exchange.

I'll go no more to the Old Exchange,
  There's no good Ware at all,
But I will go to the New Exchange,
  Called *Haberdashers Hall:*
For there are choice of Knacks and Toyes
  The fancy for to please,
For men and maids, for Girls and boyes,
  And a Trap for Lice and Fleas;
There you may buy a Holland Smock
  That's made without a gore,
You need not stoop to take it up,
  For it is button'd down before.

                                    The

The finest Fashions that are us'd,
   And Powders that excell,
And all the best and sweet perfumes
   To rarifie the smell;
The curious rich Vermilion Paint
   That maids of beauty hold,
And Alabaster driven snow
   Is there to be bought and sold.
And there, &c.

The broad-brim'd Beaver which is made
   Most curious, soft, and fine,
Will be a shadow in the face
   When as the Sun doth shine;
Fine Feathers and Ribbons you may have
   For to wear about the Crown;
Black Patches for the face also,
   O, the best in all the Town;
For there, &c.

There is curious powder'd Periwigs,
   And new-cut fashion'd gloves,
With Bodkins, Thimbles, and gold Rings,
   As men do give unto their Loves;
There's curious Books of Complements,
   And other fashions strange,
That never a place in all the Land
   Is like the New Exchange,
For there, &c.

Great Flanders-Laces, large and white,
   Are common to be sold,
And Silver Laces, very broad,
   And some that's made of Gold;
Both Knives and Sizers, sharp and keen,
   And Kerchies very fair,
Within the Change are dayly sold,
   For pretty maids to wear;
There you, &c.

Fine Silken Masks, and new French hoods,
   To shrowd the foulest face,
And every thing that costly is,
   Is present in this place;
There's Spanish Needles, Points, and Pins,
   And curious balls of Snow,
That doth perfume the stinking breath,
   And makes them wholsome too;
And there, &c.

There's precious Oyles to cleanse the teeth,
   And Purges for the Brain,
And Antidotes to make the Nose
   Both safe and sound again;
All precious Flowers may be had,
   And rich Perfumed Spice
To make your houses all
   To smell like Paradice;
And there, &c.

                              For

For one that hath a fluent tongue
    You may have medi[ci]nes good ;
And there is searching Physick too,
    To purge corrupted blood ;
You there may purifie the skin,
    And cure the tickling itch,
For he is the best esteem'd of all
    That is both free and rich ;
And there, &c.

Besides these fashions, strange and true,
    There's other things most rare.
Which are the witty, pretty maids
    All bound as Servants there :
Whose heavenly look invites the eyes
    Of gallant Gentlemen,
To buy some curious Knack or Toy,
    And then they'll come agen ;
And there, &c.

The bravest Lords and Ladies all
    Do thither much resort,
And buy the fashions that are us'd,
    And daily worn at Court ;
For Private profit, divers times,
    Some upstart Gentlemen walk,
And take new fashions up on trust,
    And nothing pay but Chalk ;
And there, &c.

         Let

Let me invite those that intend
   To follow fashions strange,
With speed to go to *Londons* pride,
   Now called the Exchange;
Where choice and store of things most rare
   For money may be had,
Besides a gallant bonny Lass
   To serve a lively Lad;
There you may have a Holland Smock
   That's made without a gore,
You need not stoop to take it up,
   For 'tis button'd down before.

A Medley.

LEt's call, and drink the Cellar dry,
   Here's nothing sober underneath the sky,
The greatest Kingdoms in confusion lye:
Since all the world grows mad, why may not I?

My fathers dead, and I am free,
He left no Children in the World, but me,
The divel drank him down with Usury,
And I'll repine in Liberality.

When first the English War began
He was, Sir Reverence, a Parliament man,
And gain'd his wealth by Sequestration,
                        Till

Till *Oliver* begun
To come with Sword in hand, & put him to the run.

Then Royallists, since you are undone
So by the Father, come home to the Son,
Whom Wine and Musick now do wait upon,
　　　We'll tipple away a Tun,
And drink our Woes away, Cavaliers come on, come
　　　　　　　　　　　　　　　　　　(on.

Heres a health to him that may
Do a trick that shall advance us all,
　　　And beget a merry Jovial day.

Fill another boule to he
That hath drank by stealth
　　　His Landlords health
If his Spirit and his Tongue agree.

The Land shall Celebrate his Fame,
All the World imbalm his name,
No Royal Right, Good Fellow,
But will Sackifie the same;
The Bells all merrily shall ring,
All the Town shall dance and sing,
More delight than I can tell ye,
When we see this Royal Spring
We'll have Ladies by the belly,
And a snatch at t' other thing.
　　　　　　　　　　　Wee's

Wee's be bonny and jolly,
Quaff, Carrouse, and Reel :
We'll play with *Peggy* and *Molly*,
Dance, and kiss, and Feel ;
Wee's put up the Bagpipe and Organ,
And make the Welch Harp to play,   (day ;
Till *Mauris* ap *Shinkin* ap *Morgan* frisk on St. *Taffie's*
Hold out *Ginny*, Piper come play us a spring,
All you that have Musick may tipple, dance, and sing.

Tet [Let] the French *Monsieur* come and swear,
      Intreut *Monsieur*,   [*Entrait*]
Dis is de ting ve long to hear so many year ;
Dancing will be lookt upon ;
Begar his dancing days be done
When de *Flower-de-luce* grows
With de English Crown and Rose ;
Dat's very good, as we suppose,
De French can live without a Nose.

A cup of old Stingo.

THere's a lusty liquor which
    Good fellows use to take,
It is distill'd with Nard most rich,
    And water of the Lake ;
Of Hop a little quantity,

                        And

And Barm to it they bring too.
Being barrell'd up, they call it a cup
   Of dainty good old Stingo.

'Twill make a man Indentures make,
   'Twill make a fool seem wise,
'Twill make a Puritan sociate,
   And leave to be precize:
;Twill make him dance about a Cross,
   And eke run the Ring too,
Or any thing that seemeth gross,
   Such vertue hath old Stingo.

'Twill make a Constable oversee
   Sometimes to serve a warrant,
'Twill make a Baylif lose his Fee,
   Though he be a Knave-Arrant;
'Twill make a Sumner, though that he
   Unto the bawd men brings too,
Sometimes forget to take his Fee,
   If his head be lin'd with Stingo.

'Twill make a Parson not to flinch,
   Though he seem wondrous holy,
But for to kiss a pretty Wench,
   And think it is no follie;
'Twill make him learn for to decline
   The Verb that's called *Mingo*,

                            'Twill

'Twill make his Nose like Copper shine,
  If his head be lin'd with stingo.

'Twill make a Weaver break his yarn,
  That works with right and left foot,
But he hath a trick to save himself,
  He'll say, there wanteth woofe to't;
'Twill make a Taylor break his thread,
  And eke his Thimble ring too,
'Twill make him not to care for bread
  If his head be lin'd with stingo.

'Twill make a Baker quite forget
  That ever corn was cheap,
'Twill make a Butcher have a fit
  Sometimes to dance and leap;
'Twill make a Miller keep his Room,
  A health for to begin too,
'Twill make him shew his golden thumb,
  If his head be lin'd with stingo.

'Twill make an Hostis free of heart,
  And leave her measures pinching,
'Twill make an Host with liquor part,
  And bid him hang all flinching;
It's so belov'd, I dare protest,
  Men cannot live without it,
And where they find there is the best,
  The Most will flock about it.

         And

And finally, the beggar poor,
  That walks till he be weary,
Craving along from door to door
  With *pre commiserere:*
If he do chance to catch a touch,
  Although his cloaths be thin too,
Though he be lame he'll prove his Crutch,
  If his head be lin'd with Stingo.

Now to conclude, here is a health
  Unto the Lad that spendeth,
Let every man drink off his Can,
  And so my Ditty endeth;
I willing am my friend to pledge,
  For he will meet me one day;
Let's drink the Barrel to the dregs,
  For the Mault-man comes a Munday.

Of the Nose.

THree merry Lads met at the Rose
  To speak in the praises of the Nose:
The Nose that stands in the middle place
  Sets out the beauty of the Face,
The Nose with which we have begun
  Will serve to make our verses run:
Invention often barren grows,
Yet still there's matter in the Nose.

The

The Nose his end's so high a prize
　　That men prefer't before their eyes,
And no man counts him for his friend
　　That boldly takes his Nose by the end:
The Nose that like *Uripus* flowes,
　　The Sea that did the wiseman pose,
　　　Invention often, &c.

The Nose is of as many kinds
　　As Mariners can reckon winds;
The long, the short, the Nose displayd,
　　The great Nose, which did fright the maid;
The Nose through which the Brother-hood,
　　Do parly for their Sisters good,
　　　Invention often, &c.

The flat, the sharp, the *Roman Snowt*,
　　The Hawkes Nose circled round about,
The Crooked Nose that stands awry,
　　The Ruby Nose of Scarlet dye,
The *brazen* Nose without a Face
　　That doth the *Learned Colledge* grace,
　　　Invention often, &c.

The long Nose when the teeth appear
　　Shews what's a Clock if day be clear;
The broad Nose stands in a Bucklers place,
　　And takes the blows for all the face;

The Nose being plain without a Ridge,
   Will serve sometimes to make a Bridge.
      Invention often, &c.

The short Nose is the Lovers bliss,
   Because it hinders not a kiss;
The toteing Nose, O monstrous thing!
   That's he that did the bottle bring,
And he that brought the bottle hither
   Will drink (O monstrous!) out of measure.
      Invention often, &c.

The Firie Nose in Lanthorn stead
   May light his Master home to bed,
And whosoever this Treasure owes
   Grows poor in purse though rich in Nose:
The *Brazen Nose* that's o'er the gate
   Maintains full many a *Latin Pate.*
      Invention often, &c.

If any Nose take this in snuff,
   And think it more than enough;
We answer them, we did not fear,
   Nor think such Noses had been here:
But if there be, we need not care,
   A nose of Wax our Statutes are.
      Invention now is barren grown,
      The Matter's out, the Nose is blown.

The Angler.

OF all the recreations which
   Attend to humane Nature,
There's nothing soars so high a pitch
   Or is of such a stature,
As is the subtil *Anglers* life
   In all mens approbation,
For Anglers tricks do daily mix
   With every Corporation,
When *Eve* and *Adam* liv'd in Love
   And had no cause of Jangling,
The Divel did the Waters move,
   The Serpent went to Angling:
He baits his hook with god-like look,
   Thought he, this will intangle her,
The woman chops, and down she drops;
   The Divel was first an Angler.

Physicians, Lawyers, and *Divines*
   Are most Ingenious Janglers,
And he that tries shall find in fine
   That all of them are Anglers;
Whilst grave *Divines* do fish for souls,
   Physicians (like Cormugeons)
Do bait with health, to fish for wealth,
   And *Lawyers* fish for Gudgeons.

A *Politician* too is one
    Concern'd in Piscatory,
He writes, he fights, unites and slights
    To purchase wealth and glory;
His Plummet sounds the Kingdoms bounds
    To make the Fishes nibble,
His Ground-bait is a past of lies
    And he blinds them with th' Bible.

Upon the Exchange 'twixt twelve and one
    Meets many a neat Intangler,
'Mongst *Merchant-men* not one in ten
    But is a cunning Angler:
For like the Fishes in the Brook
    Brother doth swallow Brother,
A Golden-bait hangs at the Hook,
    And they fish for one another.

A *Shop-keeper* I next Prefer
    A formal man in black Sir,
He throws his Angle every where,
    And cryes, what is't you lack Sir,
Fine Silks or Stuffs or Hoods or Muffs?
    But if a *Courtier* prove the Intangler,
My Citizen must look to't then,
    Or the Fish will catch the Angler.

A Lover is an Angler too,
    And baits his Hooks with kisses,

He plaies, he toyes, he fain would do,
   But often times he misses;
He gives her Rings and such fine things
   A Fan and Muff and Night-hood:
But if you cheat a City pate,
   You must bait your hook with Knight-hood.

There is no Angler like a Wench
   Stark-naked in the water,
She'l make you leave both Trout and Tench
   And throw your self in after ;
Your Hook and Line she will confine,
   Then tangled is the intangler,
And this I fear hath spoyl'd the ware
   Of many a Jovial Angler.

But if you'l Trowl for a *Scriv'ners* soul
   Cast in a rich young Gallant,
To take a *Courtier* by the pole,
   Though in a Golden Tallent :
But yet I fear the draught will ne'er
   Compound for half the charge an't,
But if you'l catch the Devil at a snatch
   You must bait him with a *Sergeant*.

Thus have I made my Anglers Trade
   To stand above defiance,
For like the Mathematick Art,
   It runs through every Science :

If with my Angling Song I can
  To Mirth and pleasure seize you,
I'le bait my hook with Wit again,
  And Angle still to please you.

Of the two Amorous Swains.

TOM and *Will* were Shepherds Swains
  Who lov'd and lived together,
Till fair *Pastora* grac'd the Plains,
  Alas! why came she thither:
Tom and *Will* fed several Flocks;
  Yet felt both one desire;
Pastora's Eyes and comely Locks
  Set both their hearts on fire.

Tom came of a gentle race
  By Father and by Mother,
Will was noble, but alass
  He was a younger Brother!
Tom was toy-some, *Will* was sad,
  No Hunts-man nor no Fowler,
Tom was held the properer Lad,
  But *Will* the better Bowler.

Tom would drink her health and swear
  The Nation could not want her,
Will would take her by the Eare
  And with his Voice enchant her:

Tom kept alwaies in her sight
   And ne'er forgot his duty,
Will was witty and would write
   Sweet Sonnets on her Beauty.

Yet which of them she loved best,
   Or whether she lov'd either;
'Twas thought they found it to their cost
   That she indeed lov'd neither:
Yet she was so sweet a she
   So pleasing in behaviour,
That *Tom* thought he, and *Will* thought he
   Was chiefest in her favour.

Pastora was a lovely Lass
   And of a comely feature,
Divinely good and fair she was,
   And kind to every Creature:
Of favour she was provident:
   And yet not over-sparing,
She gave no loose encouragment,
   Yet kept men from despairing.

When tatling fame had made report
   Of fair *Pastora's* beauty,
Pastora's sent for to the Court,
   For to perform her duty;
And to the Court *Pastora's* gone,
   It were no Court without her,

                                       The

The Queen of all her Train had none
　　Was half so fair about her.

Tom hung his Dog, and flung away
　　His Sheep hook, and his Wallet;
Will broke his Pipes, and Curst the day
　　That ere he made a Ballet;
Their Nine-pins and their bowls they brake,
　　Their Tunes were turn'd to Tears;
'Tis time for me an end to make,
　　Let them go shake their Ears.

Sweet rest in the Grave.

Wake all you dead[,] what Ho[!] what Ho[!]
　　How soundly they sleep whose Pillows lie low;
They mind not your lovers who walk above
On the decks of the world in storms of Love,
　　No whisper now, no Glance can pass
　　Through wick[et]s or through panes of Glass,
For our Windows and Doores are shut and Barr'd [;]
Lie close in the Church and in the Churchyard,
　　In every grave, make room, make room,
The world's at an end, and we come, we come.
The State is now, Loves foe, Loves foe,
Has seiz'd on his Arms, his Quiver and Bowe,
Has pinion'd his Wings, and fetter'd his feet,
Because he made way for Lovers to meet;

But oh sad chance, his Judge was old;
Hearts cruel grow, when blood grows cold [:]
No man being young, his Process would draw,
Oh Heavens that Love should be subject to Law,
Lovers go wooe the dead the dead!
Lie two in a grave, and to bed, to bed.

The Production of the Female Kind.

THere is a certain idle kind of Creature,
By a foolish name, we call a woman;
A pox upon this little old whore Nature;
That e're she brought this Monster to undo man;
Many have wondred how it came to pass,
But mark, and I will tell you how it was:

When first she brought forth man, her son and heir,
The Gods came all one day to gossip with her,
Her husband, *Lenus,* proud to see them there,
Drank healths apace to bid them welcome thither,
Till drunk to bed he went, and in the fit
He got the second child, this female Chit.

The Privy Council of the Heavens and Planets,
Whose wisdom governs all Affairs on Earth,
Held many consultations in their Senates
What should become of this prodigious Birth,

At length agreed to give these strange formallities
As many strange and correspondent quallities.

Saturn, gave sullenness; *Jove*, soveraignity;
Mars, sudden wrath, and unappeased hate;
Sol, a garish look, and a wanton eye;
Venus, desires and Lusts insatieties;   [? insatiate;]
Mercury, craft, and deep dissembling gave her;
Luna, inconstant thoughts, still apt to waver.

The Bow-*Goose.*

THe best of Poets write of Frogs,
   Some of *Ulysses* charmed Hogs,
And some of Flies, and some of Dogs
In former Ages told :
Some of the silver Swan in Prose,
Though mine be not a Swan, what though?
It was a Goose was brought from *Bow*
   To *Algate.*

As harmless, and as innocent
She was as those that with her went;
Nor do I think the watchmen meant
More sillier than She;
She gave them never a word at all,
But only rested on a stall,
And yet these Cannibals did fall,
   About her.

But

But she with silence there stood still,
Till he perceived each mans bill,
Desiring them not use them ill
That lookt so like them all :
Then they disdaining, did begin
To bring us all into a gin,
And then the Constable came in,
    And took us.

To him they straight reveal'd the case,
And vow'd each man to quit his place,
If we were suffered to disgrace
The Kings Lievtenant so :
And then the Ganders eminence
The Goose and us commanded thence,
And made us graduates commence
    The Counter.

We thither went, but then my Goose,
Which pinion'd was before, got loose,
For having her within a noose
What fear had they of her?
Then into every room we went,
And here and there our money spent
Untill the Constable had sent
    Next morning.

We summoned were for to appear
Before an Alderman, I swear,

Complete.

That might have been that very year
Lord Maior for his wit:
He tooke our Gooses case in hand,
And all things with such Judgement scan'd,
That having done, we scarce could stand
      For laughing.

For he did not only reprehend
Our follies, but did much commend
The Constable, his honest friend,
For his good service done;
How is that noble City blest
With Officers above the rest,
That now may add unto their Crest
      My Bow Goose?

But now, with grief, I'll tell you what,
My Goose that was before so fat,
That might have been accepted at
A Maior or Sheriffs own boord,
Grew lanck and lean, and straight so ill,
That from her wings she shed a Quill,
Desiring me to write her Will,
      Which I did.

Then thus my dying Goose began,
Unto the Reverend Alderman
I do bequeath my brain-sick pan,
And all that it contains:
                          And

And Master Constable, to you
My empty head, which is your due ;
My Bill I'll give the cursed crue
    Your Watchmen.

I do bequeath my bodies trunk
Unto Good Fellows for the Rump,
Desiring that it may be drunk
In Clarret and Canary :
I pray discharge your company
All such as shall Recusants be
To drink a health in memory
    O' th' Bow-Goose.

My Giblets to the City Cook
That dwels not far from Pasty-nook,
That he unto my Corps may look,
And coffin't in a Crust ;
My guts for Marshal red-face save,
To hang about his neck so brave,
That on his Palfrey the proud Knave
    May swagger.

And to my fellow prisoners all,
That now here are, or ever shall,
That come to lye within this wall,
I give my heavy heart ;
My claws and pinions I do give
Unto the Serjeants and Sheriff,

To catch and pinion them that live
    Indebted.

And furthermore, it is my will
The City Clerk shall have a quill
Such learned speeches to write still,
As his grave Lordship utters ;
And likewise Mistris Alderman
Shall have my tail to make a Fan ;
My Legs I'll give the Gentleman
    Her Usher

Because my kindred of *Bridewel*
Such asses to the Cart compel
As occupy their Trades so well,
I do forbid them all,
That they presume not for to come
Whereas my Dirges shall be sung,
For I'll have wiser in the room
    Than they are.

The Beadle and the Bell-man I
Executors do make, thereby
Such legacies to satisfie
As I have here related ;
And that all things perform'd may be,
This my last Will to oversee
I do ordain the Deputy
    Of Duck-lane.

                        There's

There's one thing more I do conceive,
Almost forgot, I do bequeath
My Tongue, which tatling cannot leave,
Unto the City Council,
That they may mediate a truce
Between the City and me their Goose,
Who wooes to be their constant Muse
      For ever.

Write on my Tombe this Epitaph,
Whereat, I pray, let no man laugh:
Here lies a Goose that could not quaff,
And yet was a good Fellow;
The coursest of our kindred must
Return with me unto the dust,
And after me who shall be first
      None knoweth.

Now let them in their Liveries call
The boys from every Hospitall
To sing my solemn funeral
With Dirges to my grave;
And when my Goose had uttered this
O then my Goose began to piss,
And sighing, with a harmeless hiss,
      Departed.

News

News.

WHite Bears are lately come to Town,
  That's no news;
And Cuckolds Dogs shall pull them down,
  That's no news
Ten Dozen of Capons sold for a Crown,
  Hey ho, that's news indeed.

A Jackanapes at a Merchants door,
  That's no news;
An Irish man in an Ale-house score,
  That's no news;
And *Gravesend* Barge without a Whore,
  Hey ho, that's news indeed.

A fizling Cur in a Ladies lap,
  That's no news;
A Feather to shake in a Fool's cap,
  That's no news;
A Lyon caught in a Mouse Trap,
  Hey ho, that's news indeed.

A younger Brother slow to thrive,
  That's no news;
A Drone to rob the poor Bees hive,
  That's no news;

A Parsons wife not apt to swive,
    Hey ho, that's news indeed.

A Taylor brisk in swaggering hose
    That's no news;
A Frenchman stradling as he goes,
    That's no news;
A Drunkard without a Copper nose,
    Hey ho, that's news indeed.

A Dutchman to be dayly drunk,
    That's no news;
A Captain to maintain a Punk,
    That's no news;
A Wardrobe in an empty Trunk,
    Hey ho, that's news indeed.

To see two Ships at sea to grapple,
    That's no news;
To see a horse that's all dapple,
    That's no news;
To see a red nose roast an apple,
    Hey ho, that's news indeed.

A Petty-fogger brib'd with fees,
    That's no news;
A Welchman cramm'd with toasted Cheese,
    That's no news;

A Lad and a Lass in bed to freeze
  Hey ho, that's news indeed.

A Sattin suit without a Page,
  That's no news;
A rayling Poet o'er the Stage,
  That's no news;
A rich man honest in this Age,
  Hey ho, that's news indeed.

A Lawyer to turn hypocrite,
  That's no news;
A Serjeant to arrest a Knight,
  That's no news;
A Court without a Parasite,
  Hey ho, that's news indeed.

Before my news be overslipt,
  That's no news,
I wish all Knaves from *London* Shipt,
  That's no news,
And all the whores in *Bridewell* whipt,
  Hey ho, that's news indeed.

*A Discourse between a Sea-man and
a Land-Souldier.*

We Sea-men are the honest boys,
    We fear no storms, nor Rocks-a,
Whose Musick is their Cannons noise,
Whose sporting is with Knocks-a.

Mars hath no Children of his own,
But we that fight by Land-a   [,]
Land-Souldiers Kingdoms up have thrown,
Yet they unshaken stand-a.

'Tis brave to see a tall Ship sail
With all her trim geer on her,
As though the divel were in her tail
Before the wind she'll run-a.

Our main Battalia when it moves
There's no such glorious thing-a,
Whose Leaders, like so many *Joves*,
Abroad their thunders fling-a.

Come let's reckon what Ships are ours,
The Gorgon, and the Dragon,
The Lyon which in field is bold,
The Bull with bloudy Flagon,

Come let's reckon what works are ours,
Forts, Bulwarks, Barricadoes,
Mounts, Gabinets, Parrapits, Counter-mines,
Casimates, and Pallizadoes,

Field-Peeces, Musquets, groves of Pikes,
Carbines, and Canoneers,
Quadrants; and Half-moons, and Ranks of Files,
And Fronts, and Vans, and Rears.

A health to brave Land-Souldiers all,
Let Cans a piece go round-a:
And to all Seamen, great and small,
Let lofty Musick sound-a.

A Song.

MY Mistris is in Musick passing skilful,
And Plaies and sings her part at the first sight,
But in her play she is exceeding wilful,
And will not play but for her own delight,
Nor touch one string, nor play one pleasing strain,
Unless you take her in a pleasing vein.

Also she hath a sweet delicious touch
Upon the Instrument whereon she plaies,
And thinks that she doth never do too much,
Her pleasures are dispers'd so many waies;

She hath such Judgement both in time and mood,
That for to play with her 'twill do you good.

And then you win her heart : but here's the spight,
You cannot get her for to play alone,
But play with her, and she will play all night,
And next day too, or else 'tis ten to one,
And run division with you in such sort,
Run ne'er so swift she'll make you come too short.

Still so she sent for me one day to play,
Which I did take for such exceeding grace,
But she so tir'd me ere I went away :
I wisht I had been in another place :
She knew the play much better than I did,
And still she kept me time for heart and bloud.

I love my mistris, and I love to play,
So she will let me play with intermission :
But when she ties me to it all the day,
I hate and loath her greedy disposition ;
Let her keep time, as nature doth require,
And I will play as much as she'll desire.

In Praise of Ale.

When the chill Charokoe blows,   [Scirocco
And Winter tells a heavy tale,

And Pies and Daws, and Rooks and crows
Do sit and curse the frost and snows,
        Then give me Ale.

Ale in a *Saxon Rumkin* then,
Such as will make grim Malkin prate,
Bids Valour bargain in't all men,   [burgeon in tall]
Quickens the Poets Wits and Pen,
        Despises Fate.

Ale, that the absent Battel fights
And forms the March of Swedish Drums,
Disputes the Princes Laws and Rights,
What's past and done tells mortall Wights,
        And what's to come.

Ale, that the Plough-mans heart up keeps,
And equals it to Tyrants Thrones :
That wipes the eye that ever weeps,
And lulls in sweet and dainty sleeps
        Their very bones.   [weary]

Grandchild of *Ceres*, *Bacchus* Daughter,
Wines emulous Neighbour, if but stale :
Ennobling all the Nymphs of Water,
And filling each mans heart with laughter,
        Oh give me Ale.

The Rebellion.

Now, thanks to the Powers below,
    We have even done our do,
The Myter is down, and so is the C——
And with them the Coronet too :
All is now the Peoples, and then
What is theirs is ours we know ;
There is no such thing as B—— or K——
Or Peer, but in name or show ;
Come Clowns, and come Boys, come Hoberde-hoys,
Come Females of each degree,
Stretch out your throats, bring in your Votes,
And make good the Anarchy ;
Then thus it shall be, saies *Alse*,
Nay, thus it shall be, saies *Amie*,
Nay, thus it shall go, saies *Taffie*, I trow,
Nay, thus it shall go, saies *Jemmy*,

Oh but the truth, good People all, the truth is such a
For it will undo both Church and State too,   (thing,
And pull out the throat of our King :
No, nor the Spirit, nor the new Light
Can make the Point so clear,
But we must bring out the defil'd coat,
What thing the truth is, and where,

Speak *Abraham*, speak *Hester*,
Speak *Judith*, speak *Kester*,
Speak tag and rag, short coat and long :
Truth is the spel that made us rebel,
And murder and plunder ding dong;
Sure I have the truth, saies *Numphs*,
Nay, I have the truth, saies *Clem*,
Nay, I have the truth, saies reverend *Ruth*,
Nay, I have the truth, saies *Nem*.

Well, let the truth be whose it will,
There is something else is ours,
Yet this devotion in our Religion
May chance to abate our Powers :
Then let's agree on some new way,
It skills not much how true,
Take *Pryn* and his club, or *Smec* and his tub,
Or any Sect, old or new;
The divel is in the pack if choice you can lack,
We are fourscore Religions strong,
Then take your choice, the Major voice
Shall carry't right or wrong;
Then let's have King *Charles*, saies *George*,
Nay, we'll have his son, saies *Hugh;*
Nay, then let's have none, saies gabbering *Jone*,
Nay we'll be all Kings, saies *Prue*.

Nay, but neighbours and friends, one word more,
There's something else behind,

And wise though you be, you do not well see
In which door sits the wind ;
And for Religion, to speak truth,
And in both Houses sence,
The matter is all one if any or none,
If it were not for the pretence ;
Now here doth lurk the key of the work,
And how to dispose of the Crown
Dexteriously, and as it may be
For your behalf and our own ;
Then we'll be of this, saies *Meg*,
Nay, we'll be of this, saies *Tib*,
Come, he'll be of all, saies pittifull *Paul*,
Nay, we'll be of none, saies *Gib*.

Oh we shall have, if we go one   [on]
In Plunder, Excise, and Blood,
But few folks, and poor, to domineer o'er,
And that will not be so good ;
Then let's agree on some new way,
Some new and happy course,
The Country is grown sad, the City is Horn mad,
And both Houses are worse ;
The Sinod hath writ, the General hath shit,
And both to like purpose, for
Religion, Laws, the Truth, and the Cause
We talk on, but nothing we do ;
Come, then let's have peace, saies *Nel*,
No, no, but We won't, saies *Meg*,   But

t I say we will, saies fiery-face *Phil*,
 will, and we won't, saies *Hodge*.

us from the rout who can expect
ght but confusion,
ice true unity with good Monarchy
gin and end in one?
then when all is thought their own,
d lies at their belief,
ese popular pates reap nought but debates
om these many round-headed beasts;
me Royallist[s,] then, do you play the men,
d Cavaliers give the word,
d now let's see what you will be
d whether you can accord;
health to King *Charles*, saies *Tom*,
 with it, saies *Ralph*, like a man,
d bless him, saies *Doll*, and raise him, saies *Moll*,
d send him his own, saies *Nan*.

t now for these prudent Wights,
at sit without end, and to none,
d their Committees in Towns and Cities
ll with confusion;
r the bold Troopes of Sectaries,
e Scots and their Partakers,
ir new Brittish States, CoL *Burges* and his mates,
e Covenant and its makers:
r all these wee'll pray, and in such a way,
        That

That if it might granted be,
Both *Jack* and *Gill*, and *Moll* and *Will*,
And all the World will agree:
Else Pox take them all, saies *Bess*,
And a Plague too, saies *Mary*,
The devil, saies *Dick*, and his Dam too, saies *Nick*,
Amen and amen say we.

How to get a Child without help of a Man.

A Maiden of late, whose name was sweet *Kate*,
Was dwelling in *London*, near to *Aldersgate*:
Now list to my Ditty, declare it I can,
    She would have a Child without help of a man.

To a Doctor she came, a man of great fame,
Whose deep skill in Physick Report did proclaim,
I pray, master Doctor, shew me, if you can,
    How I may conceive without help of a man.

Then listen, quoth he, since so it must be,   (sently
This wondrous strong medicine I'll shew you pre-
Take nine pound of thunder, six legs of a Swan,
    And you shall conceive without help of a man.

The wooll of a Frog, the juyce of a Log,
Well parboyl'd together in the skin of a hog,

With the egge of a Mooncalf, if get it you can,
    And you shall conceive without help of a man.

The love of false Harlots, the Faith of false Varlets,
With the Truth of decoys, that walk in their Scarlet,
And the Feathers of a Lobster well fry'd in a pan,
    And you shall conceive without help of a man.

Nine Drops of rain brought hither from *Spain*
With the blast of a Bellows quite over the main,
With eight quarts of brimstone, brew'd in a beer Can,
    And you shall conceive without help of a man.

Six Pottles of Lard squeez'd from a Rock hard,
With nine Turkey Eggs, each as long as a Yard,
With a Pudding of hailstones bak'd well in a Pan,
    And you shall conceive without help of a man.

These Medicines are good, and approved hath stood,
Well tempered together with a Pottle of blood,
Squeez'd from a Grashopper, and the naile of a Swan,
    To make Maids conceive without help of a man.

Love's Fancy.

After the pains of a desperate Lover,
    When day and night I had sighed all in vain,

Ah what a pleasure it is to discover,
In her eyes pitty who causes my pain,
   Chorus *Ah what,* &c.

When the denial comes fainter and fainter,
And her eyes gives what her tongue doth deny[,]
Ah what a trembling I feel when I venter,
Ah what a trembling does usher my Joy !
   Chor. *Ah what,* &c.

When with unkindness our Love at a stand is,
And both have punish'd our selves with the pain,
Ah What a pleasure the touch of her hand is !
Ah what a pleasure to touch it again ! [press]
   Chor. *Ah what,* &c.

When with a sigh she accords me the blessing
And her eyes twinkle 'twixt pleasure and pain,
Ah what a Joy ! oh beyond all expressing !
Ah what a Joy to hear it [, Shall we] again !
   Chor. *Ah what,* &c.

  Fortune's Favours distributed.

BLind Fortune, if thou want'st a Guide,
 I'll tell thee how thou shalt divide :
Distribute unto each his due,
Justice is blind, and so are you.

o Usurers this doom impart:
[ay his Scriveners break, and then his heart,
[ay his Debtors unto Beggars fall
'r what is as bad, turn Courtiers all.

nd unto Tradesmen, that sell dear,
  long vacation all the year,
evenge us thus on their deceits,
nd send them Wives light as their Weights.

ut Fortune how wil't recompence
he French mans dayly insolence?
or them I wish no greater pain,
han to be sent to *France* again.

nd lest thine Altar should want fire,
o Bridemens Votes grant their desire,
o Lovers, that will not believe
heir Sweet mistakes, thy blindness give.

nd lest the Players should grow poor,
end them *Anglauris* more and more,   ["*Aglauras*"]
nd to the Puritan more eares,
'han *Cealus* in his Garland wears.   [*Ceres* in her]

nd to Physitians, if thou Please,
end them another new Disease;
'o Scholars give if thou canst do't,
. Benefice without a suit.

                                                Unto

Unto Court-Lords, Monopolies,
And to their Wives Communities ;
Thus, Fortune, thou canst please us all,
If Lords can rise, and Ladies fall.

And unto Lawyers, I beseech,
As much for silence as for speech ;
To Ladies Ushers, strength of back,
And unto me, a cup of Sack.

If these Instructions make thee wise,
Men shall restore again thy eyes :
By a new name thou shalt commence,
Not fortune call'd, but Providence.

A Letany.

From *Mahomet*, and Paganisme,
    From Hereticks, and Sects and Schisme,
From high-way Rascals, and Cutpurses ;
From carted Bawds, Scolds, and dry Nurses,
From Glister-Pipes, and Doctors Whistles,
From begging Schollars stale Epistles,
From Turn-stile Boots, and Long lane Beavers,
From Agues, and from drunken Feavers,
    Libera nos Domine.

From all several kind of Itches,
From Pantaloons, and Cloak-bag Breeches,
From Carbinadoed Sutes on Serges,   [? of S]
From a Bastard that is the Clergies,
From thredden points, and Cap of Cruel,
From the danger of a Duel,
From a Tally full of Notches,
And from privy Seals of Botches,
    Libera nos Domine.

From a Whore that's never pleasant,
But in lusty Wine or Pheasant,
From the Watch at twelve a'clock,
And from *Bess Broughtons* button'd Smock,
From Hackney Coaches, and from Panders,
That do boast themselves Commanders,
From a Taylors tedious Bill,
And Pilgrimage up *Holborn* Hill,
    Libera nos Domine.

From damages and restitutions,
From accursed Executions,
From all new-found waies of sinning,
From the scurf, and sables Linnen,
From the Pox, and the Physitian,
And from the Spanish Inquisition,
From a Wife that's wan and meager,
And from Lice and Winters Leaguer,
    Libera nos Domine.

From a griping slavish Cullion,
From the Gout, and the Strangullion,
From a Mountibanks Potion,
From his scarrings and his Lotion,
From the Buttocks of *Prisilla*,
That diers so with *Sarsapherilla*,
From a Lecture to the Zealous,
And from the Tub of old *Cornelius*,
   Libera nos Domine.

From bawdy Courts, and Civil Doctors,
From drunken Sumners and their Proctors,
From occasions for to revel
With a Lawyer at the Divel,
From Serjeants, Yeomen, and their Maces [,]
And from false friends with double faces,
From an enemy More mighty
Than *Usquebaugh* or *Aqua vitae*,
   Libera nos Domine.

Penance.

GOD bless my good Lord Bishop,
 And send him long to raign,
In health, wealth, and prosperity,
True justice to maintain,
He beats down sin in every place,
Poor Wenches dare not do

Lest they do Penance in a sheet
  And pay their money too.

Down lately in a Garden
It was my chance to walk,
Where I heard two Sisters
That secretly did talk
Quoth the Younger to the Elder,
In faith I dare not do,
Lest I do Penance in a sheet,
  And pay my money too.

Then quoth the Eldest Sister,
You are not of my mind,
For if I meet a proper Lad
That will to me prove kind,
In faith, quoth she, I will not care
To take a turn or two,
Though I do Penance in a sheet,
  And pay my money too.

But here's the thing that vexes me,
And troubles much my brain,
If a poor man chance to get a child,
And cannot it maintain,
He must be censur'd by the Law
As Justice doth afford
He must be stript, and then be whipt,
  And brought before my Lord.

And when he comes before my Lord,
And hath no ready Tale,
His *Mittimus* is straight-waies made,
And sent unto the Jayle,
And there he must remaine
The space of half a year,
If every Wench were served so
    Then kissing would be dear.

On Good Canary.

OF all the rare juices
    That *Bacchus* or *Ceres* produces,
There's none that I can nor dare I
Compare with the Princely *Canary;*
    For this is the thing
    That a fancy infuses,
    This first got a K——
    And next the nine *Muses.*
'Twas this made old *Poets* so sprightly to sing
  And fill all the world with glory and fame on't;
They *Hellicon* call'd it and the Thispian spring,
  But this was the drink though they knew not the
                                   (name on'

2

  Our *Sider* and *Perry*
Make a man mad but not merry,
  It makes the people Wind-mill pated,
  And with crackers sophisticated,

And your *Hops, yest,* and *Malt,*
When they're mingled together
　　Makes your fancies to halt,
　　Or reeke any whither.　　　　[reel]
stuffs our Braines with *Froth* and with *Yest;*
That if one would write but a verse for a *Bellman,*
e must study till Christmas for an *Eight Shilling* Jest
These liquors won't raise but drown & o're-
　　　　　　　　　(whelm man.

3
　　Our drowsy *Metheglin*
Was only ordain'd to enveigle in
　　The Novice that knows not to drink yet;
　　But is fuddled before he can think it,
　　　And your *Clarret* and *White*
　　　Have a Gunpowder fury;
　　　They're of the French spright,
But they won't long endure you:
d your Holliday *Muscadine Allagant* and Tent.
Have only this property and virtue that's fit in't
ey'l make a man sleep till a Preachment be spent,
But we neither can warm our blood or our wit
　　　　　　　　　(in't.

4
　　The Bagrag and Rhenish
You must with Ingredients Replenish,
　　Its a wine to please Ladies & Toys with
　　But not for a man to rejoice with:
　　　But its *Sack* makes the *sport*
　　And who gaines but the *Flavour*
　　　Though an Abbesse he court

In his high shooes he'll have her :
It's this that advances the Drinker and Drawer,
　　Though his father come to Town in *Hobnailes* &
Hĕ turns it to Velvet & brings up an Heir, (*Leather*
In the Town in his Chain, in the field, with his
　　　　　　　　　　　　　　　　　　(Feathei

Loves Lunatick.

Heard you not lately of a man
　　That ran beside his wits,
And naked through the City ran,
Wrapt in his frantick fits.

My honest Neighbours it is I,
See how the people flout me ;
See where the mad man comes, they cry,
With all the Boys about me.

Tom Bedlam was a Sage to me,
I speak in sober-sadness,
For more strange Visions did I see
Than *Tom* in all his madness.

When first into this rage I hopt,
About the Market walkt I,
With Capons Feathers in my Cap,
Unto my self thus talkt I :

Saw you not Angels in her face,
Each eye a Star out-darting?
Heard you not Musick from her voyce,
Her Lips all joy imparting?

Is not her hair more pure than Gold,
Or Web of Spiders spinning?
Methinks in her I do behold
My joyes and woes beginning.

Methinks I see her in a Cloud,
The Planets round about her,
I call'd and cry'd to them aloud,
I cannot live without her.

The Bracelets which I wore of late,
Inrich'd with Pearls and Gold,
Are turn'd now to Iron Chains,
Which keep my Pulses cold.

I mused thus unto my self,
Each word with gesture acted:
The people cry'd, O look poor elfe,
See how the man's distracted.

I was a poor and harmless Wight
Till roguish *Cupid* caught me,
And till his Mother with her flight   [? slight]
Into this pickle brought me.

At which my friends they were not glad,
Pray *Jove* your Wits to cherish,
For once I was as proper a Lad
As was in all the Parish.

But whipt and stript I now must be,
Intangled now in Chains,
And for my love, you all may see,
I have this for my pains.

To Stable-straw I must go,
My time in Bedlam spending :
Good folk, you your beginning see,
But do not know your ending.

The new Medly of the Country man, Citizen, and Souldier.

FRom what-you-call't Town in what-call-you't (shire
  To *London* Cham come, what fine Volk are here
Sure thick is the place, itch smell the good chear.
Che'le knock at the Yate, then what ho : God be here
       What are you Sir ?

Cham a West Country man Zur.
Good Bumkin forbear,
Such hopnails as you are do seldom come here.
Cods sooks, here's a Vellow wo'd make a man zwear[.
Cham come to tell, Sir, with Master Lord Maior.
       What

What to do Sir?
To see his fine Doublet, his Chain, and his Ruff,
His Beaver, his Gown, and such finical stuff;
And what do you think of a kick or a cuff?
If my whip will but last, i' faith 'chil give thee enough,
      And well laid on.
Hold, hold, prethee Countriman be not so hot.
Che have a huge mind to lay a long lace on thy coat.
Prethee tell me thy name & my L. Maior shall know
My name is *Tom Hoyden*, what saiest thou to that? (it
      Tom Hoyden!

Then *Tom Hoyden* pack hence to *Croyden*,
The Country is fitter for thee.
Though you abhor us, and care not for us,
Without us you cannot be.
We can live without you and your Rustick coat, [.]
Did we not Vittle your House,
My Lady *Maries*, with all her Baries,
      Would shite as small as a Lowse.

We have money. And we have honey.
And we have the Silver and Gold.
We have fuel.
And we have Jewels.
And we have Sheep in the Fold.
We have silk enough.
And we have milk enough.
But we have the Treasure untold;

We have means, and ease.
But we have Beans and Pease,
        And Bacon, hold belly, hold.

We have Purses, and we have Horses.
And we have Powder and shot.
We have Pullets.
And we have Bullets.
And we have Spirits as hot.
We have Honours, and we have Mannors,
But we are walled about.
But when we begin
To keep our Cattle in,
In faith, you'll quickly come out.

We have Gallies.
And we have Vallies.
And we have Canons of brass;
We have Feathers.
And we have Weathers
On Mountains matted with grass.
We have Wine, and Spice, Sugar, Fruit, and Rice.
But we have good Barley and Wheat:
And, were we put to it, can better live without
Money, than you without Meat.

Cho.   Then since 'tis so that we cannot be
Without one another
        Let us two agree
                              May

May the Country prove fruitful,
And City be free
No Climate in *Europe* so happy as we.

Sol.   He that would be made by a Souldiers Trade.
Let him be encouraged by me,
For never did any men gain by the Blade
As we have since forty three.

What Fellow is that? why, it seems a Souldate;
Good morrow, good morrow to thee:
Why how now my friends, all for your ends,
Will you make up a peace without me?

You know in a word the power of the Sword,
A Canon may conquer a King:
But a sharp Sword will make a Scepter to shake;
Faith you have the World in a sling.

Compare the whole Land to the parts of a man,
The Country's the Legs and the Toes,
And without a riddle the City is the middle,
But the Souldier is the head and the Nose.

Though now we wear Blades,
We once were of Trades,
And shall be whilst Trading endures:
Our Officers are, although men of war,

Some

Some Goldsmiths, some Drapers,
           And Brewers.

Do you get increase, we'll guard you with peace,
The Sword shall not come where the Axe is,
We'll take off your cares: we'll take off your fears:
But when will you take of[f] our Taxes?

We kept Spaniards from you,
That would overcome yee,
Whilst you do plough, harrow and thresh,   (bone
The Frenchman is our own, What is bred in the
Will hardly get out of the flesh.

We quarter in Villages, Cities and Towns,
And sometimes we lie in the Fields.
But if from your Colours you offer to run,
Then you must be laid neck and heels.

Through Countries we march, & for enemies search,
And command all things in Bravadoes.
But oh, my good friend, if you do offend,
I'm sure you must have the Strappadoes.

When, Sir, the City still shall fit you
With what you do deserve,
The Country Cowman and the ploughman
Will not let you starve:
                                          With

With Buff and Beaver we will ever
Bless the back and head.

We will give thee mony enough, and Ammunition,
And seal to this condition. And so do I introth.
And I will spend my bloud Sir.
And I will spend my Treasure
To do the Souldier pleasure.
Why, now I thank you both.

(Court

Cho. Let the City, the Country, the Camp and the
Be the places of pleasure and Royal resort,
And let us observe in the midst of our sport,
That Fidelity makes us as firm as a Fort:
A Union well-grounded no malice can hurt.

[This ends Part First, in the Edition of *Merry Drollery*, 1661.]

The Indifferent Lover.

NO man Love's fiery passions can approve,
 As either yielding pleasure or promotion:
I like a mild and lukewarm zeal in love,
Although I do not like it in devotion:

For it hath no coherence with my Creed,
To think that lovers mean as they pretend:
If all that said they died, had died indeed,
Sure long ere this the World had had an end.

Some

Some one perhaps of long Consumption dried,
And after falling into love might dye,
But I dare swear he never yet had died
Had he been half so sound at heart as I.

Another, rather than incur the slander
Of true Apostate, will false Martyr prove;
I'll neither *Orpheus* be, nor yet *Leander*,
I'll neither hang nor drown my self for love.

Yet I have been a Lover by report,
And I have died for Love as others do,
Prais'd be Great *Jove* I died in such a sort,
As I revived within an hour or two.

Thus have I liv'd, thus have I lov'd, till now,
And ne'r had reason to repent me yet,
And whosoever otherwise shall do,
His courage is as little as his wit.

Loves Torment.

WHen blind God *Cupid*, all in an angry mood,
And *Cythera*, the fairest Queen of Love,
Did leave *Sylvanus* pleasant shadowed woods,
And mounted up into the Heavens above,
    Even then when *Sol*,
    Even then when *Sol*

      In water set his bed,
        Did seek to hide,
        Did seek to hide
      His golden shining head.

Like *Philomel*, all in a doleful wise,
I pass the silent coloured night in woe ;
No rest nor sleep can seize upon my eyes,
Oh cruel beauty that did torment me so !
        No one can tell,
        No one can tell
      How I in sorrows dwelt,
        Save only she,
        Save only she
      That hath like Passions felt.

The night is past all, and *Aurora* red
Begins to show her ruby-coloured face,
Leaving Old *Tytan* and his aged head,
The cloudy darkness from the skies to chase ;
        Ah my poor heart,
        Ah my poor heart
      In flames of fire doth fry ;
        I live in love,
        I love and live,
        I live, and yet I dye.

Each pretty little bird injoys his Mate,
And gently billing sits upon a Tree,
                                          And

And on the Verdant shadowed woods do prate,
Chirping their Notes with pleasant Harmony;
   I wish my Love,
   I wish my Love
  My pretty bird may be
   To ease my grief,
   To ease my grief
  And cure my malady.

The Rebel Red-coat.

COme Drawer, come fill us about more wine,
 Let us merrily tipple, the day is our own,
We'll have our delights, let the Country go pine,
 Let the King and the Kingdom groan:
For the day is our own, and so shall continue,
 Whilst Monarchy we baffle quite,
We'll spend all the Kingdoms Revenue,
 And sacrifice all to delight:
'Tis power that brings us all to be Kings,
 And we'll be all crown'd by our might.

A fig for Divinity, Lecture and Law
 And all that to Royalty do pretend, [Loyalty]
We will by our Swords keep the kingdoms in aw,
 And our power shall never have end:
The Church and the State we'll turn into liquor,
 And spend a whole town in a day,
        We'l

We'll melt all their Bodkins the quicker
  Into Sack, and so drink them away,
We'll spend the demeans o' th' Bishops & Deans,
  And over the Presbyter sway.

The nimble St. *Patrick* is sunk in a bog,
  And his Country-men sadly cry, *Oh hone, Oh hone,*
St. *Andrew* and 's kirk-men are lost in a fog,
  And we are the Saints alone:
Thus on our superiours and equals we trample,
  Whilst Jockie the stirrop shall hold,
The Citie's our Mule for example,
  While we thus in plenty are roll'd,
Each delicate Dish shall but answer our wish,
  And our drink shall be cordial Gold.

---

*Love lies a bleeding: In Imitation of
Law lies a bleeding.*

Lay by your pleading,
  Love lies a bleeding,
Burn all your Poetry, and throw away your reading.
    Piety is painted,
    And Truth is tainted,
Love is a reprobate, and Schism now is Sainted,
    The Throne Love doth sit on,
    We dayly do spit on,
                                        It

It was not thus I wis, when *Betty* rul'd in *Britain*,
    But friendship hath faultred,
    Loves Altars are altered,   (tred.
And he that is the cause, I would his neck were hal-

    When Love did nourish
    England did flourish,
Till holy hate came in and made us all so currish.
    Now every Widgeon
    Talks of Religion,
And doth as little good as *Mahomet* and his Pidgeon.
    Each coxcombe is suiting
    His words for confuting,   (puting.
But heaven is sooner gain'd by suffering than by dis-
    True friendship we smother,
    And strike at our Brother   [:]
Apostles never went to God by killing one another.

    Let Love but warm ye
    Nothing can harm ye,
When Love is General, there's Angels in the Army.
    Love keeps his quarters,
    And fears no tortures,   (tyrs.
The bravest fights are written in the Book of Mar-
    Could we be so civill
    As to do good for evill
It were the only happy way to o'recome the divel.
    The Flowers Love hath watred,
                                 Sedition

Sedition hath scattred, (of hatred.
We talk with tongues of holiness, but act with hearts

    He that doth know me,
    And love will shew me,
Hath found the nearest noble way to overcome me.
    He that hath bound me,
    And then doth wound me, (me.
Wins not my heart, doth not conquer, but confound
    In such a condition
    Love is the physitian,
True Love and Reason makes the purest politician.
    But strife and confusion,
    Deceit and delusion,
Though it seem to thrive at first will make a sad
    (conclusion.
    Love is a fewel,
    A pretious Jewel, (the duel.
'Tis Love must stanch the blood when Fury fights
    Love is a loadstone,
    Hate is a bloodstone, (stone.
Heaven is the North Point, and Love is the Load-
    Though fury and scorn
    Loves Temples have torn,
He'll keep his Covenant, and will not be forsworn.
    His Laws do not border
    On strife and disorder,
He scorns to get his wealth by perjury and murder.

What falshood drew in,
Grace never grew in,
Love will not raise him upon anothers ruine.
He can present ye
With peace and plenty, (twenty.
Love never advanceth one by throwing down of
Where Love is in season,
There Truth is and Reason,
The soul of Love is never underlaid with Treason.
He never doth quarrel
For Princely apparrel,
Nor ever fixed a chair of state upon a barrel.

Love from the dull pit
Of Follies full pit
Never took an Anvil out, and put it in a pulpit.
Love is no sinker,
Truth is no slinker,
In mending breaches Love did never play the tinker.
Where Vengeance and Lust is,
No truth nor trust is,
As will appear at last in Gods high Court of Justice.
Pity and remorse is
The strength of Loves Forces,
Paul never converted men by stables fill'd with
         (horses.
Mercy is fading,
Truth is degrading,
Love is the only cause of Plenty, Peace, & Trading.
        Love

Love is a fire
Made of desire,
Whose chief Ambition is to heaven to aspire.
It stops the gradation
Of fury and passion, (Nation.
It governs all good Families, and best can guide a
The Low Land, the high Land,
And my Land, and thy Land,
Grew all in common straight when Love had left
(this Island.
Where peace is panting,
And rage is ranting,
'Tis an undoubted sign the King of Love is wanting.
Father and Mother,
Sister and Brother,
If Love be lacking, quickly mischief one another.
Where wrath is, the rod is
That ruines our bodies;
With hate the divel is, but where Love is God is.
Then let us not doubt it,
But streight go about it,
To bring in Love again, we cannot live without it.
Then let the Graces
Crown our embraces,
And let us settle all things in their proper places.
Lest persecution
Cause dissolution,
Let all purloyned wealth be made a restitution.

   For though now it tickles,
    'Twill turn all to prickles,   (sickles.
Then let's live in peace, and turn our Swords to
   When *Noah's* Dove was sent out,
    Then Gods Pardon went out,   (it.
They that would have it so, I hope will say Amen to

A Catch.

BRing forth your Cunny skins, fair maids, to me,
  And hold them fair that I may see
Gray, Black, and blew; for your smaller skins
I'll give you Glasses, Laces, Pins :
  And for your whole Cunny
  I'll give you ready money.

Come, gentle *Jone*, do thou begin
With thy black, black, black Cunny skin,
And *Mary* then, and *Kate* will follow
With their silver'd-hair'd skins, and their yellow;
  Your white Cunny skin I will not lay by,
  Though it be fat, it is [not] fair to the Eye.

Your gray it is warm, but for my money
Give me the bonny, bonny black Coney;
Come away, fair maids, your skins will decay,
Come and take money, maids, put your ware away;
  I have fine Bracelets, Rings,
  And I have silver Pins ;

Coney skins, Coney skins,
Maids, have you any Coney skins.

A Catch of the Beggars.

FRom hunger and cold who lives more free,
    Or who lives a merrier life than we ;
Our bellies are full, and our backs are warm,
And against all Pride our Rags are a Charm ;
    Enough is a feast, and for to morrow
    Let rich men care, we feel no sorrow.

The City, and Town, and every village
Afford us [either] an Alms, or a Pillage ;
And if the weather be cold and raw,
Then in a Barn we tumble in straw :
    If fair and warm, in yea-Cock and nay-Cock
    The Fields afford us a hedge or a hey-Cock.

The Time-server.

ROom for a Gamester that plaies at all he sees,
    Whose fickle fancy fits such times as these,
One that saies *Amen* to every factious prayer,
  From *Hugh Peters* Pulpit to S. *Peters* Chair,
One that doth defie the Crosier and the Crown,
  But yet can bouze with Blades that Carrouze

Whilst Pottle-pots tumble down, dery down;
One that can comply with Surplice and with Cloak,
   Yet for his end can I depend,   [Independ
   Whilst Presbyterian broke *Britains* yoke.

This is the way to trample without trembling,
   'Tis the Sycophant's only secure,
Covenants and *Oaths* are badges of dissembling,
   'Tis the politick pulls down the pure:
To Profess and betray, to plunder and pray,
Is the only ready way to be great,
   Flattery doth the feat:
Ne'r go, ne'r stir, will venter further
Than the greatest *Dons* in the Town,
   From a Copper to a Crown.

I am in a temp'rate humour now to think well,
Now I'm in another for to drink well,
Then fill us up a Beer-boul boys, that we
   May drink it merrily,
No knavish Spy shall understand,
For if it should be known,
   'Tis ten to one we shall be trapan'd.

I'll drink to thee a brace of quarts,
Whose Anagram is call'd *True Hearts*,
If all were well as I would ha't,
   And *Britain* cur'd of its tumour,

I should very well like my Fate,
And drink my Sack at a cheaper rate,
  Without any noise or rumour,
  Oh then I should fix my humour.

But since 'tis no such matter, change your hue,
  I may cog and flatter, so may you:
Religion is a Widgeon, and Reason is a Treason,
  And he that hath a Loyal heart may bid the world
                                 (adieu.
We must be like the Scottish man,
  Who with intent to beat down Schism,
Brought in the Presbyterian,
  With Canon and with Catechism :
If Beuk won't do't, then *Jockey* shoot,
  For the *Kirk* of *Scotland* doth command,
And what hath been, since they came in,
  I think w' have cause to understand.

A Song.

GAther your Rose-buds while you may,
  Old time is still a flying,
For that Flower that smells to day,
To morrow will be dying.

That Age is best, which if she force [is the first,]
While youth and blood are warmer,

But being [spent] she grows worse and worse,
And [Times] still succeeds the former.

The glorious Lamp of Heaven, the Sun,
The higher he's a getting,
The sooner will his race be Run,
And nearer to his setting.

Then be not coy, but use your time,
And while you may, go marry,
For if you lose but once your prime
You may for ever tarry.

The Gelding of the Divel.

A Story strange I will you tell
    Of the gelding of the Divel of hell,
And of the Baker of *Mansfield* Town,
That sold his bread both white and brown;
To *Nottingham* Market he was bound,
And riding under the Willows clear
The Baker sung with a merry chear.

The Bakers horse was lusty and sound,
And worth in Judgement full five pound;
His skin was smooth, and his flesh was fat,
His Master was well pleas'd with that,
Which made him sing so merry, merrily
As he was passing on the way.

                                           But

But as he rode over the hill
There met him two divels of hell:
O Baker, Baker, then cry'd he,
How comes thy horse so fat to be?
These be the words the Baker did say,
Because his stones are cut away.

Then, quoth the divel, if it be so,
Thou shalt geld me before thou dost go;
First tye thy horse to yonder tree,
And with thy knife come and geld me;
The Baker he had a knife for the nonce
Wherewith to cut out the devils stones.

The Baker, as it came to pass,
In haste alighted from his horse,
And the divel on his back he lay,
While the Baker cut his stones away,
Which put the divel to great pain
And made him to cry out amain.

O, quoth the divel, beshrew thy heart,
Thou dost not feel how I do smart,
And for the deed that thou hast done
I will revenged be agen,
And underneath this Green-wood tree
Next Market day I will geld thee.

The

The Baker then but a little said,
But at his heart was sore afraid;
He durst no longer then to stay,
But he rode hence another way:
And coming to his Wife, did tell
How he had gelt the divel of hell.

Moreover to his Wife he told
A tale that made her heart full cold,
How that the divel to him did say,
That he would geld him next Market day:
O, quoth the good wife, without doubt
I had rather both thy eyes were out.

For then all the people far and near,
That know thee, will but mock and jeer,
And good-wives they will scold and brawl,
And stoneless Gelding will thee call;
Then hold content, and be thou wise,
And I'll some pretty trick devise.

I'll make the divel change his note,
Give me thy Hat, thy Band, and Coat,
Thy Hose and Doublet eke also,
And I like to a man will go;
I'll warrant thee next Market day
To fright the divel clean away.

When the Bakers wife was so drest,
With all her bread upon her beast,
To *Nottingham* Market, that brave Town,
To sell her bread, both white and brown,
And riding merrily over the hill,
O there she spy'd the two divels of hell.

A little divel, and another,
As they were playing both together;
Oh ho, quoth the divel, right fain,
Here comes the Baker riding amain:
Now be thou well, or be thou woe,
I will geld thee before thou dost go.

The Bakers wife to the divel did say,
Sir, I was gelded yesterday:
O, quoth the divel, I mean to see;
And pulling her coats above her knee,
And so looking upward from the ground,
O there he spy'd a terrible wound.

O, quoth the divel, now I see
That he was not cunning that gelded thee,
For when that he had cut out the stones,
He should have closed up the wounds,
But if thou wilt stay but a little space
I'll fetch some salve to cure the place.

He

He had not ran but a little way,
But up her belly crept a Flea:
The little divel seeing that,
He up with his paw and gave her a pat,
Which made the good wife for to start,
And with that she let go a rowzing fart.

O, quoth the divel, thy life is not long
Thy breath it smells so horrible strong,
Therefore go thy way, and make thy will,
Thy wounds are past all humane skill;
Be gone, be gone, make no delay,
For here thou shalt no longer stay.

The good wife with this news was glad,
But she left the divel almost mad;
And when she to her husband came,
With a joyful heart she told the same,
How she had couzned the divel of hell,
Which pleas'd her Husband wondrous well.

The Vagabond.

I Am a Rogue, and a stout one,
   A most couragious *drinker:*
I do excell, it's known full well,
   The Ratter, *Tom,* or *Tinker:*

Then

Then do I cry, Good your Worship
Bestow some small Denier a,
And bravely then at the bouking Ken
I'll bouze it all in beera.

My dainty Dames and Doxes,
When that they see [me] lacking,
Without delay, poor wretches, they
Will send the Duds a packing:
    Then do I cry, &c.

Ten miles into a Market
I go to meet a Miser,
And in the throng I'll nip a bung,
And the party ne'r the wiser:
    Then do I cry, &c.

If the Centry be coming,
Then streight it is my fashion,
My leg I'll tye close to my thigh
To move them to compassion:
    Then do I cry, &c.

When I hear a Coach come rumbling,
To my Crutches streight I hye me,
For being lame, it is a shame
Such Gallants should deny me;
    Then do I cry, &c.

My *Peg* in a string doth lead me
When I go into the Town, Sir,
For to the blind all men are kind,
And with [? will] their Alms bestow, Sir;
    Then do I cry, &c.

I' th' winter time stark naked
I go into some City,
And every man, that spare them can,
Will give me cloaths for pity;
    Then do I cry, &c.

My doublet sleeves hang empty,
And for to beg the bolder,
For meat and drink my arm I'll shrink
Up close unto my shoulder,
    Then do I cry, &c.

If any gives me lodging
A courteous knave they find me,
For in my bed, alive, or dead,
I leave some Lice behind me;
    Then do I cry, &c.

If from out the Low Countries
I hear a Captains name, Sir,
Then straight I'll swear I have been there,
And so in fight came lame Sir;
    Then do I cry, &c.

In *Pauls* Church-yard by a Piller
Sometimes you see me stand, Sir,
With a writ that shews what cares, what woes
I have past by Sea and Land, Sir ;
  Then do I cry, *&c.*

Come buy, come buy a Horn-book,
Who buys my Pins and Needles :
Such things do I in the City cry
Oftimes to scape the Beadles ;
  Then do I cry, *&c.*

Then blame me not for begging,
And boasting all alone, Sir,
My self I will be praising still,
For Neighbours I have none, Sir ;
  Then do I cry, *&c.*

The Jovial Loyallist.

STay, shut the Gate,
 T'other quart, 'faith 'tis not so late
  As your thinking,
The Stars which you see in the Hemisphere be,
Are but studs in our cheeks by good drinking ;
The Sun's gone to tipple all night in the Sea boys,
To morrow he'll blush that he's paler than we boys,
Drink wine, give him water, 'tis Sack makes us the
       (boys.
    Fill

   Fill up the Glass,
To the next merry Lad let it pass,
   Come away with't :
Let's set foot to foot, and but give our minds to't,
'Tis heretical Six that doth slay wit :
Then hang up good faces, let's drink till our noses
Give freedom to speak what our fancy disposes,
Beneath whose protection, now under the rose is.

   Drink off your Bowl,
'Twill enrich both your head and your soul
   With Canary ;
For a carbuncl'd face saves a tedious race,
And the *Indies* above us we carry :
No *Helicon* like to the juice of good wine is,
For *Phoebus* had never had wit that divine is,
Had his face not been bow-dy'd as thine is, & mine
            (is.

   This must go round,
Off with your hats till the pavement be crown'd
   With your Bevers.
A Red-coated face frights a Sergeant and his Mace,
Whilst the Constable trembles to shivers,
In state march our faces like some of the *quorum*,
While the whores do fall down, & the vulgar adore
 'um,
And our noses like Link-boys run shining before
 'um.

             Mer

MERRY DROLLERY,

Complete.

OR,

A COLLECTION

Of
{ Jovial *Poems*,
  Merry *Songs*,
  Witty *Drolleries*,

Intermixed with Pleasant *Catches*.

The Second Part.

The Answer.

Hold, quaff no more,
    But restore,
If you can, [what] you've lost by your drinking,
    Three Kingdoms and Crowns,
    With their cities and Towns,
While the King and his Progeny is sinking;
The studs in your cheeks have obscur'd his star, boys,
Your drink and miscarriages in the late war, boys
Hath brought his P[r]erogative thus to the Bar, boys.

    Throw down the Glass,
    He's an ass
That extracts all his worth from Canary:
    That valour will shrink,
    Which is only good in drink,
'Twas the Cup made the Camp to miscarry.
Ye thought in the world there was no power could
    tame ye,
Ye tipled and whor'd till the Foe overcame ye,
Cuds-nigs and ne'r-stir Sir, hath vanquisht God-
    dam:me.

    Fly from the coast,
    Or y' are lost,
And the water will run where the drink went,
    From

From hence you must slink,
  If you swear and have no chink,
'Tis the curse of a Royal Delinquent.   [? course]
We love to see Beer bowls turn'd over the thumb
    Well,
We love three fair Gamesters, four Dice and a Drum
    Well,
But you'd as live see the divel as *Oliver Cromwel*.

  Drink not the round,
    You'll be drown'd
In the source of your Sack and your Sonnets,
  Try once more your Fate
  For the Kirk against the State,   [? King]
And go barter your Bever for Bonnets:
  See how you'r charm'd by your female inchanters,
And therefore pack hence to *Virginia* for planters,
For an act and two red-coats will rout all the Ran-
      ters.

A Catch.

Had she not care enough, care enough,
  Care enough of the old man?
She wed him, she fed him,
And to the bed she led him;
For seven long winters she lifted him on:
But oh how she negl'd him, negl'd him,
Oh how she negl'd him all the night long!

A Catch.

Here's a Health unto his Majesty with a Fa la la, &c.
Conversion to his enemies with a Fa la la, &c.
And he that will not pledge this Health,
I wish him neither wit nor wealth,
Nor yet a Rope to hang himself with a Fa la la, &c.

Good Advice against Treason.

BUT since it was lately enacted high Treason
    For a man to speak truth against the head of a
    State,
Let every wise man make use of his reason,   (prate,
    To think what he will, but take heed what he
For the Proverb doth learn us,   (skin,
    He that staies from the battel sleeps in a whole
And our words are our own, if we keep them within,
What fools are we then that to prattle do begin,
    Of things that do not concern us.

Tis no matter to me who e'r gets the battel,
    The Tubs or the Crosses, 'tis all one to me,
It neither increaseth my goods nor my cattel,
    A beggar's a beggar, and so he shall be,
Unless he turn Traytor.
Let Misers take courses to hoard up their treasure,
    Whose bounds have no limits[,] whose minds have
        no measure,
                                       But

Let me be but quiet, and take a little pleasure,
    A little contents my own nature.

But what if the Kingdom returns to one of the
        Prime ones?
    My mind is a Kingdom, and so it shall be,
I'll make it appear, if I had but the time once,
    He's as happy in one, as they are in three,
If he might but enjoy it:
    He that's mounted aloft, is a mark for the Fate,
    And an envy to every pragmatical pate,
Whilest he that is low is safe in his estate,
    And the great ones do scorn to annoy him.

I count him no wit that is gifted in rayling,
    And flurting at those that above him do sit,
Whilst they do out-wit him with whipping and goaling,
    His purse and his person must pay for his wit:
But it is better to be drinking,   [:]
If Sack were reform'd to twelve pence a quart,
    I'd study for money to Merchandize for't,
With a friend that is willing in mirth we would sport,
    Not a word; but we'd pay it with thinking.

My petition shall be that Canary be cheaper,
    Without either Custom, or cursed Excize,
That the wits may have freedom to drink deeper
        and deeper,
    And not be undone whilst our Noses we baptize,
But we'll liquor them, and drench them;

If this were but granted, who would not desire,
    To dub himself one of *Apollo's* acquire? [own quire]
And then we will drink whilst our Noses are on fire,
    And the quart-pots shall be Buckets to quench them.

The feasting of the Divel[:] by Ben Johnson.

Cook-*Laurel* would needs have the divel his gues
    And bad him once into the *Peake* to dinner;
Where never the Fiend had such a Feast
    Provided him at the charge of a sinner.

His stomack was queasie (for comming there coacht)
    The jogging had caused some crudities rise,
To help it he call'd for a Puritan poacht,
    That used to turn up the whites of his eyes

And so recovered unto his wish,
    He sate him down, and he fell to eat;
Promooter in plum-broath was the first dish;
    His own privy Kitchin had no such meat.

Yet though with this he much were taken,
    Upon a sudden he shifted his trencher;
As soon as he spide the bawd, and bacon,
    By this you may note the divel's a wencher.

                                                 Six

Six pickled Taylors sliced and cut,
   Sempsters, Tire-women fit for his pallet,
With feather-men, and perfumers put,
   Some twelve in a Charger to make a grand sallet.

A rich fat Usurer stew'd in his Marrow,
   And by him a Lawyers head and Green-sawce;
Both which his belly took in like a barrow,
   As if till then he had never seen sawce.

Then carbinadoed, and cookt with pains
   Was brought up a cloven Serjeant's Face;
The sawce was made of the Yeomans brains,
   That had been beaten out with his own Mace.

Two roasted Sheriffs came whole to the board,
   (The Feast had nothing been without 'um,)
Both living and dead they were Fox'd and Fur'd;
   Their chains like Sawsages hung about 'um.

The very next dish was the Mayor of a town,
   With a pudding of maintenance thrust in his belly,
Like a Goose in the Feathers drest in his Gown,
   And his couple of Hinch boys boyl'd to a jelly.

A *London* Cuckold hot from the spit,
   And when the Carver up had broke him,
The divel chopt up his head at a bit,   (him
   But the horns were very near like to have choakt

The Chine of a Leacher too there was roasted,
  With a plump Harlots haunch and Garlick;
A Panders pettitoes that had boasted
  Himself a Captain, yet never was warlike.

A large fat Pasty of a Mid-wife hot,
  And for a cold bak't meat into the story,
A reverend painted Lady was brought,
  And coffind in crust, till now she was hoary.

To these, an over-grown-Justice of peace
  With a Clark like a gizard thrust under each arm,
And warrants for sippets, laid in his own grease
  Set over a chafing-dish to be kept warm.

The Jowle of a Jaylor served for Fish,
  A Constable souz'd with Vinegar by,
Two Alder-men Lobsters asleep in a dish,
  A Deputy tart, a Church-warden pye.

All which devoured, he then for a close,
  Did for a full draught of *Darby* call,
He heav'd the huge Vessel up to his Nose,
  And left not till he had drunk up all.

Then from Table he gave a start,
  Where banquet and wine were nothing scarce;
All which he started away with a Fart,
  From whence it was called the divels Arse.

And

And there he made such a breach with the wind,
  The hole too standing open the while,
That the scent of the Vapour before and behind,
  Hath foully perfum'd most part of the Isle.

And this was *Tobacco*, the Learned suppose,
  Which since in Country, Court, and Town,
In the divels Glister-pipe smoakes at the Nose
  Of Polcat and Madam, of Gallant, and Clown.

From which wicked weed, with swines-flesh & Ling,
  Or any thing else that's feast for the Fiend,
Our Captains and we cry God save the King,
  And send him good meat, & Mirth without end.

A Catch.

A Fig for care, why should we spare [?]
  The Parish is bound to find us,
For thou and I and all must dye,
  And leave the world behind us.

The Clerk shall Sing, the Bells shall Ring
  And the Old Wives wind us;
Sir *John* shall lay our Bones in Clay,
  Where no body means to find us.

The Virtue of Wine.

Let Souldiers fight for praise, and pay,
And Money bid the Misers wish;
Poor Scholars study all the day,
And gluttons glory in their dish;
    'Tis wine, 'tis wine revives sad souls,
    Therefore give me the chearing bowls.

Let Minions marshal every hair,
And in a Lovers lock delight,
And artificial colours wear,
We have the native red and white;
    'Tis wine, Pure wine, &c.

Take Pheasant, Puet, and Culvered Salmon,
And how to please your Pallats think:
Give me a salt Westphalia gammon,
Not meat to eat, but meat to drink; [? but meet]
    'Tis wine, pure wine, &c.

Some have the Ptysick, some the Rheume,
Some have the Palsie, some the Gout;
Some swell with fat, and some consume,
But they are sound that drink all out;
    'Tis wine, tis wine, &c.

Some men want Wit, and some want Wealth;
Some want a Wife, and some want a Punk;
Some men want Food, and some want Health,
But he wants nothing that is drunk;
  'Tis wine, 'tis pure wine, &c.

It makes the backward spirits brave,
Them lively, that before were dull;
Those grow good Fellows that are grave,
And kindness springs from Cups brim-full;
  'Tis wine, 'tis wine revives sad soules,
  Therefore give me the Charming bowles.

A Catch.

NE'er trouble thy self at the times or their turnings,
 Afflictions run Circular and wheele about,
Away with thy murmurings, & thy heart burnings,
With the juice of the Grape we'll quench the fire
         (out.

Ne'er chain nor imprison thy soul up in sorrow,
What failes us to day, may befriend us to morrow,
Let us scorn our content from others to borrow.

A Catch.

THree merry boys came out of the West,
    To make Salt-peter strong;
They turn'd it into Gunpowder,
    To charge the Kings Canon;
And so let this health go round, go round,
    And so let this health go round,
Although thy stocking be made of Silk
    Thy knee shall touch the ground.
God bless his Majesty,
    And send him Victory.
Over his Enemy's
    All or none.

A Loves Song.

CAlm was the Evening, and clear was the Skie,
    And new budding Flowers did spring,
When all alone went *Amyntas* and I
To hear the sweet Nightingale sing.
I sate, and he laid him down by me,
And scarcely his breath he could draw,
    But when with a fear,
    He began to come near,
He was dasht with a ah, ah, ah.

He blusht to himself, and lay still for awhile,
And his modesty curb'd his desire,
But streightly [I] convinc'd all his fears with a smile,
And added new flames to his fire.
Ah, *Silvia*, said he, you are cruel,
To keep your poor Lover in awe,
    Then once more he prest
    With his hands to my brest,
But was dasht with a ah, ah, ah.

I knew 'twas his passions caus'd all his fear,
And therefore I pitied his case,
I whisper'd him softly, there's nobody near,
And laid my cheek close to his face:
But as he grew bolder and bolder,
A shepheard came by us and saw,
    And just as our bliss
    Began with a Kiss:
He burst out with a Ha, Ha, ha, Ha.

The Brewers Praise.

THere's many a blinking verse was made [clinching]
    In honour of the Blacksmiths trade,
But more of the Brewers may be said,
    Which nobody can deny.

I need not else but this repeat,
The Blacksmith cannot be compleat,
Unless the Brewer do give him a heat,
    Which no body, &c.

When Smug unto his Forge doth come
Unless the Brewer doth liquor him home
Could ne'er strike my pot and thy pot *Tom*,
    Which no body, &c.

Of all the Professions in the Town,
This Brewers trade did gain renown,
His liquor once reacht up to the Crown,
    Which no body, &c.

Much bloud from him did spring,
Of all the trades this was the King,
The Brewer had got the world in a sling,
    Which no body, &c.

Though Honour be a Princess daughter,
The Brewer will woe her in bloud and slaughter,
And win her, or else it shall cost him hot water,
    Which no body, &c.

He fear'd no pouder, nor martial stops,
But whipt Armies as round as tops,
And cut off his foes as thick as hops,
    Which no body, &c.

[e div'd for riches down to the bottom,
nd cri'd, my Masters, when he had got 'um,
et every Tub stand upon his own bottom,
  Which no body, &c.

1 warlike Arts he scorn'd to stoop,
or when his party began to droop,
[e'd bring them all up as round as a hoop,
  Which no body, &c.

he Jewish Scots, who fear to eat
he flesh of Swine, our brewers beat, (treat[,]
'was the sight of their hogsheads made them to re
  Which no body, &c.

oor *Jockie* and his basket hilt
/as beaten, and much bloud was spilt,
/hen their bodies, like barrels, did run a tilt,
  Which no body, &c.

'hough *Jemmy* did give the first assault,
'he Brewer he made them at length to hault,
.nd gave them what the Cat left in the mault,
  Which no body, &c.

'hey did not only bang the Kirk,
ut in *Ireland* too they did as much work,
'was the Brewer made them surrender *Cork*,
  Which no body, &c.

        This

This was a stout Brewer, of whom we may brag,
But since he was hurried away with a hag,
We have brew'd in a bottle, and bak'd in a bag,
    Which no body, &c.

They said that Antichrist came to settle
Religion within a Cooler and a Kettle,
His Nose and his Copper were both of a mettle,
    Which no body, &c.

He had a strong, and a very stout heart,
And look'd to be made an Emperour for't,
But the Divel did set a spoke in his Cart,
    Which no body, &c.

The Christian Kings began to quake,
And said, with that Brewers no quarrels we'll make,
We'll let him alone, as he brews let him bake,
    Which no body, &c.

But yet by the way you must needs understand,
He kept all his Passions so under command,
Pride never could get the upper-hand,
    Which no body, &c.

And now may all stout souldiers say,
Farewell the glory of the Dray,
For the Brewer himself is turn'd to Clay,
    Which no body, &c.

                                       Thus

Thus fell a brave Brewer the bold son of slaughter,
Who need not to fear much what should follow after,
That dealt all his life-time in fire and water,
    Which no body, &c.

And if his Successor had had but his might,
We all had not been in that pitiful plight,
But alas, he was found many grains to[o] light,
    Which no body, &c.

Though Wine be a Juice sweet, pleasant, and pure,
This Trade doth such pleasure and profit procure,
That every Vintner in Town is turn'd Brewer,
    Which no body, &c.

But now let's leave singing, and drink off our Bub,
Let's call for a Reckoning, and every man club,
For I think I have told you a Tale of a Tub,
    Which no body can deny.

The Song of the Blacksmith.

OF all the Trades that ever I see, (be;
   There's none to the Blacksmith compared may
With so many several tooles works he,
    Which no body can deny.

The first that ever Thunderbolts made
Was a *Cyclops* of the Blacksmiths Trade,
As in a Learned Author is said,
    Which no body, &c.

When thundring like we strike about,
The fire like Lightning flashes out,
Which suddenly with water we d' out,
    Which no body, &c.

The fairest Goddess in the skies,
To marry with *Vulcan* did advise,
And he was a Blacksmith grave and wise,
    Which no body, &c.

Vulcan he to do her right,
Did build her a Town by day and by night,
And gave it a name which was *Hammersmiths* hight,
    Which no body, &c.

Vulcan further did acquaint her,
That a pretty Estate he would appoint her,
And leave her *Seacoal-lane* for a Joynter,
    Which no body, &c.

And that no enemy might wrong her,
He built her a fort, you'd wish no stronger,
Which was in the lane of *Ironmonger*,
    Which no body, &c.

Smithfield he did cleanse from durt,
And sure there was great Reason for 't,
For there he meant she should keep her Court,
    Which no body, &c.

                                                    But

But after in a good time and tide,
It was by the Blacksmith rectifi'd
To the honour of *Edmund Ironside*,
    Which no body, &c.

Vulcan after made a traine,
Wherein the God of war was tane
Which ever since hath been call'd *Pauls* chaine,
    Which no body, &c.

The common Proverb as it is read,
That a man must hit the naile on the head,
Without the Blacksmith cannot be said,
    Which no body, &c.

Another must not be forgot,
And falls unto the Blacksmiths lot,
That a man strike while the Iron is hot,
    Which no body, &c.

Another comes in most proper and fit,
The Blacksmiths justice is seen in it,
When you give a man roast & beat him with the spit
    When no body, &c.

Another comes in our Blacksmiths way,
When things are safe, as old wives say,
We have them under lock and key,
    Which no body, &c.

Another that's in the Blacksmiths books,
And only to him for remedy looks,
Is when a man's quite off the hooks,
    Which no body, &c.

Another Poverb to him doth belong,
And therefore let's do the Blacksmith no wrong,
When a man's held to it buckle and thong,
    Which no body, &c.

Another Proverb doth make me laugh,
Wherein the Blacksmith may challenge half,
When a Reason's as plain as a Pike staffe,
    Which no body, &c.

Though your Lawyers travel both near and far,
And by long pleading a good cause may mar,
Yet your Blacksmith takes more pains at the Bar,
    Which no body, &c.

Though your Scrivener seek to crush and to kill
By his counterfeit deed, and thereby doth ill,
Yet your Blacksmith may forge what he will,
    Which no body, &c.

Though your bankrupt Citizens lurk in their holes,
And laugh at their Creditors, and their Catchpoles,
Yet your Blacksmith can fetch them over the coals,
    Which no body, &c.

                                Though

Though *Jockie* in the stable be never so neat,
To look to his nag, and prescribe him his meat,
Yet your Blacksmith knows better how to give a
      Which no body, &c.   (heat,

If any Taylor have the Itch,
The Blacksmiths water, as black as pitch,
Will make his hands go thorough stitch,
      Which no body, &c.

There's never a slut, if filth o'r smutch her,
But owes to the Blacksmith for her leacher,
For without a pair of tongues there's no man will
      Which no body, &c.   (touch her,

Your roaring boy, who every one Quails,
Fights, domineers, swaggers, and rayls,
Could never yet make the Smith eat his Nails,
      Which no body, &c.

If a Schollar be in doubt,
And cannot well bring his matter about,
The Blacksmith he can hammer it out,
      Which no body, &c.

Now if to know him you would desire,
You must not scorn, but rank him higher,
For what he gets, is out of the fire,
      Which no body, &c.

Now here's a good health to Blacksmiths all,
And let it go round, as round as a ball;
We'll drink it all off, though it cost us a fall,
    Which nobody can deny.

The Gypsies, a Catch.

Come my dainty doxies,
    My Dove, my Darle, my Dear,
We have neither meat nor drink,
Yet never want good chear;
    We take no care for Candle, Rents,
    We lye, we swear, we snort in Tents,
Come rouse betimes
All you that love your dinners,
    Our store now taken
    With Pigs, Hens, and Bacon,
And that's good meat for sinners.

    At Fairs and Wakes we cuzzen
    Poor Country Folk by the dozen;
Some come to disburses,
And some to pick purses;
We for want of use
We steal both hose and shooes,
    Gilded Spurs with jingling Rowels,
    Shirts or Smocks, Sheets or Towels;
                      Come

Come live with us all you that love your ease,
  He that's a Gipsie may be drunk when he please,
    We laugh, we quaff, we roar, we snuffle
    We drink, we Drab, we cheat, we shuffle.

In imitation of Come my Daphne, *a Dialogue betwixt* Pluto *and* Oliver.

Pluto. Come Imp Royal, come away,
    Into black night we will turn bright day.
Oliver. 'Tis *Pluto* calls, what would my Syre?
Pluto. Come follow to the Stygian fire.
  Where *Ireton* doth wait to welcome thee in
                            (State.
Oliver. Were I in bed with my sweet wife,
  I'd quit those joys for such a life.
Pluto. My princely *Nol* make hast,
  For thee we keep a fast.
Oliver. In these dismal shades will I
  Unto thee unfold my Villany.
Pluto. In my bosome I'll thee lay,
  For thy sake we'll all keep holy day.

Chorus. We'll rage and roar, and fry in flames
  And *Charles* himself shall see
  How damn'dly we agree,
  Yet scorn to change our Chains
  For his Eternal diety.   [Deity]

A Catch.

                                  (for me,
THe *wise men* were but seven, ne'r more shall be
    The *Muses* were but 9, the worthies 3 times 3 :
And three merry boys, & three merry boys are we ;

The *Vertues* were but seven, & three the greater be ;
The *Cæsars* they were twelve, & the fatal Sisters three ;
    And three merry Girles, & three merry Girles are
                                            (we.

The Power of Wine.

HOw poor is his Spirit, how lost is his name?
    Deceiveth Opinion, and curtels his Fame,
When as his design turns neer to their hate,
'Twixt shall I, and shall I suspects their o[w]ne wai[gh]t,
Hath traffick't for honour, but lost the whole fraight,
He that's stout in the front, but not so in the rear,
Doth forfeit his Fame, and is cowed down by fear.

A small part of honour to him doth belong,
Consults not his glory, but faints in the throng,
That fears to embrace what his Country doth vote,
And yields up her liberty to a Red-coat ;
Sure *Midsummer* is near, and some men do doat,

                                                      I

I like the bold Romans, whose fame ever rings [,]
That kept in subjection such pitiful things.

He that will be Bug-bear'd is turn'd again Child,
A Reed than a Scepter is fitter to weild :
Examine that story, no story you'll find
Than saving that story that Cat will to kind;
The world is deluded, the Commonwealth blind,
Your false stamps of honor proves but copper mettle [,]
And Fame sounds as loud from a tinkers old kettle.

He that hath past the Pike, and found Canon-free,
Which shews that no curse from his Parents could be,
Had a soul so devout [it] made killing a trade,
And now to retreat at the scent of a blade, (made,
Doth show of what mould our Knight-errant is
He that flags in his flight when his ambition soars
Doth stab his own merit, & gives fame the lye. (high

Then *Cicero*-like you gown-men drench cares,
O'rwhelm'd with your own & your Countries affairs,
And Pulpit-men to be as ayry as he ;
Do you but preach Sack up we'll ne'r disagree
That Commonwealth's best that is the most free,
Then fret not, nor care not, when the Sack's in our
We fancy a King up, or fancy him down.   (Crown,

The

The Mad Zealot.

AM I mad, O noble *Festus*,
  When zeal and godly knowledge
Have put me in hope
To deal with the Pope,
As well as the best in the Colledge?
  Boldly I preach, hate a Cross, hate a Surplice,
    Miters, Copes, and Rochets:
    Come hear me pray nine times a day,
    And fill your heads with Crotchets.

In the house of pure *Emanuel*
I had my Education,
Where my friends surmise
I dazell'd mine eyes
With the light of Revelation,
  Boldy I preach, &c.

They bound me like a Beldam   [Bedlam]
They lasht my four poor quarters;
Whilst this I endure,
Faith makes me sure
To be one of *Foxes* Martyrs,
  Boldly I preach, &c.

These

These injuries I suffer
Through Antichrists perswasions;
Take off this chain,
Neither *Rome* nor *Spain*
Can resist my strong invasions,
    Boldly I preach, &c.

Of the beasts ten horns (God bless us)
I have knockt off three already:
If they let me alone,
I'll leave him none:
But they say I am too heady.
    Boldly I preach, &c.

When I sack'd the seven hill'd-City,
I met the great red Dragon:
I kept him aloof,
With the armour of proof,
Though here I have never a rag on:
    Boldly I preach, &c.

With a fiery Sword and Target
There fought I with this Monster:
But the sons of pride
My zeal deride,
And all my deeds misconster.
    Boldly I preach, &c.

I unhers'd the whore of *Babel*
With a Lance of Inspirations:
I made her stink,
And spill her drink
In the cup of Abominations,
    Boldly I preach, &c.

I have seen two in a Vision,
With a flying Book between them:
I have been in despair
Five times a year,
And cur'd by reading *Greenham*,
    Boldly I preach, &c.

I observ'd in *Perkins* Tables
The black Lines of Damnation,
Those crooked veins
So stuck in my brains,
That I fear'd my Reprobation,
    Boldly I preach, &c.

In the holy land of Canaan
I plac'd my chiefest pleasure,
Till I prick'd my foot
With an Hebrew root,
That I bled beyond all measure,
    Boldly I preach, &c.

I appear'd before th' Archbishop,
And all the High Commission :
I gave him no Grace,
But told him to his face
That he favour'd Superstition,
  Boldly I preach, hate a Cross, hate a Surplice,
  Miters, Copes, and Rochets :
  Come hear me pray nine times a day
  And fill your heads with Crotchets.

Drunk with Love.

I Doat, I doat, but am a Sot to shew it,
 I was a very fool to let her know it,
For now she doth so cunning grow,
And proves a friend worse than a Foe,
She will not hold me fast, nor let me go :
  She tells me I cannot forsake her,
  Then straight I endeavour to leave her,
  But to make me stay throws a kiss in my way,
  O then I could tarry for ever.

Thus I retire, salute, and sit down by her
There do I fry in frost, and freeze in fire ;
Now nectar from her lips I sup,
And though I cannot drink all up,
Yet I am Fox'd with kissing of the Cup :

         For

> For her lips are two brimmers of Clarret,
> Where first I began to miscarry,
> Her breasts of delight are two bottles of White,
> And her eyes are two cups of Canary.

Drunk, as I live, dead drunk beyond reprieve,
For all my secrets dribble through a sieve;
About my neck her arms she layeth,
Now all is Gospel that she saith,
Which I lay hold on with my fudled faith;
> I find a fond Lover's a Drunkard,
> And dangerous is when he flies out,
> With hips, and with lips, with black eyes & white
> Blind *Cupid* sure tipled his eyes out.   (thighs

She bids me rise, tells me I must be wise,
Like her, for she's not in love she cries;
This makes me fret, and fling, and throw,
Shall I be fetter'd to my foe?
I begin to run, but cannot go;
> I prethee, sweet, use me more kindly,
> You were better to hold me fast,
> If you once disengage your bird from his cage,
> Believe it he'll leave you at last.

Like Sot I sit that fill'd the Town with wit,
But now confess I have most need of it;
I have been fox'd with Duck and Deer
Above a quarter of a year

Beyond the cure of sleeping, or small beer;
    I think I can number the Months too,
    July, August, September, October,
    Thus goes my account, a mischief light on't,
    But sure I shall go when I'm sober.

My Legs are lam'd, my courage is quite tam'd,
My heart and all my body is enflam'd,
As by experience I can prove,
And swear by all the Powers above,
'Tis better to be drunk with wine than love:
    For 'tis Sack makes us merry and witty,
    Our foreheads with Jewels adorning,
    Although we do grope, yet there's some hope,
    That a man may be sober next morning.

Thus, with command, she throws me from her hand,
And bids me go, yet knows I cannot stand;
I measure all the ground by trips,
Was ever Sot so drunk with sips,
Or can a man be overseen with lips?
    I pray Madam fickle be faithful,
    And leave off your damnable dodging,
    Then do not deceive me, either love me or leave
    Or let me go home to my lodging.   (me,

I have too much, and yet my folly is such,
I cannot [leave] hold, but must have t'other touch;
Here's a health to the King: how now?
                                              In

I'm drunk and speak treason I vow,
Lovers and Fools say any thing you know;
    I fear I have tired your patience,
    But I'm sure 'tis I have the wrong on't;
    My wits are bereft, and all I have left
    Is scarce enough to make a Song on't;
    My Mistris and I shall never comply,
    And there's the short and the long on't.

A Present to a Lady.

LAdies I do here present you
    With a token Love hath sent you;
'Tis a thing to sport and play with,
Such another pretty thing
For to pass the time away with;
Prettier sport was never seen;

Name I will not, nor define it,
Sure I am you may devine it:
By those modest looks I guess it,
And those eyes so full of fire,
That I need no more express it,
But leave your fancies to admire.

Yet as much of it be spoken
In the praise of this love-token:
'Tis a wash that far supasseth

                                          For

For the cleansing of your blood,
All the Saints may bless your faces,
Yet not do you so much good.

Were you ne'r so melancholly,
It will make you blithe and jolly;
Go no more, no more admiring,
When you feel your spleen's amiss,
For all the drinks of Steel and Iron
Never did such cures as this.

It was born in th' Isle of Man
Venus nurs'd it with her hand,
She puffed it up with milk and pap,
And lull'd it in her wanton lap,
So ever since this Monster can
In no place else with pleasure stand.

Colossus like, between two Rocks,
I have seen him stand and shake his locks,
And when I have heard the names
Of the sweet Saterian Dames,
O he's a Champion for a Queen,
'Tis pity but he should be seen.

Nature, that made him, was so wise
As to give him neither tongue nor eyes,
Supposing he was born to be
The Instrument of Jealousie,

Yet here he can, as Poets feign,
Cure a Ladies love-sick brain.

He was the first that did betray
To mortal eyes the milky way;
He is the *Proteus* cunning Ape
That will beget you any shape;
Give him but leave to act his part,
And he'll revive your saddest heart.

Though he want legs, yet he can stand,
With the least touch of your soft hand;
And though, like *Cupid*, he be blind,
There's never a hole but he can find;
If by all this you do not know it,
Pray Ladies give me leave to shew it.

A Combate of Cocks.

GO *you tame Gallants, you that have the name,*
    And would accounted be Cocks of the Game,
That have brave spurs to shew for't, and can crow,
And count all dunghil breed that cannot shew
Such painted Plumes as yours; that think no vice,
With Cock-like lust to tread your Cockatrice:
Though Peacocks, Wood-cocks, Weather-cocks you be,
If y' are no fighting-cocks, y'are not for me:

I

I of two feather'd Combatants will write,
He that to th' life means to express the fight,
Must make his ink o' th' bloud which they did spill,
And from their dying wings borrow his quill.

NO sooner were the doubtfull people set[,
   The matches made, and all that would had bet,
But straight the skilful Judges of the Play,
Bring forth their sharp-heel'd Warriours, and they
Were both in linnen bags, as if 'twere meet,
Before they dy'd to have their winding sheet.
With that in th' pit they are put, & when they were
Both on their feet, the *Norfolk* Chanticleere
Looks stoutly at his ne'r-before seen foe,
And like a Challenger begins to crow,
And shakes his wings, as if he would display
His warlike Colours, which were black and gray:
Mean time the wary *Wisbich* walks and breaths
His active body, and in fury wreaths
His comely crest, and often looking down,
He whets his angry beak upon the ground:
With that they meet, not like the coward breed
Of *Æsop*, that can better fight than feed.
They scorn the dung-hill, 'tis their only prize,
To dig for Pearl within each others eyes:
They fight so long, that it was hard to know
To th' skilful, whether they did fight or no,
Had not the bloud which died the fatal floor
Born witness of it; yet they fight the more,

As if each wound were but a spur to prick
Their fury forward : lightning's not more quick
Nor red than were their eyes : 'twas hard to know
Whether 'twas bloud or anger made them so :
And sure they had been out, had they not stood
More safe by being fenced in by blood.
Yet still they fight, but now (alas) at length
Although their courage be full tried, their strength
And bloud began to ebbe; you that have seen
A water-combat on the Sea, between
Two roaring angry boyling billows, how
They march, and meet, and dash their curled brows,
Swelling like graves, as if they did intend
T'intomb each other, ere the quarrel end :
But when the wind is down, and blustring weather,
They are made friends, & sweetly run together, (low[,]
May think these champions such, their combs grow
And they that leapt even now, now scarce can go :
Their wings which lately at each blow they clapt [,]
(As if they did applaud themselves) now flapt.
And having lost the advantage of the heel,
Drunk with each others bloud they only reel.
From either eyes such drops of bloud did fall,
As if they wept them for their Funeral.
And yet they would fain fight, they come so near,
As if they meant into each others ear
To whisper death ; and when they cannot rise,
They lie and look blows in each others eyes.
                                                But

But now the Tragick part after the fight,
When *Norfolk* Cock had got the best of it,
And *Wisbich* lay a dying, so that none,
Though sober, but might venture seven to one,
Contracting (like a dying Tapre) all
His force, as meaning with that blow to fall;
He struggles up, and having taken wind,
Ventures a blow, and strikes the other blind.
And now Poor *Norfolk* having lost his eyes,
Fights only guided by th' Antipathies:
With him (alas) the proverb holds not true,
The blows his eyes ne'er see, his heart most rue.
At length by chance, he stumbling on his foe,
Not having any power to strike a blow,
He falls upon him with a wounded head,
And makes his conquered wings his Feather-bed,
Where lying sick, his friends were very chary
Of him, and fetcht in haste an Apothecary;
But all in vain, his body did so blister,
That 'twas uncapable of any Glister,
Wheresoever at length, opening his fainting bill,
He call'd a Scrivener, and thus made his Will.

INprimis, Let it never be forgot,
   My body freely I bequath to th' pot,
Decently to be boyl'd, and for its tomb,
Let it be buried in some hungry womb.
Item, *Executors I will have none,*
But he that on my side laid seven to one:

And like a Gentleman that he may live,
To him and to his heirs my comb I give;
Together with my brains, that all may know,
That often times his brains did use to crow.
Item, *It is my Will to the weaker ones,*
Whose wives complain of them, I give my stones;
To him that's dull, I do my spurs impart,
And to the Coward, I bequeath my heart:
To Ladies that are light, it is my will,
My feathers should be giv'n; and for my bill,
I'l giv't a Taylor, but it is so short,
That I'm afraid he'l rather curse me for't:
And for the Apothecaries fee, who meant
To give me a Glister, let my Rump be sent.
 Lastly, because I feel my life decay,
 I yield, and give to Wisbich *Cock the day.*

In praise of Sack.

Come faith let's frolick, fill some Sack,
  For then we shall not lack
Food for the belly, nor physick for the back,
  This Beer breeds the Chollick, let us spread
  Our Cheeks with Royal Red,
And then we'll sing, hey toss the divel's dead,
To Faction we never more will bow the knee:
Great *Britains* fate in faith 'twas long of thee.

You

You may see what Madam *England* hath been at
When we behold her Nose is faln so flat.

To Wine we'll build a Shrine,
    And an Altar divine,
High as the sign, where thy red nose and mine
    Like Tapers shall shine :
Then let's drink for the Bets, 'tis the loser that gets,
    In spight of their threats, and their Creditors nets,
We'll drink off our debts,
    Where he that's dead drunk, shall be
Laid out in state, as well as he
    Whose dignity the only objects be
Of new Idolatry.
We'll guard his corps like a Bride
    To the grave-side, so copious and wide,
With as much pride as he that lately dyed,
    The Railing set aside.

Fifty red-faces free, shall his Torch-bearers be ;
Six maudlin mourners his Coffin shall carry,
There we will tipple free unto the memory
Of our fraternity drown'd in Canary :
In the Divel-Tavern we commonly will shew him,
    We'll bury him from the divel,
    Others fair men to him.

We'll be blythe and trimmer,
We'll have Musick to[o] ——

Jews-harp, tongues and Skimmer,
Thy Cup —— my Cup ——
Bar-boy fill the other brimmer,
Fly cup —— strike up —— there boy,
    Till our eyes do grow dimmer.

Money shall be spent in Bays,
Every pen shall vent a praise
And a Monument we'll raise
    Over his bones.
Where his Epitaph shall be,
That he dyed in Loyalty,
Never gain'd by Cruelty,
    Kingdoms, nor Crowns,
That he never lived by injury,
Nor confounded men for forgery,
Neither put a prop of Perjury
    Under his thrones;
That although he drank his Cares away,
And sometimes his Loyal fears away,
Yet he never drank the tears away
    Of Orphans Groans.

Thus he shall be both frollick and free,
    Who's kindly kill'd with Canary,
With red and white, or other delight,
    If tippling makes him miscarry,
Provided he [a] Bachanel be,
    And scorns to admit of a parley,

                                        With

With Ale or Beer, or other such geer,
    Polluted with Hop or with Barley,   [:]
Good wine doth ring, like Priest and King,
    But 'tis Ale that looks like a Lay-man,
Then for the Vineyard draw your Whynyard,
    The Divel go with the Dray-man.

A Maidenhead.

WHat is that you call a Maidenhead ?
    A thing oft smothered in a bed,
Which some have now, which all have had,
Which freely given makes one sad.

'Tis got for nought with little pain ;
'Tis kept, but lost, not got again ;
'Tis that you call a Maidenhead,
By proving quick 'tis ever dead.

A lump which Lasses bear about   [lamp]
Till putting in doth put it out ;
A herb it is which proves a weed
When first the husk doth bear a Seed.

It's that a Maidenhead we call,
A thing by standing made to fall ;
It is a Maiden-head, say we,
That's kept by holding close the knee.
                        Which

Which youths were often used to lurch,
Which Brides do seldom bear to Church;
At fifteen rare, at eighteen strange,
Which either lose when two do change.

That f[l]it's when Maidens begin to reak,
When ere it parts, it makes them squeak,
And being gone, they streight repent:
This by a Maidenhead is meant.

The Night encounter.

WHen *Phoebus* had drest his course to the West
    To take up his rest below,
And *Cynthia* agreed in her glittering weed
Her light in his stead to bestow:
I walking alone, attended by none,
I suddenly heard one cry,
    O do not, do not kill me yet,
    For I am not prepared to dye.

At length I drew near to see and to hear,
And straight did appear to shew,
The Moon was so bright, I saw such a sight
It's fit no Wight should it know:
A man and a maid together were laid,
And ever she said, nay fie,
    O do not, &c.

The youth was so tough he pull'd up her stuff,
And to blindman-buff he did go,
Though still she did lye, yet still she did cry,
And put him but by with a no;
But he was so strong, and she was so young,
But she rested a while for to cry,
    O do not, &c.

Thus striving in vain, well pleased again,
She vowed to remain his foe,
She kept such a coyl, when he gave her the foyl,
The greater the broyl did grow;
For he was prepar'd, and did not regard
Her words, when he heard her cry,
    O do not, &c.

He said to the Maid, Sweet be not afraid,
Thy Physitian I will be;
If I light in the hole that pleaseth me best,
I'll give thee thy Physick free;
He went to it again, and hit in the Vein
Where all her whole grief did lye;
    O kill me, kill me once again,
    For I am prepared to dye.

At length he gave o'r and suddenly swore,
He'd kill her no more that night,
He bid her adieu, for certain he knew
She wou'd tempt him to more delight:
                                  But

But when they did part it went to her heart,
For at length he had taught her to cry,
  O kill me, kill me once again,
   For now I am prepared to dye.

The Protecting Brewer.

A Brewer may be a Burgess grave,
 And carry the matter so fine and so brave,
That he the better may play the Knave,
  Which no body can deny.

A Brewer may be a Parliament-man
For there the knavery first began,
And Brew most cunning Plots he can,
  Which no body, &c.

A Brewer may put on a *Nabal* face,
And march to the Wars with such a grace,
That he may get a Captains place,
  Which no body, &c.

A Brewer may speak so monstrous well, [wondrous]
That he may raise strange things to tell,
And so [to] be made a Colonel,
  Which no body, &c.

A Brewer may make his foes to flee,
And raise his fortunes, so that he
Lieutenant General may be,
    Which no body, &c.

A Brewer he may be all in all,
And raise his powers both great and small,
That he may be a Lord General,
    Which no body, &c.

A Brewer may be like a Fox in a Cub,
And teach a Lecture out of a Tub,
And give the wicked world a rub,
    Which no body, &c.

A Brewer by's Excise and Rate,
Will promise his Army he knows what,
And set it upon the Colledge-gate,
    Which no body, &c.

Methinks I hear one say to me,
Pray why may nor [not] a Brewer be,
Lord-Chancelour o' th' University,
    Which no body, &c.

A Brewer may be as bold as a Hector,
When he has drunk off his cup of Nectar,
And a Brewer may be a Lord Protector,
    Which no body, &c.

                                        Now

Now here remains the strangest thing,
How this Brewer about his liquor doth bring,
To be an Emperour, or a King,
    Which no body, &c.

A Brewer may do what he will,
[And] Rob the Church and State, to sell
His soul unto the divel of hell,
    Which no body can deny.

Cromwel's *Coronation*.

OLiver, *Oliver*, take up thy Crown,
  For now thou hast made three Kingdoms thine own;
Call thee a Conclave of thy whole creation,
  To ride us to ruine, who dare thee oppose :
Whilst we thy good people are at thy devotion,
  To fall down and worship thy terrible Nose.

To thee and thy Mermydons *Oliver*, we,
  Do tender thy [? our] homage as fits thy degree,
We'll pay the Exsize and Taxes, God bless us,
  With fear and contrition, as penitents should,
Whilst you, great sirs, vouchsafe to oppress us,
  Not daring so much as in private to scold.

                      (Sword.
We bow down, as cow'd down, to thee & thy
  For now thou hast made thy self *Englands* sole Lord,
                          By

By mandate of Scripture, and heavenly warrant,
   The Oath of Allegiance, and Covenant too ;
To *Charles* & his Kingdoms thou art Heir apparent,
   And born to rule over the Turk and the Jew.

Then *Oliver, Oliver*, get up and ride,
   Whilst Lords, Knights, & Gentry, do run by thy (side,
The Maulsters and Brewers account it their glory,
   Great God of the Grain-tub's compared to thee :
All Rebels of old are lost in their story,
   Till thou Plod'st along to the *Paddington*-tree.

The Drunkard.

WHen I do travel in the night
   The Brewers dog my brains do's byte,
My heart grows heavy, and my heels grow light,
   And I like my humour well, well,
   And I like my humour well.

When with upsie freeze I line my head,
My Hostis Sellar is my bed,
The worlds our own, and the divel is dead,
   And I like, *&c.*

Then I'll be talking of matters of Court,
About the taking of some Fort,
Then I'll swear a lye is true report,
   And I like, *&c.*

Then I'll be talking of matters of State,
  Of news from [the] *Pallatinate*,
What Princes are confederate,
    And I like, &c.

If my Hostis bids me pay my score,
And stand if I can, I call her whore,
I reel and tumble out of her doore,
    And I like, &c.

That I came from the War, I roar and swear
I made a fellow die for fear,
How many I killed that I never came near,
    And I like, &c.

If I meet with a Taylors Stall,
And the stones with my nose with fighting fall,
We kiss and are friends, and so there's all,
    And I like, &c.

With an Indian Chimney in my hand,
Having a Boy at my command,
Like a brave Commander up I stand,
    And I like, &c.

Then I justle with every post I meet,
I kick the dunghils about the street,
I trample the kennels about my feet,
    And I like, &c.

                                        The

The Constable I curse and ban,
That bids me stand if I be a man,
I tell him he bids me do more than I can,
  And I like, &c.

If I fall to the ground, and the watchmen see
And ask of me, if I foxed be?
I tell them 'tis my humility,
  And I like, &c.

Then home I go, and my Wife doth skold [,]
She bawls the more I bid her hold,
It is my patience makes her bold,
  And I like, &c.

Then I grope to bed, but miss the way,
Forget me where my Cloaths, I lay,
I call for drink by break of day,
  And I like my humour [well].

Song of Sir Eglamore.

SIr *Eglamore*, that valiant Knight, fa, la, la, la, la,
 He put on his Sword, & he went to fight, fa, la,
And as he rid o'r hill and dale,
All armed in his Coat of Maile,
  Fa, la, la, la, fa, la, la, lalla, la.

There

There starts a huge Dragon out of his Den, fa, la,
Which had kill'd I know not how many men, fa, la,
But when he see Sir *Eglamore*,
If you had but heard how the Dragon did roar,
    Fa, la, la, &c.

This Dragon he had a plaguy hard hide, fa, la, la,
Which could the strongest steel abide, fa, la, la,
He could not enter him with cuts,
Which vex'd the Knight to his heart bloud & guts,
    Fa, la, la, &c.

All the trees in the wood did shake, fa, la, la,
Horses did tremble, and men did quake, fa, la, la,
The birds betook them to their peeping,
'Twould have made a mans heart to fall a weeping,
    Fa, la, la.

But now it was no time to fear, fa, la, la,
For it was time to fight Dog, fight Bear, fa, la, la,
But as the Dragon yawning did fall,
He thrust his Sword down hilt and all,
    Fa, la, la.

For as the Knight in Choller did burn, fa, la, la,
He ought the Dragon a shrewd good turn, fa, la, la,
In at his mouth his Sword he sent,
The hilt appeared at his fundament.
    Fa, la, la.

Then

Then the Dragon, like a Coward, began to flee, fa, la,
Into his Den that was hard by, fa, la, la,
There he laid him down and roar'd,
The Knight was sorry for his Sword,
    Fa, la, la,

The Sword it was a right good blade, fa, la, la,
As ever Turk or Spaniard made, fa, la, la,
I, for my part, do forsake it,
[And] He that will fetch it, let him take it,
    Fa, la, la.

When all was done, to the Alehouse he went, fa, la,
And presently his two pence he spent, fa, la, la,
He was so hot with tugging with the Dragon,
That nothing would squench him but a [w]hole flagon,
    Fa, la, la.

Well, now let us pray for the King & Queen, fa, la,
And eke in *London* there may be seen, fa, la, la,
As many Knights, and as many more,
And all as good as Sir *Eglamore*,
    Fa, la, la, la, fa, la, la, la, lalla, la.

The Rump.

IF none be offended with the Scent,
  Though I foul my mouth, I'll be content,

To sing of the Rump of a Parliament,
    Which no body can deny.

I have som[e]times fed on a Rump in Souse,
And a man may imagine the Rump of a Louse;
But till now was ne'r heard of the Rump of a house,
    Which no body, &c.

There's a rump of beef, and the rump of a goose [,]
And a rump whose neck was hang'd in a noose;
But ours is a Rump can play fast and loose,
    Which no body, &c.

A Rump had *Jane Shore*, and a Rump *Messaleen*,
And a Rump had *Antonies* resolute Queen;
But such a Rump as ours is, never was seen,
    Which no body, &c.

Two short years together we English have scarce
Been rid of thy rampant Nose (old *Mars*,)
But now thou hast got a prodigious Arse,
    Which no body, &c.

When the parts of the body did fall out,
Some votes it is like did pass for the Snout;
But that the Rump should be King was never a
    Which no body, &c.   (doubt

A Cat has a Rump, and a Cat has nine lives,
Yet when her head's off, her Rump never strives;
But our Rump from the grave hath made two re-
    Which no body, &c.   (trives,

That the Rump may all their enemies quail,
They'l borrow the Divels Coat of Mayl,
And all to defend their estate in Tayl,
    Which no body, &c.

But though their scale now seen to be th' upper,
There's no need of the charge of a thanksgiving supper,
For if they be the Rump, the Armies their Crupper,
    Which no body, &c.

There is a saying belongs to the Rump,
Which is good although it be worn to the stump [,]
That on the Buttock, I'll give thee a thump,
    Which no body, &c.

There's a Proverb in which the rump claims a part,
Which hath in it more of Sence than of Art,
That for all you can do I care not a fart,
    Which no body, &c.

There's another Proverb gives the Rump for his
But Alderman *Atkins* made it a jest,   (Crest,
That of all kind of lucks shitten luck is the best,
    Which no body, &c.

There's another Proverb that never will fail,
That the good [the] Rump will do when they prevail,
Is to give us a flap with a Fox-tail,
    Which no body, &c.

There is a saying, which is made by no fools,
I never can hear on't but my heart it cools,
That the Rump will spend all we have in close-
    Which no body &c.   (stools,

There's an observation wise and deep,
Which, without an Onion, will make me to weep,
That flies will blow Maggots in the Rump of a
    Which no body, &c.   (sheep,

And some, that can see the wood from the trees,
Say, this Sanctified Rump in time we may leese:
For the Cooks do challenge the rumps for their Fees,
    Which no body, &c.

When the Rump do sit, we'll make it our moan,
That the Reason be 'nacted, if there be not one,
Why a Fart hath a tongue, and a Fiest[le] hath none,
    Which no body, &c.

And whil'st within the walls they lurk,
To satisfie us, will be a good work,
Who hath most Religion, the Rump or the Turk,
    Which no body, &c.

                              A

A Rump's a Fag end, like the baulk of a furrow,
And is to the whole like the jail to the burrough,
'Tis the bran that is left when the meal is run tho-
    Which no body, &c.   (rough,

Consider the world, the heav'n is the head on't,
The earth is the middle, and we men are fed on't,
But hell is the rump, and no more can be said on't,
    Which no body can deny.

The Red-coats Triumph.

COme Drawer, and fill us about some wine,
   Let's merrily tipple, the day is our own;
We'll have our delights, let the Country go pine,
Let the King and the Kingdom groan:
The Crown is our own, and so shall continue,
We'll baffle Monarchy quite,
We'll drink of the Kingdoms Revenue,
And sacrifice all to Delight;
'Tis power that brings us all to be Kings,
And we'll all be crown'd by our might.

A fig for Divinity Lectures, and Law,
And all that true Loyalty do pretend;
We will by the Sword keep Kingdoms in awe,
And our Powers shall never end;
The Church and the State we'll turn into liquor,
And spend a whole town in a day:

We'll melt all the Bodkins the quicker
Into Sack, and drink them away;
We'll keep the demeans of the Bishops and Deans,
And over the Presbyter sway.

Now nimble Saint *Patrick* is sunk in a bog,
And his Country-men sadly cry, *O hone, O hone;*
Saint *Andrew* and his Kirkmen are lost in a fog,
And now we are the Saints alone;
Thus on our Equals and Superiours we trample,
And *Jockie* our stirrop shall hold,
The Citie's our Mule for example,
Whilst we will in plenty be rou'ld;
Each delicate dish shall but eccho our wish,
And our drink shall be cordial Gold.

The Bulls Feather.

IT chanced not long ago, as I was walking,
  An eccho did bring me where two were a talking:
'Twas a man said to his wife, die had I rather,
Than to be cornuted, and wear the Bulls feather,

Then presently she reply'd, Sweet, art thou jealous?
Thou canst not play *Vulcan* before I play *Venus*:
Thy fancies are foolish, such follies to gather:
There's many an honest man has worn the Bulls Feather.

                                          Though

Though it be invisible, let no man it scorn,
Though it be a new Feather made of an old horn,
He that disdains it in heart or mind either
May be the more subject to wear the Bulls Feather.

He that lives discontent, or is in despair,
And feareth false measure, because his wife's fair:
His thoughts are inconstant, much like winter weather,
Though one or two want it, he shall have a Feather.

Bulls Feathers are common as *Ergo* in Schools,
And only contemned by those that are fools :
Why should a Bulls Feather cause any unrest,
Since neighbours fare alwaies is counted the best ?

Those women wh' are fairest, are likely to give it ;
And husbands that have them, are apt to believe it.
Some men though their wives should seem for to
            (tedder,
They would play the kind neighbour, and give the
            (Bulls feather.

Why should we repine that our wives are so kind,
Since we that are husbands are of the same mind ?
Shall we give them feathers, and think to go free ?
Believe it, believe it, that hardly will be.

For he that disdains my Bulls feather to day,
May light of a Lass that will play him foul play,
            There's

There's ne'r a proud gallant that treads on Cows
(Leather,
But he may be cornuted, and wear the Bulls feather.

Though Beer of that brewing, I never did drink,
Yet be not displeas'd if I speak what I think,
Scarce ten in a hundred, believe it, believe it,
But either they'll have it, or else they will give it.

Then let me advise all those that do pine,
For fear that false jealousie shorten their time :
That disease will torment them worse than any feaver:
Then let all be contented to wear the Bul[l]s feather.

Old England *turned New*.

YOu talk of *New England*, I truely believe
   Old *England* is grown new, & doth us deceive,
I'll ask you a question or two, by your leave,
   And is not Old *England* grown new?

Where are your old Souldiers with slashes and skars
That never used drinking in no time of wars,
Nor shedding of bloud in mad drunken jars?
   And is not, &c.

New Captains are come that never did fight,
But with Pots in the day, and Punks in the Night,
And all their chief care is to keep their swords bright,
   And is not, &c.

Where are your old Swords, your bills, & your bows,
Your Bucklers and Targets that never feared blows?
They are turned to Steelettoes, with other fair shews,
    And is not, &c.

Where are your old Courtiers, that used to ride
With forty blew-coats and footmen beside?
They are turned to six horses [,] a coach [,] with a
    ·And is not, &c.   (guide,

And what is become of your old fashion Cloaths,
Your long-sided breeches, and your trunk hose?
They are turned to new fashions, but what, the Lord
    And is not, &c.   knows,

Your Gallant & his Taylor some half year together,
To fit a new suit to a new hat and feather,
Of Gold, or of Silver, silk, cloath, stuff, or leather,
    And is not, &c.

We have new fashion'd beards, and new fashion'd locks,
And new fashion'd hats for your new pated blocks,
And more new diseases besides the French pox,
    And is not, &c.

New houses are built, and the old ones pull'd down,
Untill the new houses sell all the old ground,
And then the house stands like a horse in the pound,
    And is not, &c.

New fashions in houses, new fashions at table,
The old servants discharged, the new are more able,
And every old custome is but an old fable,
    And is not, &c.

New trickings, new goings, new measures, new paces,
New heads for your men, for your women new faces,
And twenty new tricks to mend their bad cases,
    And is not, &c.

New tricks in the Law, new tricks in the holds, [Rouls]
New bodies they have, they look for new souls
When the money is paid for the building of *Pauls*,
    And is not, &c.

Then talk you no more of *New-England*,
New-England is where Old *England* did stand, (man'd;
New furnish'd, new fashion'd, new woman'd new
    And is not Old *England* grown *New*.

A Merry Song.

COme Drawer, turn about the bowle
   Till every soul has made a scrowle
    As long as his arm :
Again, my boy, be filling still
Till every will has had his fill,
    Twill keep us from harm :
                      For

For he that is copious, and doth freight with Sack,
Has the world at will, and doth nothing lack;
He's richest then can drink off a Tun,
The bravest men that are under the Sun;
Now the world is so giddy, that it scarce knows
To smell out the truth now it has lost its nose:
That has left behind a Pitiful case,
It smels, you'l find, in every place.

Then since he is happiest that drinks the most,
Joy, call mine Host, that honest tost,
    He shall have his share;
For interest we'll give him drink,
Now wine is chink, yet let him think
    Our dealing is faire;
For I'll maintain his reckoning's good.
Though we had drunk on tick since *Noah's* flood,
We'll clear it all in *Platoes* year,
You'l hear we shall be *Catoes* there:
Then he's an ass will spare for Chalk
To purchase Sack; what e'r you talk,
He's not great, nor rich, nor wise;
An errant Cheat does Wine despise.

A Scottish Covenant we'll take
To burn at stake, if not forsake
    The old heresie
Of bowzing to a petticoat,
If healths of note we could not vote
    Past any she,

They

They are but blazes, and soon are gone,
Fine trifles for us to play upon:
When we have nought, or little to do,
We'll have 'um brought, and tickle 'um too:
Mean time let us drink a Carouse to those
Who are neither the French nor the Spaniards foes,
For all our treasure is there in their Mines,
There's no pleasure here but in their wines.

The Contented.

PRay why should any man complain,
   Or why disturb his breast or brain
At this new alteration?
Since that which has been done's no more
Than what has oft been done before,
And that which will be done again,
As long as there are ambitious men,
   That strive for domination.

In this mad age there's nothing firm,
All things have period, and their term,
Their rise and declination;
Those gaudy nothings we admire,
Which get above and shine like fire,
Are empty vapours raised from ground,
Their mock-shine past th' are quickly down,
   Must fall like exhalation.

                                                    But

But still we Commons must be made
A gaull'd, a lame, thin hackney Jade,
And all by turns will ride us;
This side, or that no matter which,
For both do ride with spur and switch,
Till we are tired, and then at last
We stumble. and our riders cast,
    'Cause they'd not feed nor guide us.

Th' insulting Clergy quite mistook,
Thinking that Kingdoms past by book,
Or Crowns were got by prating;
'Tis not the black coat, but the red,
Has power to make, or be the head;
Nor is it oaths, nor words, nor tears,
But Musquets and full Bandeleers
    Have power of legislating.

The Lawyers must lay by their books,
And study *Monck* much more than *Cooks;*
The Sword is the Learned Pleader:
Reports and Judgements will not do't,
But 'tis Dragoons and Horse and Foot;
Words are but wind, but Swords come home,
A stout tongued Lawyer is but a mome,
    Compared to a stout file-leader.

Such wit and valour root all things,
They pull down, and they set up Kings,

All Law is in their bosoms;
That side is alwaies right that's strong,
And that that's beaten must be wrong:
And he that thinks it is not so,
Unless he's sure to beat 'um too,
    He's but a fool to oppose 'm.

Let them impose taxes and rates,
'Tis but on them that have estates,
Not such as thou and I are:
But it concerns those wor[l]dlings which
At least are made, or else grow rich,
Such as have studied all their daies
The saving and the thriving waies,
    To be the mules of power.

If they'l reform the Church or State,
We'll ne'r be troubled much thereat:
Let each man take his opinion,
If we don't like the Church, you know
Taverns are free, and there we'l go;
And every one will be
As clearly unconcern'd as we,
    They'l ne'r fight for domination.

The indifferent.

What an Ass is he
    Waits a womans leisure
For a minutes pleasure,
And perhaps may be
Gull'd at last, and lose her,
What an ass is he?

Shall I sigh and die
'Cause a maid denies me,
And that she may try me,
Suffer patiently?
O no! Fate shall tye me,   [? no Fate]
To such cruelty.

Love is all my life,
For it keeps me doing:
Yet my love and wooing
Is not for a Wife:
It is good eschewing
Warring, care, and strife.

What need I to care
For a womans favour?
If another have her,

Why should I despair,
When for gold and labour
I can have my share.

If I fancy one,
And that one do love me,
Yet deny to prove me,
Farewel, I am gone.
She can never move me,
Farewel, I am gone.

If I chance to see
One that's brown, I love her,
Till I see another,
That is browner than she,
For I am a lover
Of my liberty.

Every day I change,
And at once love many,
Yet not tied to any,
For I love to range,
And if one should stay me
I should think it strange.

What though she be old,
So that she have riches,
Youth and Form bewitches,

But

But 'tis store of Gold
Cures lascivious itches,
So the Criticks hold.

A West-country Mans Voyage to New-England.

MY Masters give audience, and listen to me,
And streight che will tell you where che have be :
Che have been in *New-England*, but now cham come o'er,
Itch do think they shal catch me go thither no more.

Before che went o'er Lord how Voke did tell
How vishes did grow, and how birds did dwell
All one mong, t'other [,] in the wood and the water,
Che thought had been true, but che find no such matter.

When first che did land che mazed me quite,
And 'twas of all daies on a Satterday night,
Che wondred to see the strong building were there,
'Twas all like the standing at *Bartholmew* Fair.

Well, that night che slept till near Prayer time,
Next morning che wondred to hear no Bells chime,
And when che had ask'd the reason, che found
'Twas because they had never a Bell in the Town.

At last being warned to Church to repair,   (prayer,
Where che did think certain che sho'd hear some
But the Parson there no such matter did teach,
They scorn'd to pray, they were all able to preach.

The virst thing they did, a Zalm they did sing,
I pluckt out my Zalm book, which with me did bring[,]
Che was troubled to seek him, 'cause they call him by
    name,
But they had got a new Song to the tune of the same.

When Sermon was done was a child to baptize
About sixteen years old, as volk did surmise,
And no Godfather nor Godmother, yet 'twas quiet
    and still,
The Priest durst not cross him for fear of his ill will.

A Sirra, quoth I, and to dinner che went,
And gave the Lord thanks for what he had sent ;
Next day was a wedding, the brideman my friend,
He kindly invites me, so thither I wend.

But this, above all, to me wonder did bring,
To see a Magistrate marry, and had ne'r a ring ;
Che thought they would call me the woman to give [,]
But che think he stole her, for he askt no man leave.

Now this was new *Dorchester* as they told me,
A Town very famous in all that Country ;
                                                    They

They said 'twas new building, I grant it was true,
Yet methinks old *Dorchester* as fine as the new.

Che staid there among them till che was weary at
    heart,
At length there came shipping, che got leave to de-
    part:
But when all was ended che was coming away,
Che had threescore shillings for swearing to pay.

But when che saw that, an oath more che swore,
Che would stay no more longer to swear on the score;
Che bid farewel to those Fowlers and Fishers,
So God bless old *England* and all his well wishers.

A medicine for the Quartan Ague.

THe Aphorisms of *Galen* I count but as straws,
    Profound Pispot-peepers be you all mute,
The old quartan feaver breaks all Physick-laws,
To help to cure it I think it is boot:
Perusing of late a wormeaten book,
Brought hither from *Cinthia* down in *Charles's* wain;
A curious medicine out thence I took,
    To cure the quartan Feaver again.

First choose a Physitian that will not exceed
Probatum est, speaking no more than he knows,

Who hath more skill in his tongue than his head;
Who his Potions on Patients *gratis* bestows,
Three Midsummer moons in one, let him pray
To *Apollo*, and the Moon being full in the wane,
And *Scola Salerna* twice backward to say,
    And it will cure the quartan Feaver again.

His Patients water then let him cast
In a pure Urinal of old *August* Ice,
And diet him strictly, no gross meats to eat,
But feed him with fancies, and antick device,
To walk every morning some eight miles or more,
Before *Phœbus* rises, in the sunshine,
And before he be up to be seen without door,
    And 'twill cure, *&c.*

Then let him take from him nine drops and a half
Of purified bloud, but pierce not the skin,
Only open a vein in the heel of the calf,
Some half a year before the fit do begin;
To sweat eleven minutes in an Oven let him lye,
Heat with a North wind, and a shower of rain,
And sleep every night with one half of an eye,
    And 'twill cure, *&c.*

To keep his body alwaies soluble and loose,
That he shall never fear to be subject to be bound,
Let him drink Woodcocks water in the quill of a
    Goose,
                                  And

And alwaies untruss when he goes to ground;
Thus being prepared, let the Doctor proceed
With all other ingredients to conquer his pain,
And profess more Art than ere he did read,
  To cure the quartan, &c.

Then let him take the wind of the wing of a Crane,
As he flies over *Caucasus* hill,
With the precious stone was in *Gyges* his Ring,
Mix them with three turns of an honest windmil,
Boyl these altogether from a pint to a quart
In a Travellers mouth whose tongue cannot feigne,
And having new din'd give him this next his heart,
  And 'twill cure, &c.

Then three handfull take of Popes holy shadow,
When *Sol* is new entred into the dog : daies,
Three skreeches of an Owl [,] four kaws of a Jackdaw,
With the brains and the heads of three ninepenny
Fry these together within a meal-sive,   (nailes,
With the sweat of the south-side of a French bean,
And this to his Patient Morn & Even let him give,
  And 'twill cure, &c.

Take three merry thoughts of a Bride the first night
She's to lye with her Groom, to purge melancholly,
Three gingles of the silver spur of a field Knight,
Four Puritan faces, not counterfeit holy,

Take three youthful Capers of an old Oxe,
And thorough a joyned stool them let him strain,
And then drink the juice through a tail of a Fox,
    And it will cure, &c.

Moreover, because I strive to be brief,
Take three honest thrums of a weavers shuttle,
Three snips of a Taylors sheers that's no thief,
A cut-purses thumb, with his horn and his whittle,
The mind of a miller that ne'r took a corn,
More than his due in grinding of grain,
Burn these all together with Jeeny red stalks,
    And 'twill cure, &c.

And lastly, this counsel my old Author gives,
Take the bloud of a Beetle in the ayre as she flies,
Who, like a Physitian, of excrement lives,
And therewith let Empericks anoynt his quick eyes:
This being practised, he shall see soon
All natural mysteries perfect and plain,
And know as much Physick as the man in the moon
    To cure the quartan feaver again.

A Catch.

NOw I am married, Sir *John* I'll not curse,
    He joyn's us together for better, for worse;
But if I were single I tell you plain,
I would be advised ere I marri'd again.

Of

Of Levelling.

I Have reason to fly thee, & not to sit down by thee,
For I hate to behold one so sawcy and bold,
That derides and contemns his superiours;
    Your Madams and Lords,
    With such manerly words,
    With gestures that be
    Fit for our degree
    Are things that we and you
    Do claim as our due
From all those that are our inferiours,   (know,
  For from the beginning there were Princes we
  'Tis your Levellers do hate 'cause they cannot be
                                                                (so.
All titles of honour were at first in the Donors,
But being granted away by that persons stay
Where he wore a small soul or a bigger,
    There's a necessity
    That there should be a degree,
    Though *Dick, Tom,* and *Jack,*
    Will serve you and your pack,
    Where 'tis due we'll afford
    A Sir *John,* or my Lord,
Honest *Dick's* name is enough for a digger;
  He that hath a strong purse may all things be, or
  Be valiant, and wise, and religious too.   (do,
                                                                We

We have cause to adore that man that hath store
'Though a boor or a sot, there's something to be got
'Though he be neither honest nor witty,
  Make him high, let him rule,
  He'll be playing the fool,
  And transgress, then we'll squeeze
  Him for fines and for fees,
  And we shall gain
  By the vanities of his brain,
"'Tis the fools Cap that maintains the City;
 If honour be but air, 'tis in common, and as fit
 For the fool, or the Clown, as the champion or wit.

'Then why may not we be of a different degree,
And each man aspire to be greater and higher
'Than his wiser or honester brother,
  Since Fortune and Nature
  Their favours do scatter,
  This hath Valour, that Wit
  To his wealth, nor is it fit
  That one should have all,
  For then what would befall
He that is born not to one nor the other? (chattel,
 'Though honor were a prize from at first, now it's a
 And as meer huntable now as your ware, lands or
    [huntable]   (cattle.
But in this we agree to live quiet and free,
'To drink Sack and submit, and not shew your wit
By your prating, but silence and thinking;
          Let

Let the Presbyter Jews
Read Diurnals and News,
And lard their discourse
With a Covenant that's worse;
That which pleaseth me best
Is a Song or a Jest,
And my obedience I'll shew it by my drinking;
And the name I desire is an honest good fellow,
And that man hath no worth that won't some-
(times be mellow.

In praise of a Mistresse.

I Have the fairest *Non-perel*,
  The fairest that ever was seen,
And had not *Venus* been in the way,
  She had been Beauties Queen.

Her lovely looks, her comely grace,
  I will describe at large;
God *Cupid* put her in his books,
  And of this Jem took charge.

The *Grœcian Helen* was a Moore,
  Compar'd to my dear Saint,
And fair fac'd *Syrens* beauty poor,
  And yet she doth not paint.

                  Andromeda

Andromeda, whom *Perseus* lov'd,
   Was foul were she in sight,
Her lineaments so well approv'd,
   In praise of her I'll write.

Her hair not like the Golden wyre,
   But black as any Crow,
Her brows so beetl'd all admire,
   Her forehead wondrous low.

Her squinting, staring, gogling eyes
   Poor Children do affright,
Her nose is of the Sarasens size;
   O she's a matchless wight.

Her Oven-mouth wide open stands,
   And teeth like rotten pease,
Her Swan-like neck my heart commands,
   And breasts all bit with Fleas.

Her tawny dugs, like two great hills,
   Hang sow like to her waste,
Her body huge, like two wind-mills,
   And yet she's wondrous chaste.

Her shoulders of so large a breadth,
   She'd make an excellent Porter,
And yet her belly carries most,
   If any man could sort her.

No Shoulder of Mutton like her hand,
   For broadness thick and fat,
With a pocky Mange upon her wrist:
   Oh *Jove!* how love I that?

Her belly Tun-like to behold,
   Her bush doth all excell,
The thing that, by all men extoll'd,
   Is wider than a well.

Her brawny buttocks, plump and round,
   Much like a Horse of War,
With speckled thighs, scab'd and scarce sound;
   Her knees like Bakers are.

Her legs are like the Elephants,
   The calf and small both one,
Her anckles they together meet,
   And still knock bone to bone.

Her pretty feet not 'bove fifteens,
   So splay'd as never was,
An excellent Usher for a man
   That walks the dewy grass.

Thus have you heard my Mistris prais'd,
   And yet no flattery us'd,
Pray tell me, is she not of worth?
   Let her not be abus'd.

If any to her have a mind,
  He doth me wondrous wrong,
For as she's beautious, so she's chaste,
  And thus concludes my Song.

Sensual Delight.

ARe you grown so melancholly,
  That you think of nought but folly?
Are you sad, are you mad, are you worse,
Do you think want of chinck is your curse?
Do you love for to have longer life, or a grave?
  Then this will cure you.

First I would have a bag of Gold,
That should ten thousand pieces hold,
And all that in your lap would I poure
For to spend on your friend or your whore,
For to play away at dice, or to shift you from your (lice,
  And this will cure you.

Next I would have a soft bed made,
Wherein a Virgin should be laid
That will play any way you devise,
That will stick like an itch to your thighs,
That will bill like a dove, lie beneath or above,
  And this will cure you.

Next

Next the bowl that *Jove* divine
Drunk Nectar in, fill'd up with wine
And all that, like a Greek, you should quaff
Till your cheeks they look red, and you laugh,
Unto *Ceres*, and to *Venus*, unto *Bacchus*, and *Selenus*,
    And this will cure you.

Next seven Eunuchs should appear
Singing in Spheare-like manner here
In the praise of the wayes of delight,
Venus can use with man in the night,
When she seemeth to adorn *Vulcans* head with a
    And this will cure you.   (horn.

But if no gold nor women can,
Nor wine, nor Song make merry man,
Let the Batt be your mate and the Owle,
Let the pain in the brain make you howl:
Let the Pox be your friend, and the Plague be your
    And this will cure you.   (end.

On Captain Hick *his* Oxford Feasts.

Sublimest discretions, have clubd for expressions
    Which are muster'd up here by our Captaine;
Some staler, some milder, some tamer, some wilder,
    And all in clean Linnen are wrapt in:
Oxford

2

Oxford University approves her self witty,
  In Jests of more jovial concerning,
And jocose Apprehensions prefer their Inventions,
  Before all the rest of her learning.

3

Here is choice, here is store, Eight Hundred or more
  The Cream, and the Crown of all Jesting;
All brave souls be Guests at this Banquet of Jests [:]
  Lucullus had never such feasting.

4

Such wit here's exprest in every choice Jest
  They'll make *Mellanchollicus* frolick,
And all those to forget to groan, and to fret,
  That are troubled with Stone and the Chollick.

5

Will Sumners and Scoggin with Archee be Jogging[,]
  Your Quirks and your Quibbles are folly:
No such rare Antidotes, ere took flight from the
  'Gainst the poyson of black Mellancholly. (throats,

6

One reading a score did with laughter give o're
  Or his broad sides had else split in sunder;
At next Ordinary he with repeating of three
  Made the wits at the board to knock under.

7 (turnies,

These will shorten the Journeys of Clarks and At-
  With wits most refin'd Recreations,
                                        And

And when they are far remote from the Barr
   We'll cheer up their hearts in Vacations.

8
                                 (trades)
Now all you brave Blades leave your Shops & your
   Your lying and sollemn protesting,
And if ever you'll thrive cease to drink, swear, & ——
   And study the science of Jesting.

9
To Gratifie Jesters sinks Angells to Testers   [;]
   But here without fear of Expences,
You may pick, you may chuse, you may take or refuse
   As suits with the moods, and the tences.

10
At home and abroad on our walks or the Road
   These Cordials will prove Efficacious,
Search the Books of all ages, & ransack their Pages
   You will find nothing half so Solacious.

A Catch.

A Pox on the Jaylor and on his fat Jole,
   There's liberty lies in the bottom of th' Bole,
A fig for what ever the Rascal can do,
   Our Dungeon is deep, but our Cups are so too ;
Then Drink we round in despite of our foes,
   And make our hard Irons cry clink in the close :
Now laugh we and quaff we, untill our rich Noses
Grow red, and contest with our chapplets of Roses.

                T   *Phillis*

Phillis, *her Lamentation.*

MY Lodging is on the cold ground,
    And very hard is my Fare;
But that which troubles me most is
    The unkindness of my Dear:
        Yet still I cry O turn Love,
            And I prethee Love turn to me;
        For thou art the man that I long for,
            And alack what remedy!

I'll Crown thee with Garlands of straw then,
    And I'll marry thee with a Rush Ring;
My frozen hopes shall thaw then,
    And merrily we will sing,
        O turn to me my dear Love,
            And I prethee Love turn to me;
        For thou art the man that alone can'st
            Procure my libertie.

But if thou wilt harden thy Heart still,
    And be deaf to my pitiful moan,
Then I must endure the smart still,
    And tumble in straw alone:
        Yet still I cry O turn Love,
            And I prethee Love turn to me;
        For thou art the man that alone art
            The cause of my miserie.

The Song of the Pedlers.

From the fair *Lavinian* Shore
    I your Markets come to store,
Muse not though so far I dwell
    And my wares come here to sell:
Such is the secret hunger of Gold,
    Then come to my Pack,
    While I cry, what d' ye lack,
What d' ye buy? for here it is to be sold.

I have Beauty, Honour, and Grace,
    Fortune, favour, Time and Place;
And what else thou would'st request,
    Even the thing thou likest best:
First let me have but a touch of thy Gold,
    Then come to me Lad
    Thou shalt have what thy Dad
Never gave; for here it is to be sold.

Madam, come see what ye lack,
    Here's Complexion in my pack;
White and red you may have in this place
    To hide your old ill wrinkled face.
First let me have a touch of thy Gold,
    Then thou shalt seem
    Like a Wench of fifteen,
Although you be threescore year old.

Ha, Ha, Ha, Ha, Ha.

Calm was the Evening and clear was the skie,
    And the sweet budding flowers did spring,
When all alone went *Amintor* and I
    To hear the sweet Nightingale sing :
I sate, and he lay'd him down by me,
    And scarcely his breath he could draw,
        But when with a fear he began to come near,
        He was dasht with a ha ha ha ha ha ha, &c.

He blusht to himself, and laid still a while,
    'Twas his modesty curb'd his desire ;
But streight I convinc'd all his fears with a smile,
    And added new flames to his fire :
Ah ! *Silvia*, said he, you are cruel
    To keep your poor lover in awe [:]
        Then once more he prest with his hand to my bre
        But was dasht with a ha ha ha ha ha ha, &c.

I knew 'twas his passion that caused his fear,
    And therefore I Pitied his case ;
I whisper'd him softly, there's no body near,
    And lay'd my Cheek close to his Face :
But as he grew bolder and bolder
    A Shepherd came by us and saw,
        And straight as our bliss, began with [a] *kiss,*
        He laughs out with a ha ha ha ha ha ha, &c.

In praise of Sack.

FEtch me *Ben Johnsons* scull, and fill't with Sack,
   Rich as the same he drank, when the whole pack
Of jolly sisters pledg'd, and did agree
It was no sin to be as drunk as he :
If there be any weakness in the wine,
There's virtue in a Cup to mak't divine ;
This muddy drench of Ale does taste too much
Of earth, the Mault retains a scurvy touch
Of the dull hand that sows it ; and I fear
There's Heresie in Hops ; give *Calvin* Beer,
And his precise Disciples, such as think
There's Powder-treason in all *Spanish* drink ;
Call Sack an Idoll, nor will kiss the Cup,
For fear their Conventicle will be blown up
With superstition : give to these Brew-house alms,
Whose best mirth is Six shilling Beer, and Psalms :
Let me rejoyce in sprightly Sack, that can
Create a brain even in an empty pan.
Canary! it's thou that dost inspire
And actuate the soul with heavenly fire ;
That thou sublim'st the Genius [,] making wit,
Scorn earth, and such as love, or live by it ;
Thou mak'st us Lords of Regions large and fair,
Whil'st our conceits build Castles in the air :

Since

Since fire, earth, air, thus thy inferiours be,
Henceforth I'll know no Element but thee;
Thou precious *Elixir* of all Grapes!
Welcome[d] be thee our Muse begins her scapes, [by]
Such is the work of Sack; I am (me thinks)
In the *Exchequer* now, hark now it chinks:
And do esteem my venerable self
As brave a fellow, as if all the pelf
Were sure mine own; and I have thought a way
Already how to spend it; I would pay
No debts, but fairly empty every trunk,
And charge the Gold for Sack to keep me drunk; [change]
And so by consequence till [,] rich *Spains* Wine
Being in my crown, the *Indies* too were mine[,]
And when my brains are once afoot (heaven bless us)
I think my self a better man than *Crœsus*.
And now I do conceit my self a Judge,
And coughing laugh to see my Clients trudge
After my Lordships Coach unto the Hall
For Justice, and am full of Law withal,
And do become the Bench as well as he
That fled long since for want of honestie:
But I'll be Judge no longer though in jest,
For fear I should be talk'd with like the rest
When I am sober; who can chuse but think
Me wise, that am so wary in my drink!
Oh admirable Sack! here's dainty sport,
I am come back from *Westminster* to Court;

And am grown young again ; my Ptisick now
Hath left me, and my Judges graver brow
Is smooth'd, and I turn'd amorous as *May*,
When she invites young lovers for[th] to play
Upon her flowry bosome : I could win
A Vestal now, or tempt a Queen to sin.
Oh for a score of Queens ! you'd laugh to see
How they would strive which first should ravish me,
Three Goddesses were nothing : Sack has tipt
My tongue with charms like those which *Paris* sipt
From *Venus*, when she taught him how to kiss
Fair *Helen*, and invite a fairer bliss :
Mine is *Canary-Rhetorick*, that alone
Would turn *Diana* to a burning stone :
Stone with amazement, burning with loves fire,
Hard, to the touch, but short in her desire.   [? soft]
Inestimable Sack ! thou mak'st us rich :
Wise, amorous, anything ; I have an itch
To t'other cup, and that perchance will make
Me valiant too, and quarrel for thy sake
If I be once inflam'd, against thy Nose
That could preach down thy worth in small-beer
I should do miracles [as] bad, or worse,   (Prose [:]
As he that gave the King an hundred Horse :
T'other odd Cup, and I shall be prepar'd
To snatch at Stars, and pluck down a reward
With mine own hands from *Jove* upon their backs
That are, or *Charles* his enemies, or Sacks :

T 4   Let

Let it be full, if I do chance to spill
Ov'r my standish by the way[,] I will[,]
Dipping in this diviner Ink, my pen,
Write my self sober, and fall to 't agen.

A Catch.

NOw that the *Spring* hath fill'd our Veins
    With kind and active fire.
And made green liveries for the Plains
    And every Grove a Quire

Sing we this Song with mirth and merry glee,
    And *Bacchus* crown the Bowl,
And here's to thee, and thou to me
    And every thirsty soul.

Shear sheep that have them, cry we still,
    But see that none escape,
To take off this Sherry, that makes us so merry
    And plump as the lusty Grape.

The Huntsman.

OF all the sports the world doth yield
    Give me a pack of hounds in field,
Whose eccho sounds shrill through the sky,
Makes *Jove* admire our harmony,

                              And

And wish that he a mortal were,
To see such pleasures we have here.

Some do delight in Masks and plays,
And in *Diana's* Holy daies.
Let *Venus* act her chiefest skill,
If I dislike I'll please my will ;
And choose such as will last,
And not to surfeit when I taste.

Then I will tell you of a scent,
Where many a horse was almost spent,
In *Chadwel* Close a Hare we found,
That led us all a smoaking round ;
O'r hedge and ditch away she goes,
Admiring her approaching foes.

But when she felt her strength to waste,
She parleys with the Hounds in haste.
The Hare.   You gentle dogs forbear to kill
A harmless beast that ne'r did ill :
And if your Masters sport do crave,
I'll lead a scent as they would have.

The Hounds.   Away, away, thou art alone,
Make haste we say, and get thee gone ;
We'll give thee leave for half a mile,
To see if thou canst us beguile :

But

But then expect a thundering cry,
Made by us and our company.

The Hare. Then since you set my life so light,
I'll make Black lovely turn to White,
And *York-shire* Gray, that runs at all,
I'll make him wish him in his stall;
And Sorrel, he that seems to fly,
I'll make him sickly ere I die.

Let *Burham-Bay* do what he can,
And *Barton Gray*, Which now and then
Doth strive to winter up my way;
I'll neither make him sit nor play,
And constant *Robin*, though he lie
At his advantage, what care I?

But here *Kit Bolton* did me wrong,
As I was running all along;
For with one pat he made me so,
That I went reeling too and fro:
Then, if I die[,] your masters tell,
That fool did ring my passing-Bell.

But if your masters pardon me,
I'll read them all to *Througabby*;   [? lead]
Where constant *Robin* keeps a room
To welcome all the Guests that come,

To laugh, and quaff in Wine, and Beer,
A full Carouze to their Career.

The Hounds.   Away, away, since 'tis our nature
To kill thee, and no other Creature,
Our Masters they do want a bit,
And thou wilt well become the spit :
They eat the flesh, we pick the bone,
Make haste, we say, and get thee gone.

The Hare.   Your Masters may abate their cheer,
My meat is dry ; and Butter dear ;
And if with me they'd make a friend,
They had better give a Puddings end :
Besides, once dead, then sport they'l lack,
And I must hang on th' Huntsman's back.

The Hounds.   Alas poor Hare [!] we pity thee,
If with our nature 'twould agree ;
But all thy doubling shifts we fear
Will not prevent thy death so near,
Then make thy Will, for it may be that
May save thee ; else, we know not what.

The Hare's   Then I do give my body free,
   Will.   Unto your Masters courtesie ;
And if they'l spare till sport be scant,
I'll be their game, when they do want :
                                    But

But when I'm dead each greedy hound
Will trail my entrails on the ground.

The Hounds.   Were ever Dogs so basely crost?
Our Masters call us off so fast,
That we the scent have almost lost;
And they themselves must lose the roast,
Wherefore, kind *Hare* we pardon you:
The Hare.   Thanks gentle *Hounds,* and so Adieu.

A Catch.

O The wily wily *Fox*, with his many wily mocks,
   We'll Earth him if you'l but follow,
And now that we have done't, to conclude our mer-
   Let us roundly whoop and hollow: (ry hunt,
      Prethee drink, prethee drink, prethee, prethee drink,
      That the Hunters may all follow.

A Song.

SHe lay all naked in her bed,
   And I my self lay by;
No Vail nor Curtain there was spread,
   No covering but I:
Her head upon one shoulder seeks
   To hang in careless wise,

All

All full of blushes were her cheeks,
    And wishes were her eyes.

Her bloud lay flushing in her face,
    As ['t]on a message came,
To say that in some other place
    It meant some other Game;
Her neather Lip moyst, plump, and fair,
    Millions of kisses crown'd,
Which ripe and uncropt dangled there,
    And weighed the branches down.

Her breasts, that lay swell'd full and high,
    Bred pleasant pangs in me,
And all the world I did defie
    For that felicity;
Her thighs and belly, soft and plump,
    To me were only shewn:
To have seen such meat, and not to have eat,
    Would have angred any one.

Her knees lay up, but stoutly bent,
    And all was hollow under,
As if on easie terms they meant
    To fall unforc'd asunder:
Just so the *Cyprian* Queen did lye,
    Expecting in her bower;
When too long stay, had kept the boy
    Beyond his promis'd hour.

                                      Dull

Dull Clown, quoth she, why dost delay
   Such proffered bliss to take?
Canst thou find no other way
   Similitudes to make?
Mad with delight I thundred in,
   And threw mine arms about her,
But a pox upon 't 'twas but a dream,
   And so I lay without her.

Of a Good Wife and a Bad.

Some Wives are Good and some are Bad,
   (Reply.) *Methinks you touch them now,*
And some will make their Husbands mad,
   (Cho.) *And so will my Wife too:*
      And my Wife and thy Wife,
      And my Wife so will do.

Some Women love to breed discord,
   Methinks, &c.
And some will have the latter word,
   (Cho.) *And so will my wife too:*
      And my Wife, &c.

Some Women will Spin, and some will Sow,
   Methinks, &c.
And some will to the Tavern go,
   (Cho.) *And so will my Wife too:*
      And my Wife, &c.

                        Some

Some Women will say they'r sick at Heart,
>> *Methinks,* &c.
And some will let a rousing Fart,
> (Cho.) *And so will my Wife too :*
>> *And my Wife,* &c.

Some Women will ban and some will curse,
>> *Methinks,* &c.
And some will pick their Husbands Purse,
> (Cho.) *And so will my Wife too :*
>> *And my,* &c.

Some Women will Brawle, and some will Scold,
>> *Methinks,* &c.
And some will make their Husbands Cuckold,
> (Cho.) *And so will my Wife too :*
>> *And my,* &c.

Some Women will drink, and some will not,
>> *Methinks,* &c.
And some will take the t'other Pot,
> (Cho.) *And so will my Wife too :*
>> *And my Wife,* &c.

Some Women are sick, and some are sound,
>> *Methinks,* &c.
And some will take it on the Ground,
> (Cho.) *And so will my Wife too :*
>> *And my,* &c.

Thus

Thus of my song I'll make an end,
  Methinks, &c.
Hoping all women will amend,
  (Cho.) *And so will my Wife too:*
  And my Wife, &c.

A Catch.

CAll *George* again boy, call *George* again,
  And for the love of *Bacchus* call *George* again.
George is a good boy, and draws us good wine,
Or fills us more Clarret our wits to refine;
George is a brave Lad, and an honest man,
If you will him know, he dwells at the *Swan*.

A Song.

POx take you Mistris I'll be gone,
  I have friends to wait upon;
Think you I'll my self confine,
To your humours (Lady mine :)
No, your louring seems to say:
'Tis a rainy drinking day,
To the Tavern I'll away.

There have I a Mistris got,
Cloystered in a Pottle pot:

Brisk

Brisk and sprightly as thine eye,
When thy richest glances fly,
Plump AND bounding, lively, fair,
Bucksome, soft, and debonair :
And she's call'd Sack, my DEAR.

Sack's my better Mistris far,
Sack's my only beauty-star ;
Whose rich beams, and glorious raies,
Twinkle in each red rose and face :
Should I all her vertues shew,
Thou thy self would love-sick prove,
AND she'd prove thy Mistris TOO.

She with no dart-scorn will blast me ;
But upon thy bed can cast me ;   [? my]
Yet ne'er blush herself too red,
Nor fear of loss of Maiden-head :   [a loss]
And she can (the truth to say)
Spirits into me convey,
MORE than thou canst take AWAY.

Getting kisses here's no toyl,
Here's no Handkerchief to spoyl ;
Yet I better Nectar sip,
Than dwells upon thy lip :   [can dwell]
And though mute and still she be,
Quicker wit she brings to me,
Than e'er I could find in THEE.

If I go, ne'er think to see
Any more a fool of me;
I'll no liberty up give,
Nor a Maudlin-like love live,
No, there's nought shall win me to 't,
'Tis not all thy smiles can do 't,
Nor thy Maiden-head to BOOT.

Yet if thou'lt but take the pain
TO be good but once again;
If one smile then call me back,
THOU shalt be that Lady Sack:
Faith but try, and thou shalt see
What a loving Soul I'll be,
WHEN I am drunk with nought but thee.

The Answer.

I Pray thee, Drunkard, get thee gone,
  Thy Mistris Sack doth smell too strong:
Think you I intend to wed,
A sloven to be-piss my bed?
No, your staining me's to say,
You have been drinking all this day.
Go, be gone, away, away.

Where you have your Mistris Sack,
Which hath already spoy'ld your back,

                                              And

And methinks should be too hot,
To be cloystered in a pot.
Though you say she is so fair,
So lovely, and so debonair,
She is but of a yellow hair.

Sack's a whore which burns like fire,
Sack consumes and is a dryer ;
And her waies do only tend
To bring men unto their end :
Should I all her vices tell,
Her rovings and her swearings fell,
Thou wouldst dam her into Hell.

Sack which no dart-scorns will blast thee,
But upon thy bed still cast thee :
And by that impudence doth shew,
That no vertue she doth know :
For she will, the truth to say,
Thy body in an hour decay,
More than I can in a day.

Though for kisses there's no toyl,
Yet your body she doth spoil :
Sipping Nectar whilst you sit,
She doth quite besot your wit :
Though she is mute, she'll make you loud :
Brawl and fight in every croud,
When your reason she doth cloud.

Nor do you ever look to see
Any more a smile from me,
I'll [yield] no liberty, nor sign,
Which I truly may call mine.
No, no sleight shall win me to't,
Tis not all thy parts can do't;
Thy Person, nor thy Land to boot.

Yet if thou wilt take the pain,
To be sober once again,
And but make much of thy back,
I will be instead of Sack.
Faith but try, and thou shalt see,
What a loving soul I'll be:
When thou art drunk with nought but me.

A Catch.

She that will eat her breakfast in her bed,
   And spend the morn in dressing of her head,
And sit at dinner like a Maiden-bride,
And nothing do all day, but talk of pride;
Jove of his mercy may do much to save her,
But what a case is he in that shall have her.

St. George

St. George for England.

WHy should we boast of *Arthur* and his Knights,
Knowing so many men have endured hot fights;
Besides King *Arthur*, and Sir *Lancelot du Lake*,
Sir *Tristram de Lionel*, that fought for Ladies sake,
Read old Histories, and then you shall see,
That St. *George*, St. *George* did make the Dragon flee;
   St. *George* for *England*, St. *Dennis* for *France*,
   Sing *Hony soit qui mal y pense*.

Mark how father *Abraham*, when first he rescued *Lot*,
Only by his household what conquest there they got;
David elected a Prophet and a King,
He slew great *Goliah* with a stone and a sling;
These were no Knights of the Table round,
But St. *George*, St. *George* the Dragon did confound;
   St. *George*, &c.

Joshua and *Gideon* did lead their men to fight,
They conquered the *Amorites*, and put them to flight;
Hercules labour's upon the Plains of *Bass*,
And *Sampson* slew a thousand with the jaw bone of
Besides a goodly Temple there he did spoyl, (an ass,
But St. *George*, St. *George* the Dragon he did foyl;
   St. *George*, &c.

The wars of the Monarchs they were too long to tell[,]
And next of all the Romans, for they did far excell,
When *Hannibal* and *Scipio* so many fields did fight,
Orlando Furioso was a worthy Knight;
Remus and *Romulus*, that first *Rome* did build,
But St. *George*, St. *George* did make the dragon yield,
    St. *George*, &c.

Many have fought with proud *Tamberlain*,
And *Cutlax* the *Dane*, great wars did maintain,
Rowland, and *Bryan*, and good Sr. *Oliveer;*
In the forrest of *Arden* there slew both Bull & Bear,
Beside the noble Hollander, Sir *Goward* with his bill,
But St. *George*, St. *George* the dragons bloud did spill;
    St. *George*, &c.

Bevis conquered *Askupart*, and after slew the bore,
And then he crost beyond the seas to combate
      with a Moor,
Sir *Isinbrass* & *Egleman* they were Knights bold[,]
And good Sir *John Mandevil* of travels much have told
These were all English Knights that pagans did convert.
But St. *George*, &c. pluckt out the Dragons heart.
    St. *George*, &c

The noble *Alphonso*, that was the Spanish King,
The order of the red scarfs and bedrowl he did bring,
He had a troop of mighty Knights, when first he did,
    begin,
                              That

That sought adventures far and nigh what conquest
    they might win,
The ranks of the Pagans full oft he put to flight,
But St. *George*, St. *George* did with the Dragon fight ;
    St. *George*, &c.

The noble Earle of *Warwick*, that called was Sir *Guy;*
The Infidels and Pagans much he did defie,
He slew the Gyant *Brandemoor*, & after was the death
Of the most gastly dun Cow, the divel of *Dunsmore*
    heath,
Besides other noble Deeds he did beyond the seas,
But St. *George*, St. *George* the Dragon did appease ;
    St. *George*, &c.

Valentine and *Orson* of King *Pipins* blood,
Alfred and *Henry* they were Knights good;
The four Sons of *Amon* that fought for *Charlemain*,
Sir *Hugo de Bourdeaux*, and *Godfrey de Bullaign*,
These were all french Knights that lived in that age,
But St. *George*, St. *George* the Dragon did asswage ;
    St. *George*, &c.

When at the first K. *Richard* was King of this Land,
He gorged a Lyon with his naked hand ;
The noble Duke of *Austria* nothing he did fear,
He killed his Son with a box on the ear,
Besides other noble deeds done in the holy-Land,
But St. *George*, St. *George* the Dragon did withstand ;
    St. *George*, &c.

When as the third King *Edward* had conquered all
    France,
He quartered their Arms his honour to advance,
He ransack'd their Cities, threw their Castles down,
And garnished his head with a double double Crown,
He thumped the *French*, & homeward then he came,
But St. *George*, St. *George* the Dragon he did tame;
    St. *George*, &c.

St. *David* of *Wales* did the Welchmen much advance,
St. *James* for *Spain*, that never yet broke Lance,
St. *Patrick* for *Ireland*, that was St. *Georges* Boy,
Seven years he kept his horse, & then stole him away,
For which filthy act a slave he doth remain,
But St. *George*, St. *George* the Dragon he hath slain;
    St. *George* for *England*, St. *Denis* for *France*,
    Sing *Hony soit qui mal y pense.*

Arthur of Bradly.

SAw you not *Pierce* the Piper,
    His Cheeks as big as a Myter,
Piping among the Swains
    That's down in yonder Plains:
Where *Tib* and *Tom* doth tread it,
    And Youths the hornpipe lead it,
With every one his carriage
    To go to yonder Marriage,
                                    For

For the honour of *Arthur* of *Bradly*,
   Oh brave *Arthur* of *Bradly*, O fine *Arthur* of *Bradly*,
   O brave *Arthur* of *Bradly*, oh.

Arthur hath gotten a Lass,
   A bonnier never was;
The chiefest youths in the Parish
   Come dancing in a *Morris*,
With Country Gambols flouncing,
   Country Wenches trouncing,
Dancing with mickle pride,
   Every man his wench by his side,
For the honour of *Arthur*, &c.

But when that *Arthur* was married,
   And his Bride home had carried;
The Youngsters they did wait
   To help to carry up meat:
Francis carried the Furmety,
   Michael carried the Mince-pye,
Bartholomew the Beef and the Mustard,
   And *Christopher* carried the Custard,
Thus every one went in this Ray,
   For the honour of *Arthur* of *Bradly*, Oh fine, *&c.*

But when that dinner was ended,
   The Maidens they were befriended;
For out stept *Dick* the Draper,
   And he bid pipe up scraper;

Better to be dancing a little,
   Than into the Town to tipple;
He bid him play him a Horn-pipe,
   That goes fine of the Bagpipe:
Then forward Piper, and play
   For the honour of *Arthur* of *Bradly*, Oh fine, *&c.*

Then *Richard* he did lead it,
   And *Margery* she did tread it;
Francis followed them,
   And after courteous *Jane*:
And every one after another,
   As if they had been sister and brother,
That 'twas a great sight to see
   How well they did agree,
And then they all did say,
   Hay for *Arthur* of *Bradly*, oh fine, *&c.*

When all the Swains did see
   This mirth and merry glee,
There was never a man did flinch,
   But every man kist his Wench:
But *Giles* was greedy of gain,
   And he would needs kiss twain;
His Lover, seeing that,
   Did rap him on the pate,
That he had not one word to say
   For the honour of *Arthur* of *Bradly*, oh fine, *&c.*
                             The

The Piper look'd aside,
   And there he spide the Bride;
He thought it was a hard chance
   That none would lead her a dance:
For never a man durst touch her,
   But only *Will.* the Butcher;
He took her by the hand
   And danc'd whilst he could stand;
The Bride was fine and gay,
   For the honour of *Arthur* of *Bradly*, Oh fine, &c.

Then out stept *Will.* the Weaver,
   And he swore he'd not leave her;
He hopt it all of a Leg,
   For the honour of his Peg,
But *Kester* in *Cambrick* Ruffe,
   He took that in snuff:
For he against that day
   Had made himself fine and gay;
His Ruff was whipt over with blew,
   He cryed a new dance, a new;
Then forward Piper and play,
   For the honour of *Arthur* of *Bradley*, Oh fine, &c.

Then 'gan the Sun decline,
   And every one thought it time
To go unto his home,
   And leave the Bridegroom alone.

To 't [,] to 't, quoth lusty *Ned*,
   We'll see them both in bed :
For I will jeopard a joynt
   But I will get his codpiece point :
Then strike up Piper and play,
   For the honour of *Arthur* of *Bradly*, oh fine, &c.

And thus the day was spent,
   And no man homeward went,
That there was such crouding and thrusting,
   That some were in danger of bursting,
To see them go to bed :
   For all the skill they had,
He was got to his Bride,
   And laid him close by her side,
They got his Points and Garters,
   And cut them in peeces like quarters ;
And then they bid the Piper play,
   For the honour of *Arthur* of *Bradley*, oh fine, &c.

Then *Will.* and his sweet heart
   Did call for *Loath to depart*,
And then they did foot it and toss it,
   Till the Cook had brought up the posset,
The Bride-pye was brought forth,
   A thing of mickle worth,
And so all at the bed-side
   Took leave of *Arthur* and his Bride,
                            And

And so they went all away
From the wedding of *Arthur* of *Bradley*, oh, &c.

On the Printing of the Oxford *Jests*.

1

I Tell thee *Kit*, where I have been,
Where I the rarest Jests have zeen,
  O Jests without compare,
Zuch Jests again cannot be shewn,
In *Oxford* no nor *Cambridge* town;
  They be so very rare.

2

I yesterday did go to buy
A book, (thou know'st) for thee and I,
  Of zomething that was pretty,
And when poor *Robins* Jests I zaw,
Methoughts they were old, and lean, and raw,
  Not like his Almanachs witty.

3

I then did ask for the *Oxford* Jests,
Which *Kit* thou knowest came from the Brests,
  Of our University;
The man to me did then confess,
They were not yet come out o' th press,
  Quoth I [,] the more's the pitty.

At

4

At last he shew'd the very coppy,
Of that i'th press, I'm a very puppy
   Kit, if e'er the like was zeen;
Before I half a score had read,
With laughing (if it may be zed)
   I'd like to have broke my spleen.

5

I then did point to read 'um o'er,
Zuch Jests I never heard before,
   Fore *George* tis true our *Kit;*
And e'er that I had read 'um half
I found I was so great with laugh,
   I thought my zides would split.

6

Then hey for *Oxford* now I zay   [!]
Evaith I long to see the day
   That they shall printed be;
Then thee and I will each buy one,
For our two sweet hearts *Nell* and *Jone*,
   For Mirth and Mellodie,

A Catch.

There was three Cooks in *Colebrook*,
   And they fell out with our Cook,
And all was for a pudding he took,
And from the Cook of *Colebrook*.

                                             There

There was swash Cook, and flash Cook,
And thy Nose in my Narse Cook,
And all was for a pudding he took,
And from the Cook of *Colebrook*.
Then they fell all upon our Cook,
And numbled him so, that he did look
As black as the pudding which he took,
And from the Cook of *Colebrook*.

The Blacksmith.

OF all the Sciences beneath the Sun.
    Which have been since the world begun,
The Smith by his art great praise hath won,
    Which no body can deny.

The fairest Goddess in the skies
To marry with him did devise,
That was a cunning Smith and wise,
    Which no body, *&c.*

Then *Mars* came down for *Venus* sake,
The Smith he did his armour make,
In love together he did them take,
    Which no body, *&c.*

The first that ever Musick made
Was *Tubal* of the Blacksmiths Trade,

By hammering strokes as it was said,
    Which no body, &c.

He did invent continually
The Iron work for the Country,
A Smith for mirth and husbandry,
    Which no body, &c.

What Occupation can you name,
But first the Smith must help the same,
With working tools their work to frame?
    Which no body, &c.

What horse can post to carry news,
But first the Smith sets on his shooes,
With Spur and Stirrop for mens use?
    Which no body, &c.

What Ship upon the Sea can sail,
If Iron work in her do fail,
Though Anchor hold 'twill not prevail?
    Which no body, &c.

What can you build with lime or stone
If Iron-work therein be none?
Smiths make for houses many a one,
    Which no body, &c.

How can you go to Plough or Cart,
Except the Smith do play his Part,
With Coulter and Shaire made well by Art,
    Which no body, &c.

                              The

The Axletree Pin, the plowing Chain,
The Bill, the Axe, the Wedges twain,
The Pitchfork, and the Dung-fork plain,
    Which no body, &c.

The Butchers Axe, the Shooe-makers Awl,
The cutting knives on every stall,
That lies to cut and carve withall,
    Which no body, &c.

The Coopers Adds, the Brewers Slings,
The Carpenters Tools for many things,
The plyers for the Goldsmiths Rings,
    Which no body, &c.

Your Tongs, your Spits, Trevits, and Racks,
And many other things that lacks,
And for your houses pretty Knacks,
    Which no body, &c.

Weights and Skales to buy and sell,
A thousand things I need not tell,
The Smith hath match'd all things so well,
    Which no body, &c.

I could rehearse a thousand things,
Of iron Bars, Bolts, and Pins,
Latches, Catches, Staples, Rings,
    Which no body, &c.

He makes all several kinds of Locks,
For horses, for doors, for Chest, for Box,
For houses, and for Churches Clocks,
 Which no body, &c.

Your fire Irons, small and great,
Your pothooks, and forks so fine and neat,
Your Jack that turns your spits of meat,
 Which no body, &c.

Your Paviours Pickax, great and small,
Your Pattens for women, low and tall;
Your Shovel and Spade to work withall,
 Which no body, &c.

Your branding Iron to brand your Kine,
Your Clappers for Bells to ring and chime,
Your stamps for Gold and Silver fine,
 Which no body, &c.

The horses Bits, that finely gingle,
The Barbers Tools, that is so nimble,
The Taylors sheer, his Bodkin and thimble,
 Which no body, &c.

And for all weapons for the fight
The Smith I am sure makes such a sight,
So long, so strong, so fair, so bright,
 Which no body, &c.

          Bills

Bills, Pikes, Dags and Guns,
Halberts, Spears, and many things,
Through the hammer of the Smith all come,
 Which no body, *&c.*

To love the Smith all Trades are bound,
Which make him thus to be renown'd,
For which his hammers they are crown'd,
 Which no body, *&c.*

Of Smiths now living at this hour,
There was a Smith within the Tower
Which might be counted for a flower,
 Which no body, *&c.*

Thus of my Song I make an end,
The Smith is every bodies friend,
He seeks his Country to defend,
 Which no body can deny.

A North Country Song.

WHen Ise came first to *London* Town,
 Ise wor a Novice, as other men are;
se thought the King had liv'd at the Crown,
 And the way tol heaven had been through the star.

Ise set up my horse, and Ise went to *Pauls*,
    Good Lord, quoth I, what a Kirk been here?
Then Ise did swear by all Kerson souls,
    It wor a mile long, or very near,

It wor as high as any Hill,
    A Hill, quo I, nay as a Mountain,
Then went Ise up with a very good will,
    But glad wor I to come down again.

For as Ise went up my head roe round.
    Then be it known to all Kerson people,
A man is no little way fro the ground,
    When he's o' th' top of all *Pauls* steeple.

Ise lay down my hot, and Ise went to pray,
    But wor not this a pitious case,
Afore I had done it wor stolen away,   (place?
    Who'd have thought theeves had been in that

Now for my Hot Ise made great moan,
    A stander by unto me said,
Thou didst not observe the Scripture aright,
    For thou mun a watcht, as well as pray'd.

From thence Ise went, and I saw my Lord Mayor,
    Good lack [!] what a sight was there to see,
My Lord and his horse were both of a hair,
    I could not tell which the Mare should be.

                                      From

From thence to *Westminster* I went,
   Where many a brave Lawyer I did see,
Some of them had a bad intent,
   For there my purse was stoln from me.

To see the Tombs was my desire,
   I went with many brave fellows store [,]
I gave them a penny that was there hire,
   And he's but a fool that will give any more.

Then through the rooms the fellow me led,
   Where all the sights were to be seen,
And snuffling told me through the nose,
   What formerly the name of those had been.

Here lies [,] quoth he, *Henry* the Third,
   Thou li'st like a knave, he saies never a word;
And here lies *Richard* the Second interr'd,
   And here stands good King *Edwards* Sword.

Under this Chair lyes *Jacobs* stone,
   The very same stone lies under the Chair,
A very good jest, had *Jacob* but one,
   How got he so many Sons without a pair?

I staid not there, but down with the tide
   I made great haste, and I went my way;
For I was to see the Lions beside,
   And the Paris-garden all in a day.

When Ise came there, I was in a rage,
   I rayl'd on him that kept the Bears,
Instead of a Stake was suffered a Stage
   And in Hunkes his house a crue of Players.

Then through the Brigg to the Tower Ise went,
   With much ado Ise entred in,
And after a penny that I had spent,
   One with a loud voice did thus begin.

This Lyon's the Kings, and that is the Queens,
   And this the Princes that stands here by,
With that I went neer to look in the Den   [:]
   Cods body, quoth he, why come you so nigh?

Ise made great haste unto my Inne,
   I supt, and I went to bed betimes,
Ise slept, and I dream'd what I had seen,
   And wak'd again by Cheapside Chimes.

The Merry Goodfellow.

WHy should we not laugh and be jolly,
   Since all the World is mad?
And lull'd in a dull melancholly;
   He that wallows in store
   Is still gaping for more,
   And that makes him as poor,
As the wretch that ne'er anything had.

                                 How

How mad is that damn'd money-monger?
That to purchase to him and his heirs
Grows shriviled with thirst and hunger;
  While we that are bonny,
  Buy Sack with ready-money,
And ne'er trouble the Scriveners, nor Lawyers.

Those guts that by scraping and toyling,
Do swell their Revenues so fast,
Get nothing by all their turmoiling,
  But are marks of each taxe,
  While they load their own backs
  With the heavier packs,
And lye down gall'd and weary at last.

While we that do traffick in tipple,
Can baffle the Gown and the Sword,
Whose jaws are so hungry and gripple,
  We ne'er trouble our heads
  With Indentures or Deeds,
And our wills are compos'd in a word.

Our money shall never indite us,
Nor drag us to Goldsmiths Hall,
No Pyrats nor wracks can affright us;
  We, that have no Estates,
  Fear no plunder nor rates,
  We can sleep with open gates,
He that lies on the ground cannot fall.

We laugh at those fools whose endeavours
Do but fit them for Prisons and Fines,
When we that spend all are the savers;
      For if the thieves do break in,
      They go out empty agin,
Nay, the Plunderers lose their designs.

Then let us not think on to morrow,
But tipple and laugh while we may,
To wash from our hearts all sorrow;
      Those Cormorants which
        Are troubled with an itch,
      To be mighty and rich,
Do but toyl for the wealth they do borrow.

The Mayor in our Town with his Ruff on,
What a pox is he better than me?
He must vail to the man with his Buff on;
      Though he Custard may eat
      And such lubbardly meat,
Yet our Sack makes us merrier than he.

The Rebels Reign.

Now we are met, in a knot, let's take t'other pot,
    And chirp o'r a Cup of Nectar;
Let's think on a charm to keep us from harm,
  From the Fiend, and the new Protector.

                         Heretofore

Heretofore at a brunt a Cross would have done 't,
   But now they have taken courses,   (left
With their Laws and their theft, there's not a cross
   In the Church, nor the Farmers purses.

They're with you to bring for a stuffing at a King,
   For now you must make no dainty,
To have your nose ground on a stone turned round
   By *Nol*, and one and twenty.

But our Rights are kept for us in *Oliver's* store-house
   'Twere as good they were set in the stocks ;
They are just in the pickle in the thirtieth Article,
   Like *Jack* in a Juglers box.

We are loth to look for the Saints in a book,
   But would not a man be vext,
To see them so rough with the blades and their buff,
   But not a word on't in the Text.

We have been twelve years together by the ears
   To prepare for a spiritual raign :
Men were never so spic'd with the Scepter of Christ
   In the hands of a Saint in grain.

'Twas brew'd in their Hives by Citizens wives,
   Who ventured their husbands far,
With *Robin* the fool there was ne'r such a tool
   To lead in the womens war.

                                           He

He was ill at Command, but worse at a stand,
   So they sought out another more able:
Then *Fair.* undertakes, but *Nol* keeps the stakes,
   And sends away *Fox* with a bauble.

Wil, Conqueror the second, without his host reck-(on'd,
   And so did *Brown* billet his Mate:
They made a great noise mongst women and boys,
   But now they are both out of date.

Cowardly *W*——— had but a foule Fortune,
   And wanted a knife to scrape it,
When his Oriphice ran there was no mortal man,
   But *omnibus horis sapit*

Bradshaw, the Knave, sent the King to his grave,
   And on the bloud Royal did trample,
For which the next *Lent* he was made President,
   And ere long may be made an example.

Dorislaus did steer to *Hans mine beer*,
   And *Askew* to *Don* at *Madril*,
Ere a man could have scratcht they were both dis-(patcht,
   Yet there they lye Leger still.

Martin and St. *Johns*, and more with a vengeance,
   Had each a finger i'th' pye:
Some for the money, and some for the Conny,
   And some for they knew not why.

                                            The

The Parliament sate as snug as a Cat,
   And were playing for mine and yours :
Sweep-stakes was their Game till *Oliver* came,
   And turn'd it to knave out of doors.

Then a new one was cast, and made up in hast,
   But alas [!] they could do no more
Than empty our purse, and empty us worse
   Than e'r we were marred before.

But in a good hour they gave up their power
   To one that was wiser than they ;
By common consent 'twas the first Parliament
   That ever was *felo de se*.

After all this Jeer we are never the near,
   There sits one at the helm commanding ;
One that doth us nick with a trick for our trick,
   And the stone in our foot notwithstanding.

He'l not relax one groat of the Tax
   Though it come to more than he need,
He may keep it in store till his need be more,
   'Tis an Article of our new Creed.

So well he hath wrought, that now he hath brought
   The Realm to the manner he meant it ;
The Fishes, and the fowl, and the divel and all
   And the monthly pay his high rent.

All this we must bear, but 'twould make a man swear
  When they call us a reformed Nation :
It can never sink into my head for to think
  That this is a Reformation.

'Tis the man in the Moon, or the divel as soon,
  Our Laws are asleep upon shelves :
Our Charter and Freedom we may bid God speed 'um,
  'Tis well we can beg for our selves.

Since *Nol* hath bereft us, and nothing hath left us,
  Not a Horse or an Oxe to plough land ;
Let *Oliver* pass, come fill up my glass,
  And here's a good health to *Rowland*.

A Catch.

HAve you observ'd the wench in the street,
  She's scarce any hose or shooes to her feet ;
And when she cries, she sings,
  I have hot Codlings, hot Codlings.

Or have you ever seen or heard,
  The mortal with his Lyon tauny beard !
He lives as merrily as heart can wish,
  And still he cries, Buy a brush, buy a brush.

                                    Since

Since these are merry, why should we take care?
   Musitians, like Camelions, must live by the Aire;
And let's be blithe and bonny, & no good meeting
   balk,   (Chalk.
What though we have no money, we shall find

A new Medley.

The English.   L Et the Trumpet sound,
                       And the Rocks rebound,
Our English Native's coming;
        Let the Nations swarm,
        And the Princes storm,
We value not their drumming.
'Tis not *France*, that looks so smug,
Old fashions still renewing,
It is not the *Spanish* shrug,
Scottish Cap, or *Irish* rug;
Nor the *Dutch-mans* double jug
Can help what is ensuing;
Pray, my Masters, look about,
For something is a Brewing.

He that is a Favorite consulting with Fortune,
If he grow not wiser, then he's quite undon;
In a rising creature we daily see certainly,
He is a retreater that fails to go on:
                                          He

He that in a builders trade
Stops e're the roof be made,
By the Air may be betray'd
   And overthrown :
He that hath a race begun,
And lets the Goal be won ;
He had better never run.
   But let 't alone.

   Then plot rightly,
   March sightly,
Shew your glittering Arms brightly :
   Charge hightly ;
   Fight sprightly ;
Fortune gives renown.
   A right riser
   Will prize her,
She makes all the world wiser ;
   Still try her,
   We'll gain by her,
A Coffin or a Crown.

If the *Dutchman* or the *Spaniard*
   Come but to oppose us,
We will thrust them up at the main-yard
   If they do but nose us :
Hans, Hans, think upon thy sins,
And then submit to *Spain* thy Master ;
For though now you look like friends,
                       Yet

Yet he will never trust you after;
Drink, drink, give the *Dutchman* drink,
And let the tap and kan run faster;
For faith at the last I think
A Brewer will become your Master.

Let not poor Teg and Shone
Vender from der houses,
Lest dey be quite undone
In der very Trouses:
And all der Orphans bestow'd under hatches,
And made in *London* free der to cry matches;
St. *Patrick* wid his Harp do tun'd wid tru string
Is not fit to unty St. *Hewson's* shooe-strings.
   Methinks I hear
   The welch draw near,
And from each lock a louse trops;
  Ap Shon, ap LLoyd,
   Will spend her ploot,
For to defend her mouse-traps:
  Mounted on her *Kifflebagh*
  With cott store of *Koradagh,*
The Prittish war begins.
  With a hook her was overcome her,
  Pluck her to her, thrust her from her,
By cot her was break her shins.
   Let Taffie fret,
   And welch-hook whet
          And

And troop up petigrees,
        We only tout
           Tey will stink us out,
Wit Leeks and toasted Sheeze.

But *Jockie* now and *Jinny* comes,
Our Brethren must approve on't;
For pret a Cot dey bert der drums
Only to break de Couvenant.
Dey bore Saint *Andrew's* Cross,
Till our army quite did rout dem,
But when we put dem to de loss,
De deal a Cross about dem:
The King and Couvenant they crave,
Their cause must needs be further'd   [,]
Although so many Kings they have
Most barbarously, basely murthered.

The French.   The Frenchman he will give consent,
Though he tickle in our veins;
        That willingly
          We may agree,
To a marriage with grapes and grains:
        He conquers us with kindness,
        And doth so far entrench,
That fair, and wise, and young, and rich,
        Are finified by the *French:*
He prettifies us with Feathers and Fans,
With Petticoats, Doublets, and Hose,
                  And

   And faith they shall
   Be welcome all
If they forbear the nose.
   For love or for fear,
   Let Nations forbear;
If Fortune exhibit a Crown,
   A Coward he
   Must surely be,
That will not put it on.

A Catch.

SHew a Room, shew a Room, shew a Room,
 Here's a Knot of Good fellows are come,
That mean for to be merry
With Clarret and with Sherry;
Each man to mirth himself disposes,
And for the Reckoning tell *Noses;*
Give the *Red-Nose* some *White,*
And the *Pale-Nose* some *Clarret,*
But the *Nose* that looks *Blew,*
Give him a Cup of Sack, 'twill mend his hew.

The Contented.

WHy should a man care, or be in despair,
 Should Fortune prove never so unkind?

    Y   [Or]

Or why should I be sad for that I never had,
Or foolishly trouble my mind?
For I do much hate to pine at my Fate,
There's none but a fool will do so:
I'll laugh and be fat, for care kills a Cat,
  And I care not howe're the world go.

Though I am poor, and others have store,
Why should I repine at their bliss?
For I am content with what God hath sent,
And I think I do not amiss:
Let others have wealth, for I have health,
And money to pay what I owe,
I'll laugh, and be merry, and sing hey down, down
  For I care not, &c.   (derry

Some men do suppose, even by their gay Cloaths,
For to be in great request;
Though mine be but bare, I am not o' th' show,
And I think myself honestly drest;
Though every man cannot say so,
I like that I wear, though it cost not so dear,
  For I care not, &c.

Your Epicure eats of the best sort of meat
And wine of the best he doth drink,
And laies him to rest, and thinks himself blest,
On heaven he never doth think;
          Though

Though my fare be but course, I am not the worse,
My health is the better I know;
Though plain be my food, my stomach is good,
    And I care not, &c.

Your flattering Curs, that fawn upon Furs,
And hang at Noble mens ears,
If once they do fall, away they run all,
And this is their flattering fears:
Dissembling I scorn, for I am free born,
My happiness lies not below;
Though my words want Art, I speak from my heart,
    I care not, &c.

Some men do strive, and mightily thrive,
And some for Offices wait,
Much money they spend, and to little end,
And repent then when it's too late;
Low shrubs are secure, when Cedars endure
Great storms and tempests below,
Let others look high, for so will not I,
    And I care not howe're the world go.

How to live happy.

HE that a happy life would lead
    In these times of distraction,
Let him listen to me, and I will read
A Lecture without faction;

Let him want three things, whence misery springs,
They all begin with a letter,
Let him bound his desires to what nature requires,
And with reason his humour fetter.

Let not his wealth prodigious grow,
For that breeds cares and dangers;
Makes him envied above and hated below,
A constant slave to strangers;
They are happiest of all whose estates are but small,
Though but enough to maintain them,
They may do, they may say, having nothing to pay,
It will not quit cost to arraign them.

Nor would I have him clogg'd with a wife,
For household cares incumber,
Nor to one place to confine his life,
Cause he can't remove his Lumber;
They are happiest far who unmarried are,
And forrage, and all in common,
From all storms they can flye, or if they should die,
They ruine no child nor woman.

Let not his brains or'flow with wit,
That capers o'r discretion,
It's costly to keep, and hard to get,
And dangerous in the possession;
They are happiest men that can scarce tell ten,

And beat not their brains about reason,   (serve,
They may speak what will serve themselves to pre-
And their words are not taken for treason.

But of all fools there's none to the wit,
 For he takes pains to shew it,
His pride and his drink bring him into a fit,
 Then streight he turns a Poet:
His jests he flings at States, or at Kings,
 Or at Plays, or at Bays, or at shadows,
Thinks a Verse serves as well as a Circle or Cell,
 Till he rimes himself to the Barbadows.

He that within these Lines can live,
 May baffle all disasters,
To Fortune and Fate commands he can give,
 Who[m] Wor[l]dlings call their Masters;
He may sing, he may quaff, he may drink, he may
May be mad, may be sad, may be jolly,   (laugh,
He may sleep without care and speak without fear,
 And laugh at the world and its folly.

A Catch.

WHat Fortune had I, poor Maid as I am,
 To be bound in eternal vow,
For ever to lye by the side of a man,
 That would, but knows not how?

          Oh

> Oh can there no pity
> Be in such a City,
> Where Lads enough are to be had.

Unfortunate Girl, that art wed to such woe,
    Go seek thee a lively Lad,
And let the poor that hath nothing to shew
    Go seek for another as bad ;
> Then call for no pity [,]
> Thou dweltst in a City,
Where Lads enough were to be had.

Advice to Batchelors.

HE that intends to take a Wife,
    I'll tell him what a kind of life
        He must be sure to lead ;
If she's a young and tender heart,
Not documented in Loves Art,
        Much teaching she will need.

But where there is no path, one may
Be tir'd before he find the way,
        Nay, when he's at his treasure,
The gap perhaps will prove so straight,
That he for entrance long may wait,
        And make a toyl of's pleasure.

Or if one old, and past her doing,
He will the Chamber-maid be wooing,
    To buy her ware the cheaper,
But if he chuse one most formose,
Ripe for't, she'll prove libidinous,
    Argus himself shan't keep her.

For when those things are neatly drest,
They'l entertain each wanton guest,
    Nor for their honour care,
If any give their pride a fall,
Th' have learn'd a trick to bear withal,
    So you their charges bear.

So if you chance to play your game
With a dull, fat, gross, heavy Dame,
    Your riches to encrease,
Alas! she will but jear you for't,
Bid you to find out better sport,
    Lie with a pot of grease.

If meager —— be thy delight,
She'l conquer in venerial fight,
    And waste thee to the bones:
Such kind of girles, like to your Mill,
The more you give, the more crave they will,
    Or else they'l grind the stones.

If black, 'tis ods she's dev'lish proud,
If short, *Zantippe* like, too loud,
      If long, she'l lazy be,
Foolish (the Proverb saith) if fair,
If wise and comely, danger's there,
      Lest she do cuckold thee.

If she bring store of money, such
Are like to domineer too much,
      Prove Mistris, no good wife,
And when they cannot keep you under,
They'l fill the house with scolding thunder
      What worse than such a life;

But if her Dowry only be
Beauty, farewel felicity,
      Thy fortunes cast away.
Thou must be sure to satisfie her
In belly, and in back-desire,
      To labour night and day.

And rather than her pride give o'r,
She'l turn perhaps an honoured whore,
      And thou'lt *Acteon'd* be,
Whilst like *Acteon* thou maist weep,
To think thou forced art to keep
      Such as devour thee.

If being noble thou dost wed
A servile Creature, basely bred,
    Thy Family it defaces;
If being mean, one nobly born,
She'l swear t' exalt a Courtlike horn,
    Thy low descant it graces.

If one tongue be too much for any,
Then he who takes a wife with many,
    Knows not what may betide him;
She whom he did for learning honour,
To scold by book will take upon her,
    Rhetorically chide him.

If both her Parents living are,
To please them you must take great care,
    Or spoyl your future fortune,
But if departed th' are this life,
You must be parent to your wife,
    And father all, be certain.

If bravely drest, fair fac'd and witty,
She'l oft be gadding to the City,
    Nor may you say her nay,
She'l tell you (if you her deny)
Since women have Terms, she knows not why,
    But they still keep them may.

If you make choice of Country ware,
Of being Cuckold there's less fear,
      But stupid honesty
May teach her how to sleep all night ;
And take a great deal more delight
          To milk the Cows than thee.

Concoction makes their blood agree
Too near, where's consanguinity ;
      Then let no kin be chosen :
He loseth one part of his treasure,
Who thus confineth all his pleasure
          To th' arms of his first Couzen.

He'll never have her at command,
Who takes a wife at second hand ;
      Then chuse no widdowed mother :
The first cut, of that bit you love,
If others had, why mayn't you prove
          But taster to another ?

Besides, if she bring children many,
'Tis like by thee she'l not have any,
      But prove a barren Doe ;
Or if by them, she ne'r had one,
By thee 'tis likely she'l have none,
          Whilst thou for weak back go.

For there where other Gard'ners have been sowing
Their seed, but ne'r could find it growing   [,]
      You must expect so too ;
And where the *Terra incognita*
S' o'rplow'd, you must it fallow lay,
      And still for weak back go.

Then trust not to a maiden face,
Nor confidence in widdows place,
      Those weaker vessels may
Spring-leak, or split against a rock,
And when your Fame's wrapt in a smock,
      'Tis easily cast away.

Yet be she fair, foul, short, or tall,
You for a time may love them all,
      Call them your soul, your life,
And one by one them undermine,
As Courtizan, or Concubine,
      But never as married wife.
He who considers this, may end the strife,
Confess no trouble like unto a Wife.

A Catch.

IF any so wise is, that Sack he despises,
  Let him drink small beer, and be sober,
Whilst we drink Sack and sing, as if it were spring,
He shall droop like the Trees in *October*.
But be sure if over night this dog do you bite,
You take it henceforth for a warning,
Soon as out of your bed, to settle your head,
Take a hair of his tail in the morning.
And be not so silly to follow old *Lilly*,
For there's nothing but Sack that can tune us,
Let his *Ne-assuescas* be put in his cap case,
And sing *bi-bi-to vinum Jejunus*.

A Mock Song.

WHen I a Lady do intend to flatter
  Oh, how I do begin to chatter;
    I swear and vow
  How much I'd do,
  That I might once get at her ———

I say to kiss her only is a Feast,
A *Cupids* Beaver at the least,
        Whilst silly she
    Believeth me,
    And thinks I love her best.

With those fair phansies which most comely are,
I oft her Ladyship compare;
        I say the Rose
    And Lilly, when it blowes,
    Are nothing near so fair.

Yet gazing on her face I've spent some hours,
Consulted with each cheek, and all its powers,
        But there none grew,
    Unless below,
    In pleasures garden - spring her flowers.

Oft have I call'd her Jewel, oft have I
Call'd true, the false pearls of her eye,
        Yet precious stone
    She will have none,
    Until with me she lie.

With what pure whiteness is her bosome blest,
Oft cry I, yet I do but jest;
        For sure I'm still,
    She never will,
    Untill I s—— her have a milk white breast.
                              Then

Then tell her by the rowling of her eyes,
I gues her secret rarities,
   Swear he who enjoyes
  Those pleasant toyes,
 Ought much to esteem the prize.

Thus Ladies have I learn'd in *Cupids* schools,
My Master *Ovids* Grammer Rules:
   Thus can I prove
  I am in love,
 And thus I make ye fools.

FINIS.

The Contents of the First Part.

	[Edition 1691,]	Page
Now *I confess I am in love*… …	[7]	5
Be merry in sorrow, why are you so sad	[9]	7
Amerillis *told her swaine* … …	[10]	8
Call for the Master oh this is fine …	[11]	9
Once was I sad till I grew to be mad …	[12]	10
When first Mardike *was made a Prey*…	[14]	12
Of all the Crafts that I do know … …		17
The thirsty Earth drinks up the Rain… …		21
To friend and to foe … … … …		23
The Fashions [: *The Turk in linen,* &c.] …		25
Tobacco that is withered quite … … …		26
There was a Jovial Tinker … … …		27
Now Gentlemen if you will hear … …		29
The Hunt is up… … … … …		30
Of an old Souldier of the Queen … …		31
If thou wilt know how to chuse a shrew …		32
Come my delicate bonny sweet Betty … …		34
Nay, prethee dont fly me, &c. … … …		36
A fox a fox up Gallants to the field … …		38
Ah Ah come see what's here … … …		40

Let

The Contents.

Let dogs and divells dye	41
A young man that in Love &c,	42
There dwelt a maid &c....	46
The spring is coming on and our bloud &c,	47
Doctors lay by your Irksome books	48
There was an old man &c.	52
Come Jack *lets drink, or the Cavaleers complaint*	52
The Answer to it [: *I marvel,* Dick, &c.]	54
All in the land of Essex	56
My Mistris is a Shittle-Cock	60
Will you hear a strange thing &c	62
Of nothing a new song [: *I'le sing you a Sonnet*]	66
Bacchus I am come from &c.	69
Be not thou so foolish nice	69
Aske me no more [*why there appears*] &c.	70
A Sessions was held the other day	72
I came unto a Puritan to woe	77
Good Lord what a pass is this world &c	79
Walking abroad in a morning	81
In Eighty Eight &c.	82
Nay out upon this fooling for shame	84
If every woman was serv'd in her kind	85
Some Christian People all give ear	87
Come my Daphne *come away*	91
Cast your Caps and cares away	92
When first the Scottish war began	93
My Brethren all attend	95
Come let's drink the time invites	97
In the merry month of May	99

Roome

The Contents.

Roome for the best of Poets Heroick 100
I tell thee Dick *where I have been* 101
How happy is the prisoner &c. 107
I met with the divel in the shape of a Ram ... 109
The world's a bubble, &c 110
The Proctors are two and no more 111
My Mistris whom in heart &c. 113
Tis not the Silver nor Gold 115
After so many sad mishaps 118
Come lets purge our brains 121
What though the [*ill*] *times* 124
Lay by your pleading [*Law lies,* &c.]... ... 125
I am a bonny scot 127
I'll tell thee a story, &c. 131
I'll go no more to the old Exchange 134
Lets call and drink the Celler [*dry*] 138
There is [*a*] *lusty Liquor* 140
Three merry lads met at the Rose 143
Of all the Recreations which ... ... [146] 130
Tom *and* Will *were shepherds* 149
Wake all you dead what O ... ... [151] 131
There [*is*] *a certain idle kind of creature* [152] 155
The Bow Goose [*: The best of Poets,* &c.] ... 153
News[*:*] *White Bears,* &c ... ... [159] 153
We seamen are the bonny boys 162
My Mistris is in Musick passing, &c ... 163
When the Chill charakoe blows 164
Now thanks to the powers below 166
A maiden of late &c 170

z   *After*

The Contents.

After the pains of a desperate Lover	171
Blind fortune if thou want s[t]	172
From Mahomet and Paganisme	174
God bless my good Lord [Bishop]	177
Of all the rare sciences	178
Heard you not lately of a man	180
The Medly of the Country man Citizen and souldier	182
No man loves fiery passion can approve	187
When blind God Cupid &c.	188
Come Drawer come fill us &c.	190
Lay by your pleading [Love lies, &c.]	191
Bring forth your Cunny skin	196
From hunger and cold &c.	197
Roome for a Gamester	197
Gather your Rose buds	199
A story strange I will you tell	200
I am a Rogue and a stout one	204
Stay shut the Gate	207

The Second Part.

Hold quaffe no more	210
Had she not care enough	211
Here's a health to his Majesty	212
But since it was [lately] enacted high Treason	212
Cock Laurel *[would needs have:] by* Ben Johnson	214
A fig for care [why should we spare]	217
Let Souldiers fight for praise, &c.	218

Neer

The Contents.

Ne'er trouble thy self at the times	219
Three merry boys came out of the West	220
Calm was the Evening	220
There's many a blinking Verse &c	221
The Blacksmith [: Of all the Trades]	225
Come my dainty doxes	230
Come Imp Royal &c. ...	231
The Wisemen [were but seven]	232
How poor is his spirit, &c	232
[Am] I am mad O noble Festus	234
I dote I dote but am a fool &c.	237
Ladies I do here present	240
The Combate of Cocks [: Go you tame Gallants]	242
Come let's frollick fill some Sack	246
What is that you call a Maidenhead	249
When Phœbus *addrest* &c.	250
A Brewer may be a Burgess grave	252
Oliver Oliver [take up thy crown]	254
When I do travell in the night.	255
Sir Eglamore *[that valiant Knight]*	257
If none be offended &c...	259
Come drawer and fill us &c	263
The Bulls feather [: It chanced not long ago]	264
You talk of new England	266
Come drawer turn about the Bowle	268
Pray why should any man complain	270
What an ass is he	273
My masters give audience	275
The Aphorismes of Galen	277

The Contents.

Now I am merrier [i.e. married] Sir John	280
I have reason to fly thee	281
I have the fairest Non-perel	283
Are you grown so melancholly	286
Sublimest discretions have climb'd &c	288
A pox on the Jaylor	289
My lodging is on the cold ground	290
From the fair Lavinian shore	291
Fetch me Ben Johnsons *scull* &c.	293
Now that the spring &c.	296
Of all the sports in the world	296
The wily wily Fox	300
She lay all naked &c.	300
Some wives are good &c.	301
Call George *again*	304
Pox take your Mistris	304
The Answer [: *I pray thee, Drunkard,*]	306
She that will eat her breakfast	308
St. George *for* England [: *Why should we,* &c.]	309
Arthur *of* Bradley [*Saw you not* Pierce]	312
On the Oxford *Feasts* [: *I tell thee,* Kit,]	317
There were three Cooks in Colebrook	318
The Blacksmith [: *Of all the Sciences*]	319
When Ise came first to London *Town*	323
The merry good fellow [: *Why should we not laugh*]	326
The Rebels Reign [: *Now we are met*]	326
Have you observ'd the wench in the street	332
A new Medley [: *Let the trumpet sound*]	333
Shew a Room shew a Room &c.	339

Why

The Contents. [357]

Why should a man care or be in despair	...	*ibid*
He that a happy life would lead	... ...	339
What fortune had I, poor maid that I am	...	341
He that intends to take a wife... ...	...	342
If any so wise is, that Sack he despises	...	347
A mock Song [: When I a Lady, &c.]	...	348

[The Editor felt compelled to retain the present Table of Contents, since it appeared in the original, although it is less convenient than A Table of First Lines alphabetically arranged. But such a table (marking, by distinct class of type, which songs appeared only in the 1661 edition) will be given in the next volume, for the present work inclusive.]

Books

Books Printed for, or sold by *Simon Miller*, at the Star at the West-end of St. *Pauls*.

Quarto.

PHysical Experiments, being a Plain Description of the Causes, Signs, and Cures of most Diseases incident to the body of man; with a Discourse of *Witchcraft*. By *William Drage*, Practitioner of Physick at *Hitchin* in *Hartfordshire*.

Bishop *White*, upon the Sabbath.

The Artificial Changeling.

The life of *Tamerlain*.

The *Pragmatical Jesuite*. A Play by *Richard Carpenter*.

Large Octavo.

Mr. *Shepherd*, on the Sabbath.

The Rites of the Crown of *England*, as it is established

blished by Law; By *E. Bagshaw* of the *Inner-Temple*, An Enchiridion of fortification.
Merry Drollery Compleat.

Small Octavo.

Butler, of War.
Ramsey, of Poysons.
Artimedorus, of Dreams.
Record, of *Urines*.
The History of *Fortunatus*.
The History of *Daphnis* and *Cloe*.

Large Twelves.

Oxford Jeasts.
Dr. *Smith's* Practice of Physick.
The third part of the *Bible* and *New* Testament.
The duty of every one that will be saved? being Rules, Precepts, Promises, and examples, Directing all Persons of what degree soever, how to govern their Passions, and to live virtuously and soberly in the World. Dr. *Spurstow's* Meditations.

Small Twelves.

The understanding - Christians - Duty.
A Help to Prayer.
Hell Torments Shaken.
A New Method of Preserving and Restoring Health, by the vertue of Coral and Steel.
David's Sling.

Appendix.

APPENDIX.

Notes, Various Readings, and Emendations of Text,

(NOW FIRST ADDED).

———o———

N.B.—The great bulk of the 1691 edition of *Merry Drollery, Complete*, renders it expedient that we limit the present series of Notes within the smallest convenient space. Many important Notes and Illustrations are consequently reserved for a COMPANION VOLUME, which will also give the thirty-four Songs and Poems that appeared in the 1661 edition; not reprinted when the work gained the addition of twenty-six Songs, as mentioned in our Introduction, p. v. By the help of a Table of First Lines, arranged in strictly alphabetical order, to be added afterwards, the reader will discern at one glance in what editions each song appeared.

The twenty-six Additional Songs, not in the 1661 edition, are those that begin respectively on our pages 8, 9, 21, 66, 99, 143, 146, 149, 151, 171, 178, 211, 212, 217, 219, 220 *(bis)*, 232, 287, 289, 290, 291, 292, 293, 302, and 317. To all the others the date 1661 (or earlier) applies. Some of the twenty-six were not written until about 1670.

In the same volume we hope to be able to give the Additional Songs that were inserted in the 1674 edition of WESTMINSTER DROLLERY; with Notes to them.

MERRY DROLLERY, COMPLETE.

Part 1st. Page 8 [10]. *Amarillis told her Swain.*
This is Maria's Song, in THOMAS PORTER's tragedy, The Villain, 1663, Act ii. The music is given in Wm. Chappell's excellent "Popular Music of the Olden Time,"

Time," p. 284. The tune was also known as "Phillis on the new-made Hay." In Roxburghe Coll., ii. 85.

Page 9 [11].   *Call for the Master: oh, this is fine!*

Also in Windsor Drollery, p. 102. A history might be written of the various gangs of Roysterers who have successively made night hideous in London by their noise. In Dean Swift's time they were styled Mohawks, or Mohocks, from their imitating the Indian war-whoop. At beginning of this century they were Tom and Jerry men. Here we have them as Hectors. But, as Charles Mathews would say, "It's the same—drunk, Master." Verrinus seems to have been superfine tobacco. John Philips, in his *Splendid Shilling* (of which we possess the earliest edition, 1701) speaks of the hero's discomfort:—

> But I . . . . from Tube as black
> As winters chimney, or well polish'd Jett,
> Exhale Mundungus's ill-perfuming smoak.

Page 12. [14]   *When first Mardyke was made a prey.*

With music, in Pills v. 65. Loyal Garland (13th ed., 1686). Roxb. Coll., ii. 431, printed for P. Brooksby. Bagford Coll., i. 69. The date of Dunkirk being taken was June 26, 1658. But Mardyke, or Moerdyke, which seems to have been considered the key to Dunkirk, had been captured in the previous campaign, 1657, by the French conjoined with the English under Reynolds. Charles II. afterwards selling Dunkirk to King Lewis, in 1662, was felt as a sore disgrace.

Page 21.   *The thirsty Earth drinks up the Rain.*

This paraphrase of an ode by the bard of Teos is by ABRAHAM COWLEY, who died in 1667. All of Cowley's Anacreontiques are charmingly airy and graceful. Given in Wit & Mirth, 1684; in Ritson's English Sgs., ii. 24; and as an appropriate finale to his Introduction on Festive Sgs., by W. Sandys, Percy Soc., xxiii.

Page 23.   *To Friend and to Foe.*

In Wit & Mirth, 1684, p. 104, and in the Hive, ii. 176, as "The Married Man's Items."   Page

Page 25. *The Turk in linnen wraps his head.*

This favourite song on the Englishman's fickle whims regarding dress, aping his neighbours, is by THOMAS HEYWOOD, in his "Challenge for Beauty," 1636, and also in his "Rape of Lucrece," before 1638 (first edit., 1608?) Beginning omitted, as also from the Percy Folio MS., iv. 77. It should commence thus :—

> *The Spaniard loves his ancient slop;*
> *The Lombard his Venetian;*
> *And some like breechless women go,*
> *The Russe, Turk, Jew, and Grecian.*
> *The threysly Frenchman wears small waist,*
> *The Dutch his belly boasteth;*
> *The Englishman is for them all,*
> *And for each fashion coasteth.*
>
> *The Turk,* &c.

Rubrick beer is corruption of *Lubeck* beer. Chippin, for Choppine: mentioned in Hamlet, ii. 2. A later reading (inferior) for "Comely Fro," *i.e.,* Frau, has "lovely Erse," or Gael. Fairholt gives the song, under "English Mutability in Dress," Percy Soc., xvii. 141 (Costume); and a picture of the "Monmouth Cap" (2nd verse) on p. 115.

Page 26. *Tobacco that is withered quite.*

William Chappell refers to this from the 1670 edition, but it is also in that of 1661, p. 16. He gives us from a MS Collection, time of James I., belonging to J. P. Collier, a copy of the earliest known form of this song, beginning "Why should we so much despise:" Pop. Music, ii. 563. It bears the initials G. W., possibly for GEORGE WITHER, a tedious rhymester in his later days when sanctimonious, and continually in trouble, but a genuine son of Apollo, as shown by his earlier poems. His "Shepherd's Hunting," his "Mistress of Phil'arete," and even the bitter satire, "Abuses stript and whipt," possess poetry enough to float a dozen "England's Hallelujah" hulks.

With music, as "Tobacco is but an Indian weed," it is
in

in Pills, 315 (1699); iii. 292 (1719); as also in Chappell, 564. Compare a vulgarized " This Indian weed, now withered quite," in Bds. and Sgs. of the Peasantry, R. Bell's edit, p. 40.

Page 27. *There was a Jovial Tinker.*

With music to it, in the Pills, v. 62.

Page 29. *Now Gentlemen, if you will hear.*

Earlier than 1660, as it is in " Le Prince d'Amour" of that date, p. 178. Probably before 1649. P. d'A. reads *"thieves"* in line 9th; *Bazingstone.* Line 28, cp. Chaucer: "It *snewed* in his house of meate and drink," C. T.

Page 30. *The Hunt is up.*

We know not of this particular " Hunt is up" occurring elsewhere, but J. P. Collier gives from MS. " The King's Hunt is up," (? 1570), six stanzas, beginning

> The Hunt is up, the hunt is up,
> And it is well nigh daye,
> And Harry our king is gone hunting
> To bring his deere to baye," &c.
>   *Extr. Registers Stat. Comp.* (1848) i. 129.

J. P. C. *(loc. cit)* also gives opening stanza of a religious parody, and one from a love serenade; all begin with the same common line. He believed the one he transcribed might be [William] Gray's, mentioned by Puttenham, 1589. But Dr. Rimbault gives Gray's in his Little Book of Sgs. & Bds., p. 69. Also the beginning of one in Rawlinson Collection, Oxford.

Page 31. *Of an Old Souldier of the Queens.*

Tune, " The Queens old Courtier " (for which see Prince d'Amour, 1660; and, with music also Chappell, Pop. M., 300). Cp. Wit and Drollery, "Of old soldiers the song you would hear," and "With a new beard," 1682, pp. 165, 282. Page

Page 34. *Come my delicate bonny sweet Betty.*

Not found elsewhere as yet. Some corruption of text apparently, which baffles us. In line 8, may not the right word be *Vulcan?* The *Æolus* in third verse shows a likelihood of such mythologic allusions as to *Tellus* the Earth, and *Vulcan*.

Page 36. *Nay, prithee don't fly me.*

For the answer to this, "I have reason to fly thee," see page 281. Both are by ALEXANDER BROME. As "The Leveller," among his Sgs. (3rd edit., 1668), 12. Also in Rump Collect. (1662), i. 265; Loyal Sgs. (1731), i. 158. "Grinning honour" is a phrase borrowed from Falstaff, Henry IV. Pt. i. Act v. Sc. 3.

Page 52, 53. *Come, Jack, lets drink,* and *I marvel, Dick,* &c.

See introduction, p. xxi. In Bagford Coll. Bds., iii. 23, a copy "printed for N. Butter, 1660" [-61?]. Antidote ag. Melancholy (1661), 49, 51. Dryden's Misc. Poems, vi., 352. Percy Soc., iii., 257, 259. Wilkins' Pol. Bds., i. 162, 165.

Page 56. *All in the Land of Essex.*

Date before 1653-4. It is satisfactory to remember that SIR JOHN DENHAM, the reputed author of this objectionable but clever ballad, was afterwards rendered sufficiently uncomfortable (when he had married a young wife, handsome and unprincipled), by his fits of jealousy and by the attacks made against him by infuriated mobs, who could not sympathise with him for the amiable weakness he was suspected to have shown in poisoning Elizabeth Lady Denham. She seems well to have deserved her fate, despite her voluptuous beauty; but perhaps that is scarcely extenuation. We see her portrait among Sir Peter Lely's Court Beauties, and read the history in De Grammont and elsewhere, Mrs. Jameson not shirking the difficulties. Denham was a strange
                                                                mixture

mixture of dirt and precious metal. His "Lines on the death of Cowley" dispose us to love him, and the way in which he saved George Wither is a perfection of humour. This "Colchester Quaker" is also in the Rump, early edition, 1660, p. 6; 1662, i. 354; Loyal Sgs., i. 231, the editions of Denham and of CLEVELAND. Tune, Tom of Bedlam, like "Am I mad?" Compare "All you that have two," &c., and "All Christians and Lay Elders too," in the Rump, i. 358; i. 350.

Page 60. *My Mistris is a shittle-cock.*
In Wit and Drollery, 1661. Tune, "To all you Ladies."

Page 62. *Will you hear a strange thing*, &c.
See Introduction, p. xviii. Date, April, 1653. It is also in the Rump Coll., i. 305. Loyal Sgs. i. 189. Wilkins Polit. Bds., i. 100. Compare Carlyle's Cromwell.

Page 66. *I'le sing you a Sonnet*, &c.
Tune, "The Blacksmith," giving it the popular burden of "Which no body can deny;" in Pills iii. 138. Old Bds., 1727, iii. 187. Windsor Drollery, 1672, p. 93.

Page 69. *Bacchus, I am* [,] *come from*, &c.
This (not found elsewhere) is a parody on John Fletcher's song, in "The Mad Lover," Act iv. Sc. 1 —

>   Orpheus *I am, come from the deeps below,*
>   *To thee, fond man, the plagues of love to show.*
>   *To the fair fields where loves eternal dwell* [&c.
>   *There's none that come, but first they pass through hell,*

It is sung by Stremon, disguised as Orphèus, to sooth the Mad Lover, Memnon. Date before 1625, but not printed until 1647.

Page 69. *Be not thou so foolish nice.*
Before 1656, as it is in *Musarum Deliciæ*, p. 58; 1873 Reprint, p. 75. Page

APPENDIX. 369

Page 70. *Aske me no more why there appears.*
Asserted to have been written in 1642, and not improbably by THOMAS JORDAN. It is in his "Royal Arbor of Loyal Poesie" (1664); p. 84 of J. P. Collier's Reprint. Rump (1662), i. 68. Loyal Sgs., i. 41.

Page 72. *A Session was held the other day.*
By SIR JOHN SUCKLING. Written about 1637; and found, with a few variations, but always the one broken verse, in all editions of his poems. Compare other Sessions, viz., "Apollo concerned to view the transgressions," Poems on State Affairs, i. 206; Rochester's, or Villiers's "Since the sons of the Muses;" R.'s, and V.'s Poems; and "One night the great Apollo pleased with Ben," (With Notes to each of these, *and to the present poem*, in our forthcoming Reprint) in the rare "Choice Drollery," 1656.

Page 77. *I came unto a Puritan to woo.*
Also in Rump Coll., i. 194, and Loyal Sgs., i. 122.

Page 82. *In Eighty Eight, e'er I was born.*
Also in Choice Drollery, 1656, p. 38, the earliest printed version known to us. We gave the Harleian MS. version, No. 791, fol. 59, in *Appendix to Westminster Drollery*, p. 38. Cp. the very different re-casting, "Some years of late, in eighty eight," in same vol., Part I. p. 93; and in J. O. Halliwell's Naval Bds., Percy Soc., ii. 18.

Page 85. *If every woman were serv'd*, &c.
With music in Pills (1700 and 1719), iv. 110. Also in Windsor Drollery, 57. As Hamlet puts it, "Give every man after his dessert, and who shall 'scape whipping?"

Page 87. *Some Christian people all give ear.*
See Introduction, p. ix., for modern condensation of this burlesque. Tune, Chevy Chase. Given with music
in

A A

in Pills, iv. 1. 1719. Dr. Wagstaffe quotes first verse of modernization, before 1726, in his " Character of Richard St[ee]le, Esq."

Page 91.   *Come, my Daphne, come away.*

By JAMES SHIRLEY, whom Charles Lamb designates "the last of a great race, all of whom spoke nearly the same language, and had a set of moral feelings and notions in common." We sadly need a fresh edition of Shirley (and of Middleton), Dyce's work of 1833 having become scarce. The present song was set to music by William Lawes. It belongs to Shirley's tragedy, "The Cardinal," Act v. Sc. 3, 1652. It appears, with the music, the same year, in Playford's Select Ayres, ii., p. 6. Title, song of Strephon and Daphne. In Windsor Drollery, 115. Acad. Compl., 1670, p. 206. Wit's Academy, 79. Dyce's Shirley, v. 344.

Page 92.   *Cast your Caps and cares away.*

By JOHN FLETCHER, in "Beggar's Bush," Act ii. Sc. i.; before 1625. Given in Windsor Drollery, 87. Sgs. of Dramatists, 125.

Page 93.   *When first the Scottish War began.*

Compare Bagford Coll., ii. 96. In Rump, i. 228; Loyal Sgs. (1731), i. 58.

Page 95.   *My Brethren all attend.*

See Introduction, p. viii. The final verse touches the same chord that vibrates so sweetly in Mrs. Hemans' poem, to which her sister set the music. We would gladly give the entire poem, though men ought to know it by heart. The Mayflower Pilgrim Fathers belong to all of us, and the story of their landing and of their early privations is perhaps as dear even as that of the Pitcairn Islanders. Involuntarily, there breaks through the burlesque of Merry Drollery something not unallied to earnestness in the "Zealous Puritan." Read the final verse, and compare

pare the song which has become a national hymn on the shores of America :—

> "*Not as the flying come,*
> *In silence and in fear,—*
> *They shook the depths of the forest gloom*
> *With their hymns of lofty cheer.*
>
> *Amid the storm they sang,*
> *And the stars heard, and the sea!*
> *And the sounding aisles of the dim woods rang*
> *To the anthem of the free.*"

Page 97. *Come, let us drink, the time invites.*
In Loyal Garland, 1686. Repr. by Percy Soc., xxix. 28. Old Bds., iii. 159.

Page 99. *In the merry month of May.*
By NICHOLAS BRETON, about 1580. In "England's Helicon," 1600. With music by Dr. John Wilson, in Playford's Select Ayres, 1659, p. 99. Also among Madrigals by Michael Este, 1604. In Pills, iii. 51. Percy's Reliques, iii. Bk. I. No. 10. Calliope (music, 1788), 309. Ritson, Engl. Sgs., i. 235.

England's Helicon reads :—*In* a morne ;. *Forth I walked by* the *wood-side ; his* pride ; *Phillida ; God* wot, He *would* love & she *would* not. *She said neuer man* was true, *He said, none was* false to you ; *haue* no wrong. Till they *did ; shepheard* call ; witness *truth :* Never loved a *truer* youth. Was *made* the lady, &c.

Page 100. *Room for the best Poets heroic!*
This first appeared among "Certain [Satyrical] Verses, written by several of the Author's friends, to be reprinted with the second edition of Gondibert." [April 30] 1653. Another poem from the same volume is given on our page 118, beginning "After so many sore mishaps." These scurrilous lampoons on Sir William D'Avenant (whose mode of spelling his name was sneered at,) were followed

lowed by another volume, entitled, "The Incomparable Poem of Gondibert Vindicated," &c. Isaac D'Israeli, in an interesting paper entitled "D'Avenant and a Club of Wits" (in his "Quarrels of Authors," pp. 403-414, edit. 1867), gives ample evidence that this second volume was by the same or similar malicious wits as the "Four Esquires" who concocted the "Certain Verses." The received error is that the Vindication came from the author: even Maidment and Logan, recently editing D'Avenant, seem to think thus, they having probably, like ourselves, been unable to see the later publication. Aubrey mentions George Villiers, D. of Buckingham, as being responsible; but the Four are understood to have been Sir John Denham and John Donne, Sir Allan Broderick and Will Crofts.

Page 101. *I'll tell thee, Dick, where I have been.*

This unequalled "Parley between two West Countrymen," "On the sight of a Wedding," is to be found in the Antidote against Melancholy, 40; Pills iii. 132 (with the music); Dryden's Misc. Poems, i. 154 (ed. 1716); and all editions of its author, SIR JOHN SUCKLING. The wedding referred to was that of Roger Boyle, Lord Broghill, afterwards first Earl of Orrery, with the beautiful Lady Margaret Howard, daughter of Theophilus, Earl of Suffolk. Suckling wrote another poem on the occasion, beginning "In bed, dull man, when Love and Hymen's revels are begun." The exact date of the marriage (Tho. Morrice, in memoir of Boyle, does not give it), 1641, fixes that of the poems. Suffolk house with its grand staircase "at Charing Cross," where men sold their hay, has been lately destroyed: the massive Northumberland House. The mutilation of the ballad, in 1836, by the Rev. Alfred Suckling (who went against the proverb, and tried to dirty his own family nest in the Memoir) is inexcusable. Wm. Chappell gives the music, Pop. M., p. 360.

For Imitations of this Ballad, see Additional Note, and the Appendix to *Westminster Drollery*, pp. lxviii.-ix.; "Now that Love's Holyday," &c., was by John Cleveland, before 1658.

Page

Page 107. *How happy is the Prisoner who conquers his fate.*

This song appears in the play called "Cromwell's Conspiracy," among the Thomason pamphlets, dated 1660, as sung by Musicians in Act iii. Sc ii. But we find it earlier, in "Choice Drollery," 1656, p. 93, *q. vide.* Probably the 1660 "Cromwell's Conspiracy," which is anonymous, " by a Person of Quality," was the extension of an earlier drama, with the final scenes of the Rump-burning and Restoration added. The song is repeated in Windsor Drollery, 74, and in the Loyal Garland of 1686.

We feel certain that the above must have been remembered by the author of an excellent song, "Diogenes surly and proud," in "Wine and Wisdom; or, the Tippling Philosophers," 1710, to which music was set by Richard Leveridge, from whose rich voice it doubtless came rolling blithly. This song was originally only six verses (fifty-four were in the author's *Lyrick Poem.*) We possess seventeen additional verses to these six, in various early Song-books of last century. The resemblance to "How happy is the Prisoner," in regard to Aristotle, Copernicus, and Diogenes are far too close to be accidental. Thus of the latter we read:—

> *But growing as poor as a Job,*
> *And unable to purchase a flask,*
> *He chose for his mansion a Tub,*
> *And liv'd by the scent of the cask.*

And of Copernicus, indulging in wine:—

> *Then fancied the world, like his brains,*
> *Turn'd round like a chariot wheel.*

Page 109. *I met with the Divel in the shape of a Ram.*

An old proverb says that the Smith and his penny are both black. So we need not expect that a Sowgelder's song will be cleanly. The present is sung by Higgen, exalting his trade, in JOHN FLETCHER's Comedy, "The Beggar's Bush," Act iii., Sc. i. Date probably about 1622, or earlier. In Wit Restored, 1658, p. 172; (Reprint, 1873,

1873, p. 294). Also, with music by Thomas Wroth, in the Pills, v. 330. Not in the 1647 folio of Beaumont and Fletcher; and only imperfect in the 1811 quarto. Sometimes printed " He ran at me first in the shape of a Ram."

Page 110. *The World's a bubble, and the life of man."*

Attributed to JAMES USHER, Archbishop of Armagh, who died in 1658. Dr. Johnson quotes it (Tour to the Hebrides) as by Bacon; and Dr. Robert Carruthers erroneously annotates that the reference is to the Rev. Phanuel Bacon : who was not born until about 1700. The poem appeared as by " Bishop Usher, late Lord Primate of Ireland," in H. W.'s " Miscellanies," 1708. See Notes and Queries, 5th, S. III. pp. 313, &c., 1875.

Page 115. *'Tis not the Silver nor Gold for itself.*

This clever satire on the times (applicable to most other times, alas !) is in the Rump, i. 230, and Loyal Songs, i. 60.

Page 118. *After so many sad mishaps.*

See our note on the other poem (p. 100 of *M. D. C.*) from the same " Certain Verses," April 30, 1653. Two examples of the same class of burlesque may be named; one, by W. M. Thackeray, on the " Sorrows of Werter." The other, in the " Melbourne Punch," was entitled " Enoch Arden Boiled Down." It follows Tennyson closely (by the way, he made no acknowledgment of having borrowed the story from Adelaide Anne Procter's earlier-printed " Homeward Bound," in *Legends and Lyrics*, p. 34, edit. 1866; but which had first appeared as part of Dickens' Christmas Story, " The Wreck of the Golden Mary," 1856). It ends thus, after seven stanzas :

> " Yet reflecting on the subject,
>   He determined to atone
> For his lengthened absence from her
>   By just leaving well alone.

Taking

*Taking to his bed, he dwindled
   Down to something like a shade;
Settled with his good landlady,
   Next the debt of nature paid.*

*Then, when both the Rays discovered
   How poor Enoch's life had ended,
They came out in handsome style, and
   Gave his corpse a fun'ral splendid.*

*This is all I know about it,
   If it's not sufficient, write
By next mail to Alfred Tenny-
   Son, P.L., the Isle of Wight."*

The satirist hits the blot, in the penultimate verse, as A. T. marred the grandeur of his hero's death, by unnecessarily adding, for conclusion :—

"*So past the strong heroic soul away.
And when they buried him the little port
Had seldom seen* a costlier funeral ! ! ! "

What an Undertaker's bathos, and from a true poet.

Page 121. *Come, let's purge our brains,* &c.

More disparagement of malt and hops, associated with "The Brewer," Oliver Protector. Also in Loyal Garland, 1686; Percy Soc. Reprint, xxix. 53.

Page 124. *What though the ill times do run cross,* &c.

Also in Rump, i. 234; and Loyal Songs, i. 65. Compare "What though the Times produce effects," in 1661 edit. of Merry Drollery, p. 161. (Next volume.)

Page 125. *Lay by your pleading, Law lies a bleeding.*

Date about 1658. Music in Chappell, Pop. M., p. 431; and in the Pills, vi. 191. Words in the Rump, i. 333; Loyal Songs, i. 223; Wilkins' Political Bds., i. 86; and Mackay's Cavalier Sgs., 67, from the Loyal Garland, 1686. Additional Note in next volume.

Page

Page 127. *I am a bonny Scot, Sir,* &c.

In the Antidote against Melancholy, 1661, p. 59; J. P. Collier's Reprint, p. 73.

Page 131. *I'll tell you a story that never was told.*

Additional Note in next volume. Also given in the Rump, i. 340; Loyal Sgs. ii. 2.

Page 134. *I'll go no more to the Old Exchange.*

Music to this in Chappell P. M., p. 317. Additional Note in our next volume. In "Wit Restored," 1658 (Repr. pp. 139-45) are The Burse of Reformation, beginning "We will go no more to the *Old* Exchange," and an Answer to it, "We will go no more to the *New* Exchange." Compare, also, in Wit and Drollery, 1656, pp. 110, 60, "I'll go no more to the *New* Exchange," and "I'll go no more to Tunbridge Wells." In the Pills, vi. 145, we find another song, with music, on the "Buttoned Smock," so entitled, beginning "Sit you merry."

Page 138. *Let's call and drink the Cellar dry.*

Compare Roxburghe Collection, ii., 372, The Noble Prodigal. The six ayres are, "The Jew's Corant," "Princess Royal," "Come hither my own Sweet Duck," &c.

Page 140. *There's a lusty liquor which,* &c.

With music, given by Wm. Chappell, P. M., 308. His remarks are as usual of great value. The tune is known as "Stingo, or Oyl of Barley" (1650), as "The Country Lass" (Martin Parker's hearty ballad), and "Cold and Raw" (D'Urfey's Song, 1688, in the Pills, ii. 167).

Page 143. *Three merry Lads met at the Rose.*

In "Wit Restored," 1656, p. 162; Reprint, 294. Also in "Antidote ag. Melan.," 33. The Rose Tavern was in Russell Street, Covent Garden, and bore a bad repute.

In

In Shadwell's "Scourers," 1691, we read, "In those days a man could not go from the Rose Tavern to the Piazzi once, but he must venture his life twice" *(Hist. Signboards*, p. 125). Hogarth shows a room of the Rose in the supper orgie of Rake's Progress. Other Rose Taverns, however, were near Temple Bar, and in Wood Street, &c.

Page 146. *Of all the Recreations which,* &c.

This was sung to the tune "Amarillis" *(vide ante,* p. 8; but in Pills, iii. 126, we meet these words to the music of a tune "My Father was born before me"). It is in Vocal Companion, ii. 242. "The Royal Recreation of Jovial Anglers" is the title attached to it in J. P. Collier's excellent 4to., A Book of Roxburghe Ballads, 1847, p. 232; from a broadsheet printed by F. Coles, T. Vere, W. Gilbertson, and J. Wright. He believed it to be not older than 1653. We guess it to be of ten years later date, remembering Porter's "Villain." Tom Hudson, early in his Nineteenth Century, wrote an amusing song on the same theme (we have a copy of it, beginning "We're all fishing in Country and in Town").

Page 149. *Tom and Will were shepherd swains.*

Evidently alluding to some recent rivals; town gossip, now difficult to follow, but possible, if worth the labour. The earliest other copy yet seen is of same date (as our second edition) 1670; in Acad. Compl., p. 180. The music is given in Pills, iii. 112; p. 130 of 1699 edition. It is in Old Ballads, ii. 179.

Page 151. *Wake all you dead, What ho!* &c.

This is Viola's song, by SIR WILLIAM D'AVENANT, in his "Law against Lovers," Act iii. Sc. i., 1662. Paterson's edit. of D. (Dramatists of the Restoration) has it in Vol. v. p. 152. The play, which Pepys records having seen and liked, in his Diary, 18th February, 1661-2, is composed from a mixture of "Measure for Measure" and "Much Ado about Nothing." Properly, the song should be divided into stanzas, the second beginning "The State is," &c. Page

Page 152. *There is a certain idle kind of creature.*

We find this, signed "Philo-balladus" in the Roxburghe Collection of Bds., i. 466; printed for Francis Grove [abt. 1620-55], Snow Hill; to a pleasant new tune. 15 verses.

Page 159. *White Bears are lately come to town.*

Also in Wit and Mirth, 1684, p. 39. We have an impression that this is by the author of "Some wives are bad," &c., p. 302.

Page 162. *We seamen are the honest boys.*

Included by J. O. Halliwell (Phillips) in his Naval Bds., for Percy Soc., ii. 36. We meet it first in 1656, *Wit and Drollery*, p. 31, as "We Sea-men are the *bonny* boys;" with variations :—up have *blown ;* She fore the wind will run a ; Gabions ; counter*murs ;* and an additional verse (the 7th) :—

> The Bear, *the* Dog, *the* Fox, *the* Kite,
> *That stood fast on the* Rover,
> *They chas'd the* Turk *in a day and night,*
> *From* Scandaroon *to* Dover.

Page 164. *When the chill Charokoe blows.*

Not later than 1656, being in "Wit and Drollery" of that date, p. 154. With music, in "Calliope," 1788, p. 452. Also in Acad. Compl., 1670, p. 241. Dryden's Misc. Poems, vi. 358. Ritson's Engl. Sgs., ii. 57. Percy Soc. (Festive Sgs.), xxiii. 67. At commencement of Antidote ag. Melancholy, 1661, is a long "Ex-Ale-tation of Ale," worth our quoting hereafter.

Page 166. *Now [that] thanks to the powers below.*

Date 24th Oct., 1648. Title, The Anarchie; or, the Blessed Reformation Since 1640; to a rare new tune. It is in the Rump, i. 291; Loyal Songs, i. 174; Wilkins' Polit. Bds., i. 32; Wright's ditto (Percy Soc., iii.), 112.

Page 170. *A maiden of late, whose name was sweet Kate.*

With music, as "The Maiden's Longing," in Pills, iv. 2. Also in Windsor Drollery, 131; and in Dryden's Misc. Poems, iv. 101.

Page 171. *After the pains of a desperate lover.*

By JOHN DRYDEN; in "An Evening's Love," Act ii. 671. General reading, "pangs." Music by Alphonso Marsh, in Playford's Choice Ayres, 1676, Bk. i. p. 4. Music also set later by Galliard, in Watts' Musical Misellany, i. 100, 1729; and in Merry Musician, ii. 87. It is in Windsor Drollery, 139; and in Hive, iv. 143, entitled "The Transport."

Page 178. *Of all the rare juices,* &c.

Another song by ALEXANDER BROME, died 1665. In 1668 ed. of his songs, p. 74.

Page 180. *Heard you not lately of a man.*

By HUMFREY CROUCH. It is in Roxburghe Collection, i. 264; and ii. 362. (Probable date, 1635-42):—

"*The Mad Man's Morrice; wherein you shall finde
His trouble and grief, and discontent of his minde;
A warning to young men to have a care,
How they in love intangled are.*"

This motto precedes in the Roxb. broadsheet, which is reprinted for our Ballad Society, annotated by Wm. Chappell, in Roxb. Bds., ii. 153. It is also in the Bagford Coll., i. 50, ii. 117; the Euing, Nos. 201, 202; and the Ouvry (formerly J. P. Collier's), two copies. The stanzas are printed as eight lines, this being the second not in *M. D. C.*):—

> " *Into a pond stark nak'd I ran,*   [line 9]
>   *And cast my cloathes away, Sir,*
> *Without the help of any man,*
>   *Made shift to run away, Sir.*

How

> *How I got out I have forgot,*
> *I do not well remember;*
> *Or whether it was cold or hot,*
> *In June, or in December.*

And this, Roxb. Bd. fourth verse, not in our's, but needed to introduce the thought of his Lady, love for whom has crazed him:

> *" Did you not see my Love of late,*   [line 25]
>   *Like Titan in her glory?*
> *Do you not know she is my mate,*
>   *And I must write her story*
> *With pen of gold on silver leafe?*
>   *I will so much befriend her;*
> *For why, I am of this belief,*
>   *None can so well commend her.*
>
> *Saw you not angels in her eyes,*   [var. of M.D.C.
>   *While that she was a speaking?*
> *Smelt you not smells like paradise,*
>   *Between two rubies breaking?*
>
> *Is not a dimple in her cheek?*   [line 41]
>   *Each eye a star that's starting*   [var. of M.D.C.
> *Is not all grace install'd in her?*   p. 181]
>   *Each step all joys imparting?*
> *Methinks I see her in a cloud,*   [variation]
>   *With graces round about her;*
> *To them I cry and call aloud,*
>   *I cannot live without her."*

These broadside ballads, when not originally long enough to give sufficient for the two-pence, or to satisfy the milkmaids and apprentices, who loved them, with enough "piling up of the agony," were frequently lengthened out. But Humfrey Crouch, being a genuine balladist, probably grew his own redundancies. The 3 vols. for Novels are still orthodox: a second part to Street Ballads was a *sine qua non* in the 17th century. We shall give it in the companion volume (along with " CHOICE DROLLERY.")

Our ninth half-verse does not appear at all in the

Crouch" broadsheet. The others are varied and
transposed, from what was, probably, the original; viz.,
the Roxburghe Ballad. It was worth comparing, as being
an elaborate specimen of those Mad Songs in which our
nation especially delighted of old. See Notes on pp. 234
and 290.

Page 187. *No man Love's fiery passions can approve.*
Wit and Drollery, 1656, p. 70; "Academy of Complements," 1670, p. 185. An Answer to it, in *Oxford Drollery*,
1671, p. 114, begins :—

> Some men Love's fiery passions can resist,
> That either values pleasure or promotion :
> I hate Luke-warmness in an Amorist,
> It is as bad in Love as in devotion.

Seven verses follow this.

Page 190. *Come Drawer, come fill us, &c.*
A third song by ALEXANDER BROME; written in 1648.
In the 1688 edition of his Songs, p. 73. Rump, i. 270.
Loyal Sgs., i. 164. Properly, "Come, Drawer, *and
fill*," &c.

Page 191. *Lay by your pleading, Love lies a bleeding.*
We have hitherto met this excellent song nowhere but
here. Wm. Chappell gives only a few disconnected
scraps of the verses, along with the music, in Popular M.
of the Olden Time, p. 431. Compare previous note on p.
25 (App., 375).

Page 196. *Bring forth your Cunny-Skins*, &c.
Hare-skin and rabbit-skin collectors have always been
queer characters. This Catch is by JOHN FLETCHER,
in his "Beggar's Bush," Act iii. sc. 1; where it is sung
by Clause his boy. Clause the vagabond beggar was a
popular favourite, reproduced in Drolls. We see him
represented in the frontispiece of "The Wits" by Kirkman
and

and Cox; now given to our readers. The Song is in Windsor Drollery, abt. p. 88; Acad. Compl. 1670, p. 173; and, *with the Music*, in Pills, v. 303.

Page 197.   *From hunger and cold, &c.*

By RICHARD BROME, in his "Jovial Crew," Act i. 1641. Music to this Song of the Jovial Beggars in Playford's Select Ayres, 1659, p. 64. The play has always been, deservedly, a favourite. When it was revived, in 1731 with many additional songs to popular tunes, converted into a Ballad Opera by Roome and Sir William Young almost every song found its way to Collections, and kept a place in them. The present editor possesses several editions, some being in manuscript with the music, showing how songs were introduced, almost *ad libitum*. Tom Moore's "Evelyn's Bower" makes its appearance for one. Richard Brome deserves esteem. There was something boastful, *more suo*, in Ben Jonson's addressing him, "I had you for a servant once, Dick Brome," &c., but the two men understood and liked each other.

Page 197.   *Room for a Gamester, who plays, &c.*

Also in the Rump, i. 252; Loyal Sgs., i. 142; Loyal Garland (1686). Mackay's Cavalier Sgs., 278.

Page 199.   *Gather your Rosebuds while you may.*

By ROBERT HERRICK, in his Hesperides, 164. Also in Wit's Recreations, Reprint, p. 474, *with Music*, by Wm. Lawes in Playford's Select Ayres, 1659, p. 101. Our text is wofully corrupt; but is a little set to rights in the margin by bracketted corrections. Date, before 1645.

Page 200.   *A Story strange I will you tell.*

Of a date at least as early as 1656, see "Choice Drollery," p. 31. Sometimes printed "A pretty jest I will," &c., as in Roxb. Coll., ii. 192; iii. 330; Bagford ditto, i. 55; ii. 128. Also, as "Now listen a while, and I will you tell," &c.: in Wit & Mirth, 1684, p. 40. The humour is extremely

tremely coarse, but evidently found acceptance among a multitude, for it was frequently reproduced. In old broadsheets (especially one of the Bagford copies) the rude woodcut almost out-Herods Herod in offensiveness, the style of engraving being moreover extremely primitive and Catnachish.

Page 204. *I am a Rogue, and a Stout One.*

The music to this is one of the favourite Tom o' Bedlam tunes, and is found in John Gamble's MS., as we learn from Chappell, P. M., pp. 332, 779. We know no other print of this vigorous song, exposing the cheats of mendicants, except one with variations in *Wit and Drollery*, 1682, p 74. It is entitled The Blind Beggar." By it we correct our text :—*Bousing* Ken; *Gentry* folk (v. 4.); *Dog* in a string [but our " Peg " may be correct] ; and four additional verses,—viz. 2, 5, 10, 14, of which we append the two of any value :—

> *If a Bung be got by the High-way,* [verse 2]
> *Then streight I do attend them,*
> *For if Hue and Cry*
> *Do follow, I*
> *A wrong way soon do send them,*
> *Still do I cry, &c.*

> *I pay for what I call for,* [verse 5]
> *And so perforce it must be,*
> *For yet I can*
> *Not know the Man,*
> *Or Hostess that will trust me.*
> *Still do I cry, &c.*

Page 207. *Stay, [stay], Shut the Gate !*

A fourth song by ALEXANDER BROME, written before 1658. With the music, in Pills, v. 85. In Loyal Garland (1686, 13th edit.) is an additional verse, as fifth. Among A. Brome's " Songs and other Poems," 3rd edit. 1668, p. 55; with an additional verse, by "M. C. Esquire."

5.
Call, call, honest Will,
Hang a long and tedious bill,
It disgraces;
When our Rubies appear,
We justly may swear,
That the reckoning is true by our faces.
Let the Bar-boy go sleep, and the drawers leave roaring,
Our looks will account without them, had we more in,
When each pimple that rises will save a quart scoring.

This is answered, by T. J., in the next page of A. Brome's Songs, as it is in "*Merry Drollery,*" though divided, in *M. D. C.*, 1691, by it commencing the Second Part.

MERRY DROLLERY, COMPLETE.
PART SECOND.

Page 210. *Hold, [hold,] quaff no more!*

This "Mock Song," or Answer, from the more sober and thoughtful kind of Cavalier, to those who by debauchery ruined themselves and the cause they were supposed to love, bears the initials "T. J." as author, in A. Brome's volume of Songs, p. 57. Perhaps it may be by THOMAS JORDAN, a staunch Royallist versifier, although it seems higher and nobler in tone than his acknowledged productions. Also in Mackay's Cavalier Sgs., 114.

Page 211. *Had she not care enough,* &c.

With the music, this is given in Walsh's Catch Club (no date, but about 1704), ii. 43, No. 69, as "On a Widow who Married an Old Man." An Answer to it appears in *Oxford Drollery*, Pt. 1st, p. 66, by Capt. Willm. Hicks, 1671,

Was he not kind enough, kind enough, kind enough,
Was he not kind enough to his young Bride?
From her Childhood he bred her, then he fed her,
And he led her, to the Church where he wed her,
Then lay by her side: But

But Oh how he push't her, and crush't her,
And thrust her, and like to a burst her
With long lying on.
And Oh how she panted, and ranted,
Being scanted, of the thing that she wanted
All the night long!

See Later, p. 396; and *Westminster Drollery* Appendix, for Note on CaptainWilliam Hicks, p. 76.

Page 212. *Here's a Health unto his Majesty.*

Music, by Jeremiah Saville in Playford's Musical Companion, 1667, given by Chappell, Pop. M., 492. Words in Mackay's Cav. Sgs., 251.

Page 212. *But since it was lately enacted High Treason.*

A fifth song by ALEXANDER BROME, and full of character; written in 1646. Among his Sgs., 1668, p. 63. Loyal Garland, Percy Soc. Reprint, xxix. 25. Mackay, Cav. Sgs., 283.

Page 214. *Cook Laurel would needs have the divel,* &c.

By BEN JONSON, in his Masque, "The Gipsies Metamorphosed," acted in August, 1621. It is in the Percy Folio MS., iv. 40; in the Antidote against Melancholy, 9; in Dryden's Misc. Poems, ii. 142, and, with the music, in Pills, iv, 101. There can be no question as to whose favour Ben Jonson wished to propitiate by this delectable ditty (coarse, but of sustained humour and rollicking fun). It was suited to the taste of James I., whom Ben could please far better than "our gentle Willy"—who indeed died more than five years before. Charles I. appreciated him better, as we know. Even the final verse gives evidence that to James was this "Banquet in the Peak" directed; as the royal author of the "Counterblast against Tobacco" (reprinted in Dec., 1869, by Edward Arber, to whom we all owe so much gratitude) gives, as fitting diet for his Satanic Majesty, a poll of ling, a side (flitch) of bacon, and a pipe of tobacco for digestion. And
"the

"the Scottish Solomon" was not far wrong in his apportionment; for, prejudice apart, when we see the ever-growing evils of inordinate smoking, what a curse it is, drying the juices, gradually paralysing the intellect, and making its slaves selfishly indifferent to the discomforts of all who are forced to be in contact with them, we are not indisposed to agree with Ben Jonson and his Royal patron. Shakespeare (almost alone, of all the Elizabethan writers) avoids mention of tobacco. It cannot possibly be by accident. And if he had loved the weed " not wisely, but too well," we may be sure he would have indicated it, as he has done almost every other imaginable thing. Was it that he disliked and wondered at the infatuation; but, in his fine tolerance of human weakness, and genial sympathy with all "humours," he yet abstained from uttering a word of scorn? We may never know. In the Genuine Works of Charles Cotton, 6th edit., 1771, illustrating his poem of " The Wonders of the Peake," in Derbyshire, is a copper-plate representing the remarkable cavern bearing the vulgar title " The Devil's Arse, near Castleton." The versical description is precise, but almost interminable. There are many variations in the printed copies of Ben Jonson's Cook Laurel.

Page 218. *Let souldiers fight for praise and pay.*

In Antidote ag. Melancholy, 39. With music, by Henry Lawes, 1653, in his Ayres, Book i. Part 2, p. 9, where the author is stated to be MR. TOWNSHEND. In Pills, v. 145, with music, it is printed "By Ben Jonson." In Old Ballads, iii. 164. Vocal Companion, ii. 159. Ritson's Engl. Sgs., ii. 42. Tea Table Misc., iii. 250, &c. The true commencement (as in Lawes' copy) is :—

" *Bacchus, Iacchus, fill our brains,*
As well as bowls, with sprightly strains,
Let Souldiers fight for pay or praise, &c."

Given thus, as "A Bacchanal" in Wit's Interpreter, 1655, 116. Also in Wit and Mirth, 1684, p. 100.

Page 220. *Calm was the evening, and clear was the sky.*

By JOHN DRYDEN, in " An Evening's Love," Act iv. Sc. i.,

i., 1671. Music by Alphonso Marsh, in Playford's "Choice Ayres," 1786, i. 8. Also in Pills, iii. 161. In Bagford Collection, ii. 147, printed for W. Thackeray, T. Passenger, and W. Whitwood; where it is entitled "Amintas and Claudia; or, the Merry Shepherdess." With the carelessness habitual in old collections of songs, we find this one repeated on page 292.

Page 221. *There's many a [clinching]*, &c.

Written in 1657. With music, in Pills, iii. 24; but earlier, in 1661, in Antidote ag. Melancholy, 62; in the Rump, i. 336; Loyal Sgs., i. 227; Wit and Mirth, 1684, p. 25; and Percy Soc. (Political Ballads) i. 130. Of course the allusions in the ballad are to Oliver Cromwell. See Introduction, p. xv. But compare page 252 for a later and more severe characterization.

Page 225. *Of all the Trades that ever I see.*

Most probably by DR. JAMES SMITH, the friend of Sir John Mennis, or Menzies, and his fellow-labourer in *Musarum Deliciæ*, 1656; and also (it is thought) in "Wit Restored," 1658, where extra verses are found of the Blacksmith Song. It is there given "*As it was sung before* Ulysses *and* Penelope *at their feast, when he returned from their* Trojan Warrs, *collected out of* Homer, Virgil, *and* Ovid, *by some of the Modern Familie of the Fancies.*" (Wit Restored, reprint, p. 278.) It follows, and is avowedly introduced by Dr. James Smith's "Innovation of Ulysses and Penelope." London, October, 1658. Smith died in June, 1667.

"' Sing me some Song made in the Iron Age.'
' The Iron Age?' quoth he that used to sing,
' This to my mind the Black-Smith's Song doth bring.'
' The Black-Smith's?' quoth Ulysses, *and there holloweth*,
' Whoope! is there such a Song? Let's ha't.' It followeth," &c.

Chief various (and earlier) readings :—3rd verse, 1st line, *Thunderingly* we *lay;* did *devise; Mulciber* to do her *all right;*

right; Which *afterwards* he Hammersmith ; our verses 6 and 7 transposed from 7 and 6, &c. ; v. 8 refers to the notorious Turnemill Street, in a line "*It stood very near to Venus Court)* :" [Wit Rest., verse 17th.]

> " Another proverb does seldome fayle,
> When you meet with naughty bcere or ale,
> You cry it is as dead as a dore nayle.   Which, &c.
>
> If you stick to one when fortune's wheele   [verse 18]
> Doth make him many losses feele,
> We say such a friend is as true as steele.   Which, &c.
>
> There is a lawe in merry England   [verse 21]
> In which the Smith has some command,
> When any one is burnt in the hand ;   Which, &c.
>
> Banbury ale a halfe-yard-pott,   [verse 22]
> The Devill a Tinker dares stand to't ;
> If once the tost be hizzing hott.   Which, &c.

Other additional verses follow, concerning the Sullen woman, the snuffling Puritans, St. Dunstan, the Blacksmith's Vice, Hæresies, Sergeants' at Law, a Commander's look, Soldiers, Lawes, and these (before our final verse, with which compare) :—

> *Though Ulysses himselfe has gon[e] many miles* [v. 37]
> *And in the warre has all the craft and the wiles,*
> *Yet your Smith can sooner double his files.*   Which, &c.
>
> *Sayst thou so, quoth Ulysses, and then he did call*   [38]
> *For wine to drinke to the* Black-Smiths *all,*
> *And he vowed it should go round as a Ball,* Which, &c.
>
> *And cause he had such pleasure ta'ne,*   [39]
> *At this honest fidlers merry straine,*
> *He gave him the Horse-Shoc in Drury-lane,* Which, &c.
>
> *Where his posterity ever since*   [40]
> *Are ready with wine, both Spanish and French,*
> *For those that can bring in another Clench* [;] Which, &c.
>
> *The song being don[e,] they drank the health, they rose,*
> *They wo'd in verse, and went to bed in prose.*

Our

APPENDIX.

Our text agrees virtually with Antidote ag. Melancholy, 1661, p. 11. With the music it is in Pills, iii. 20; the tune being a modification of "Green Sleeves" (given, both arrangements, in Chappell, P. M., pp. 233, 230). In Wit and Drollery, 1656, p. 6; the earliest book-copy we know. In Roxb, Coll. i. 250; Pepys, iv. 264; Rawlinson, 191. Ballad Soc. Roxb. Bds. ii. 127. The popularity of the song is incontestable.

Page 230. *Come, my dainty Doxies.*

By THOMAS MIDDLETON, in his "More Dissemblers beside Women," Act iv. Sc. i. Dyce's Middleton, iii. 606. Earlier than 1623, in which year Sir Henry Herbert enters the comedy as an "old play." But it was not printed, we are told, until 1657. It appears, however, probably before that date in the Percy Folio MS., iii. 313, where, as usual, there is no guide given to the authorship. We have found many of the manuscript songs elsewhere, apparently not known to the editors as being in print. They explain "Doxy" as a mistress, and "dill" as much the same as darling; which "*darle*" certainly seems to be. R. Bell gives "*dell*" as a cant term for "an undefiled girl." Among variations we note the line "Our store now taken" reads in Middleton and P. Fol. "Our store *is never* taken." Instead of "Some come to disburses," they read, "*If one have money he* disburses, *While some tell fortunes*, some pick purses," &c. "He that's a gipsy, May be drunk or tipsy, At any hour he please; roar, we *scuffle;* we *filch*, we shuffle.

Page 231. *Come, Imp Royal, come away.*

In the Rump, i. 339; and "Loyal Songs," commencing the second volume. For "Come, my Daphne!" See M. D. C., p. 91, and Note.

Page 232. *The Wise Men were but seven.*

Also in Antidote against Melancholy, 1661, p. 69; J. P. C. Reprint, 85. In Universal Songster, iii. 95. Compare the Droll on former page, 113, final verse. The Nine Worthies

Worthies were Joshua, David, Judas Maccabæus; Hector, Alexander, Julius Cæsar; King Arthur, Charlemagne, and Godfrey of Bulloigne. Sometimes Hercules and Pompey were substituted; as in *Love's Lab. Lost*, Act v. The Muses were Clio, Euterpe, Thalia, Melpomene, Terpsichore, Erato, Polyhymnia, Urania, and Calliope. The Seven Wise Men were Solon, Chilo, Pittacus, Bias, Periander (or Epimenides), Cleobulus, and Thales. The Three Fatal Sisters, or Parcæ, were Clotho, Lachesis, and Atropos.

Page 232. *How poor is his spirit*, &c.

In the Rump, i. 326, and Loyal Songs, 1731, i. 214.

Page 234. *Am I mad, O noble Festus.*

This memorable Mad-Song and burlesque is by DR. RICHARD CORBET, successively Bishop of Oxford and of Norwich. (Concerning him see Appendix to *Westminster Drollery*, pp. xxxv. xxxvi. By the way, we have again read "The Times Whistle," in E. T. Soc., and feel disinclined to believe that worthy Bishop Corbet wrote it.) This is sometimes entitled "A Song of the Hot-headed Zealot, otherwise the Distracted Puritan." It is in the Percy Folio MS., iii, 269; in Prince d'Amour, 171; Antidote against Melancholy, 35; Rump, i. 237; Corbet's Poems, 3rd edit., 1672, p. 106; Loyal Songs, i. 69; Percy's Reliques. ii. B. 3, No. 18, and elsewhere. Corbet has no malice in his caricature of the Puritan. "Pure *Emanuel*" refers to Emanuel College, at Cambridge, founded in 1584 by Sir Walter Mildmay, a patron of the Puritans, designing it "as a nursery for that party. He did little more than lay the foundation; saying therefore of it, that he had set an acorn, which, he hoped, in time might become an *oak*." What sort of a triple-tree it became we pretty well know; small thanks to him. Elsewhere we read who it was that sowed tares in the field, and without disguise that an Enemy had done it. Nevertheless, some eminent men came from Emanuel's. Among them, Dr. Joseph Hall, whose Satires are quite as coarse

as

as anything in the Drolleries (the book was interdicted and ordered to be burnt; "but that's not much," as Othello says). Verse 3, *Foxes* Martyrs : the first edition of John Fox's "History of the Acts and Monuments of the Church" appeared in a folio volume, 1553. Verse 9 refers to some exposition of Zechariah, v. 1, Bp. Percy thinks to Coppe's "The fiery flying Roll," &c. He also mentions Greenham's Works, folio, 1605, one tract being "A sweet comfort for an afflicted conscience." And as to verse 10, he guides us to Perkins's Works, fol., 1616, i. 11; where is a large half-sheet folded, containing "A Survey, or table declaring the order of the causes of salvation and damnation, &c.," the pedigree of damnation being distinguished by a broad zig-zag line. Verse 11 alludes to a not defunct error that study of Hebrew encourages heresy. Some folks become heretics without studying any ancient language, or even understanding their own. Verse 12 refers to Laud; his predecessor, Archbishop Abbott, having favoured the Puritans. Laud's primacy began in 1633, and since Corbet died in 1635, we fix the date of the ballad to 1633-5, which is tolerably close. Probably 1633.

Page 237. *I doat, I doat, but am a sot to show it.*

Probably by the gallant Cavalier WILLIAM CAVENDISH, first Duke of Newcastle (see Introduction, p. xxix). Certainly two scraps of the song are sung by Sir John in his "Triumphant Widow," Act iii., which we believe to have been written before 1660. Other songs, known to be his, are of similar gaiety. There are good things found in my Lady Duchess's ponderous folios.

Page 240. *Ladies, I do here present you.*

In Wit and Drollery, 1656, p. 103, is a similar song :—

Ladies, here I do present you
With a dainty dish of fruit; &c.

Page 242. *Go you tame Gallants.*

In the Antidote against Melancholy, 1661, p. 44, where it

is

is stated to be "by T. R.," but in the Pills, iii. 329 (1719) is given as "by Dr. R. W." It also appears in the 1684 edition of Wit and Mirth, p. 62. The initials probably refer to Thomas Randolph (often printed Randall), who died in 1635); and to DR. ROBERT WILDE, whose *Iter Boreale*, celebrating General Monk's progress, attained popularity in 1660. We believe this powerful "Combat of Cocks" to be by him. It is also in *Wit and Drollery*, 1656, p. 70, as by "T. R."

Page 249. *What is that you call a Maidenhead?*

Also in "Wit's Interpreter," 255, 1655, and (p. 280) 1671.

Page 250. *When* Phœbus *had drest his course*, &c.

This is a corruption of "When *Phœbus addrest* his course," &c. It is in Wit and Drollery, 1656, p. 35; and in the Percy folio MS., vol. iv. p. 7 (imperfect version, deficient verses iv. and v). Mr. Wm. Chappell notes that the tune "O doe not, doe not kill me yet" (given in Pop. Music, p. 194) is printed under the title of the burden, in J. J. Starter's "Boertigheden," Amsterdam, 4to, 1634, with a Dutch song, written to the tune. So "When Phœbus," &c., is certainly as early as 1634, or before it. Tune afterwards known as "Drive the cold winter away." Other reading, 2nd verse:—did appear *a show*.

Page 252. *A Brewer may be a Burgess grave.*

Written in 1657; this is one of the many references to Oliver Cromwell as having been a brewer. If nothing worse could be charged against him, he could afford to smile, although the connection between malt and a "copper nose" might seem pressed home ungenerously. It is said that the other "Brewer" song (p. 221) was not considered severe enough; therefore, the present ditty was framed. It occurs in the Rump, i. 33; Loyal Songs, i. 221. Wilkins mutilates it, in his Political Bds., i. 132, and such castrated scraps are worthless.

APPENDIX. 393

Page 254. *Oliver, Oliver, take up thy Crown.*

In the Rump, i. 335; Loyal Songs, i. 225. See Additional Note in ensuing volume of the Drolleries.

Page 255. *When I do travel in the night.*

This first meets us as Pride's Song, beginning "As I was walking in the night," &c., in the play of "Cromwell's Conspiracy," Act iii. Sc. 5, where is an extra verse, the twelfth:—

> *I prithee Sweet-heart do thou be civil,*
> *Ore I'le take a course to cure this evil,*
> *By beating out of the scolding Devil.*
> *And I like my Humour well, well, &c.*

The play is anonymous, "By a person of Quality," and dated Aug. 8, 1660. Compare the abbreviated version in Westminster Drollery, i. 108, "As we went wandering all the night," &c.

Page 257. *Sir Eglamore, that valiant knight.*

Like the still-later burlesque, "More of More Hall and the Dragon," (beginning "Old stories tell how Hercules," &c., Pepy's Coll., and Pills, iii. 10., on which "honest Harry" Carey founded his operetta "The Dragon of Wantley," 1738;) this grotesque account of a knight errant was long popular. We meet it in the 1656 edition of Wit and Drollery, p. 128. Again, in Antidote against Melancholy, 25; Dryden's Misc. Poems, iv. 104; Evan's Bds. i. 365; as a broadsheet, in Roxb. Coll., ii. 81, 1672; in Bagford Coll., ii. 18. With music, it is given in Playford's Musical Companion, 1687, Pt. ii.; in the Pills, iii. 293 (where the dragon is a dragoness): Busby, Hist. Music, ii. 203, and Chappell, P. M., 276, also give the music. The earliest appearance of it known to us is in SAMUEL ROWLAND's "Melancholie Knight," p. 27, 1615. Political parodies were written on it, one concerning Gen. Monk, Rump, i. 371, &c. Another in Percy Soc., ii. 205.

Page

Page 259. *If none be offended with the scent.*

In the Rump, ii. 1; Loyal Songs, ii. 37; Loyal Garland, 1686; Percy Soc. Reprint, xxix. 80. Tune, the Blacksmith. Variations in versions.

Page 263. *Come, Drawer, and fill us about some wine.*

Another by ALEXANDER BROME. Written in 1648. Title, "The Independents Resolve." It has already appeared, on p. 190; see Note thereon.

Page 264. *It chanced not long ago, as I was walking.*

In Wit and Mirth, 1684, p. 34; Loyal Garland, 1686, sg. 78 (omitted from Percy Soc. Reprint). In Roxb. Collect. of broadside Bds. ii. 20, printed by F. Coles, &c.

Page 266. *You talk of New England; I truly believe.*

Music in the Pills, iii. 19. In Wit and Drollery, 1661 edition, p. 81, it reads "You talk of Old England, but I do believe." In Wit and Mirth, 1684, p. 35, and in Dr. Rimbault's Little Book of Sgs., 183.

Page 270. *Pray why should any man complain?*

By ALEXANDER BROME, his seventh here. Among his Sgs., 1668, p. 10. Also, as "On Sir G. B—— his defeat," in the 4to. Collection of Diverting Songs, p. 401.

Page 275. *My Masters, give audience.*

Not yet found elsewhere (as, indeed, also the others left specially unannotated). Compare Introduction, p. viii., and the following ballad (date before Nov., 1643) :—

> *New England is preparing a-pace,*
> *To entertain King* Pym, *with his grace,*
> *And* Isaac *before shall carry the mace :*
>   For Roundheads Old *Nick* stand up now!
>   *No*

No Surplice, nor no Organs there,
Shall ever offend the eye or the ear ;
But a spiritual preach, with a three hours pray'r ;
   For Roundheads, &c.

All things in zeal shall there be carried,
Without any porredge read over the buried,
No crossing of infants, nor rings for the married :
   For Roundheads, &c.

The swearer there shall punish'd be still,
But drunkenness private be counted no ill,
Yet both kinds of lying as much as you will :
   For Roundheads, &c.

Blow winds, hoist sails, and let us begone,
But be sure we take our plunder along,
That Charles may find little when as he doth come ;
   For Roundheads, &c.

Page 277. *The Aphorisms of Galen I count, &c.*

With this accumulation of impossible ingredients, not devoid of humour, compare "A Maiden of late," &c., p. 170.

Page 280. *Now I am married, Sir John, &c.*

Also in the Antidote against Melancholy, 70 (J. P. C. Reprint, 86). Music by Willm. Webb, in John Hilton's *Catch that Catch Can*, 1652, p. 72.

Page 281. *I have reason to fly thee, &c.*

By ALEXANDER BROME; among his Sgs., 1668, p. 78. In the Rump, i. 267; Loyal Sgs., i. 161. It is the Answer to " Nay, prithee don't fly me ! " given on p. 36.

Page 283. *I have the fairest Non-perel.*

Also in Wit and Drollery, 1656, p. 26; where Syrens is printed *Hyrens*, in 3rd verse. Cf. *Westm.* Droll. Appendix, p. xxxii., note on p. 74. The present mocker concedes that his beauty was "chaste." Probably (as even
the

the ugliest meet temptation: thus compare John Skelton's delightful book, "A Campaigner at Home," p. 114), in the same way that another Lady merited the title:—

> *I had a Love, and she was chast,*
>   *Alack the more's the pity:*
> *But wot you how my love was chaste?*
>   *She was chaste quite through the City.*
>   (Wit and Drollery, 1656, p. 89.)

Page 286. *Are you grown so melancholy?*

With the music, in Pills, v. 118, as "A Cure for Melancholy."

Page 287. *Sublimest discretions have clubbed, &c.*

By E. EDWARDS, of London; this poem is in laudation of Captain William Hicks, his Oxford Jests. Compare pp. 317, 408, and the Appendix to our Westminster Drollery, pp. ii., iii., xlv., xlvi. Verse 5. Will Summers or Sommers was a favourite Jester to Henry VIII. His portrait, as behind a lattice, is (we believe) at Hampton Court: a small copy, after Dalarem, is in G. Daniel's "*Merrie England,*" chapter 30. Archibald Armstrong, or Archee, disliked by Laud, was Jester to Charles I., and latest of Court-Fools. Under the Hanoverians the office was put into commission. "Scoggin's Jests" may be found in W. C. Hazlitt's reprints. "Antidotes" refers to the *Ant. against Melancholy,* made up in Pills, 1661.

It is also prefixed to Oxford Jests, edition 1684.

Page 289. *A Pox on the Jaylor, and on, &c.*

Music to this by Henry Lawes. It is by WILLIAM CARTWRIGHT, who died about 1639; in his "Royal Slave," Act i. Sc. i. (p. 91 of the earliest edition of his works, 1651.

Page 290. *My lodging is on the cold ground.*

Celania's song, by SIR WILLIAM D'AVENANT, in his play, "The Rivals" (an adaptation of "The Two Noble Kinsmen")

Kinsmen") Act v., about 1664. Music by Matthew Locke,
in Chappell's Pop. M., 526. The air also given in Vocal
Mag., 1798, II, Sg. 100. As "The Fair Bedlamite" in
Hive, i. 88; as "The Mad Shepherdess" in Evans' Bds.,
v., 195. It was sung by Mary Davis (see Introduction
to our Westminster Drollery, p. xxxii. note); Downes
says "She performed that so charmingly, that, not long
after [1668], it raised her from her bed on the cold ground
to a Bed Royal." (*Rosc. Anglicanus*, 32, edit. 1781). In
Roxb. Coll., ii. 423, is the same song, lengthened to a
broadside ballad, entitled "The Slighted Maid; or, the
Pining Lover," beginning "Was ever Maiden so scorned
by one that she loved so dear?" given complete, by
Chappell, 527-8.

Page 291. *From the fair* Lavinian *shore.*

With music by Dr. John Wilson, in Playford's Select
Ayres, 1659, p. 95; and P.'s Musical Companion, 1673,
p. 115. It is in the Percy Folio MS., iii. 308, 311, *q. vide,*
as "The Lavinian Shore," reading "From the *rich*," &c.
Also in Windsor Drollery, 2; and Le Prince d'Amour,
1660, p. 177. It is attributed to WILLIAM SHAKESPEARE,
but with only manuscript evidence. (See our Additional
Note in next volume.) Compare the opening couplet of
A Song :—

A gentle breeze from the Lavinian *Sea,*
Was gliding o'er the Coast of Sicily;
When, lull'd with soft repose, a prostrate Maid
Upon her bended arm had rais'd her head:
Her Soul was all tranquile and smooth with rest,
Like the harmonious slumbers of the Blest;
Wrapp'd up in Silence, innocent she lay,
And press'd the flow'rs with touch as soft as they. &c.

(Pills to P. M., 1699, p. 221 ; iii. 213.)

Page 292. *Calm was the evening, &c.*

Given already, on p. 220. See note in Appendix, p. 386.
Nothing better shows the careless hap-hazard ways of
these

these compilers than the frequency with which, in all the longer Drolleries, songs are repeated in the same volume

---

Page 293.   *Fetch me Ben Jonson's scull, &c.*

By Dr. Henry Edwards. Although absent from the 1661 edition of Merry Drollery, it was certainly then in existence, for it appears at that date in the Antidote against Melancholy, p. 57, with "By Dr. H. E." prefixed. Again, it is in Wit and Mirth, 1684, p. 59, and in Pills, iii. 327, as "The Virtue of Sack." It is one of the best Bacchanalian Rhapsodies in praise of that liquor, and is admirably sustained throughout, while the varying whims gain mastery.

Page 296.   *Now that the Spring hath fill'd our veins.*

In the Antidote against Melancholy, 66; J. P. Collier's Reprint, 81. Music by John Hilton, in his *Catch that Catch Can*, 1652, p. 1.

Page 300.   *O the wily, wily Fox.*

Also in the Antidote against Melancholy, 69; Repr., 86. With music, by Edward Nelham, it had appeared in John Hilton's "Catch that Catch can," 57, 1658.

Page 300.   *She lay all naked in her bed.*

Also in the 1656 edition of Wit and Drollery, p. 54; to this is added, in the 1661 edition, 58 (as also in Merry Drollery, same date, ii. 116) an offensive and quite unnecessary Mock, "She lay up to," &c. We learn from illuminated manuscripts, that it was the custom to sleep without night gear. See illustration on p. 278, vol. i. of "Chaucer's England."

Page 302.   *Some wives are good, and some are bad.*

With the music in Pills, iv. 181. Robert Jamieson quotes this in his Popular Bds., 1806, ii. 316.

APPENDIX.

Page 304. *Call* George *again boy, Call* George *again.*
This excellent Catch is also in Antidote against Melancholy, 67; Reprint, 82. Music by Jn. Hilton, M.C., 26.

---

p. 304, 306. *Pox take you*; and, *I pray thee, Drunkard.*
Also in Wit and Drollery, 1656, pp. 84, 89; where the peculiarly drunken look of the promiscuously mingled capitals meets us. Like David Copperfield's running his words together (*i.e.*, " Amigoarawaysoo" and " Lorblessner!") which Thackeray speedily imitated, it is suggestive of "How came you so?"

Page 308. *She that will eat her breakfast in her bed.*
Music (by John Hilton) in Walsh's Catch-Club, Pt. ii. p. 42, No. 68. Words in Wits Recreations, 1640, No. 66; Wits Interpreter, 1655, p. 115; Antidote ag. Melancholy, 68; and Musa Madrigalesca, 300, from Hilton's 'Catch that Catch can," p. 23, 1652.

Page 309. *Why should we boast of* Arthur, &c.
The variations and additional verses are so numerous, that we reserve them for the companion volume. The song was popular, from about 1612, and meets us (sometimes as "Why do we boast," &c.) in Antidote ag. Melanc., 26; Wit and Mirth, 1684, p. 29; Pills (with music), iii. 116; Old Bds., 1723, i. 24; Percy's Reliq., ii. 3, No. 14; Bagford Coll., ii. 16, &c. A Second Part, by John Grubb, beginning "The Story of King Arthur it is very memorable," meets us in Pills, 1699, p, 303; 1719, iii. 315. An earlier second part, political, leads off with " Now the Rump is confounded ;" March 7, 1659-60; in the Rump, ii. 159; Loyal Sgs., ii. 249.

Page 312. *Saw you not* Pierce *the Piper.*
One other early copy of this meets us in Antidote against Melancholy, same date, 1661, p. 16; J. P. C. Repr., 21. Ritson gives it in his Robin Hood, ii. 210. Wm. Chappell

pell (to whom we all owe a debt of gratitude for his Popular Music of the Olden Time, and other works alike scholarly to satisfy the antiquary, and yet so genial in tone that they form delightful reading to the general lovers of literature), gives us the music, and first verse only, in P. M., p. 540. We find the words of the lively modern version, "The Wedding of Arthur O'Bradley" (attributed, in this re-cast, to one Taylor, a comic singer and actor at beginning of the 19th century), in Bds. of the Peasantry, annotated edit., p. 139; It begins, "Come neighbours, and listen awhile." The bridegroom is of a Petrucio cast, in disposition and attire. We suspect that Taylor had got some traditional fragment of the earlier Arthur O'Bradley to build on; such as was referred to by Elizabethan dramatists. A different ballad entitled "Arthur O'Bradley," printed about the end of last century, is in Roxburghe Coll., iii. 283; the end is lost, but it begins,

> "*All in the merry month of May,*
> *The maids a May pole they will have;*
> *Your helping hand I do crave;*
> *For there's never a Man shall sup*
> *Till I have drank my cup,*
> *For I am beloved by all,*
> *The great and the small,*
> *For my name it is Arthur o' Bradley, O,*
>   *O rare Arthur o' Bradley O,*
>   *O fine Arthur o' Bradley O.*

> "*And as I went forth one day,*
> *I met a maid by the way,*
> *I took her by the hand,*
> *Desiring her to stand;*
> *For 'tis Love conquers Kings,*
> *And a sorrowful heart brings;*
> *For if you lov'd your mother,*
> *Love me and no other,*
>   *For my name,*" &c.

Six other irregular verses follow. (See Additional Note in next volume of the Drolleries).

In the Sixth Scena of the ancient Interlude entitled the "Contract of a Marriage between Wit and Wisdom" (mentioned as already existing, in the play "Sir Thomas More," about 1590); printed in 1846 for the Shakespeare Society, edited by J. O. Halliwell; we find "Idlenis," the Vice, alluding to the proverbial Arthur O'Bradley, thus:—

> *This is a world to see how fortune changeth,*
> *This shalbe his luck which like me rangeth,*
>   *and raingeth;*
> *For the honour of Artrebradle,*
> *This age wold make me swere madly!*
> *Give me one peny or a halfpeny, &c.* (P. 49.)

See, also, J. P. Collier's Bibl. Account, i. 26, where he remarks "the character of the drama carries us back to the reign of Edward VI., or even earlier."

Page 317. *I tell thee, Kit, where I have been.*

By T. FRANKLIN, Oxon. Tune of Sir John Suckling's ballad, "I tell thee, Dick." Also prefixed to the "Oxford Jests, 1684, and entitled "Two Swains near Oxford that came to London."

Page 318. *There were three Cooks in Colebrook.*

Also in Antidote ag. Melancholy, 70; Repr. 87; Acad. Compt., 1670, p. 185. With music in Walsh's Catch-Club, ii. 43.

Page 319. *Of all the Sciences beneath the Sun.*

We know of no other copy. Compare (probably) Dr. James Smith's "Blacksmith," on p. 225, which preceded this one, we believe.

Page 323. *When I'se came first to London town.*

In 1656 this appeared in Wit and Drollery, p. 75; in 1684 in Wit and Mirth, 37. Also, with music by Akeroyd, n the Pills, iv. 96.   Page

C C

Page 326. *Why should we not laugh, and be jolly?*

By ALEXANDER BROME, before 1655, when it appears in Wit's Interpreter, p. 61 (edit. 1671, p. 167); in Wit and Drollery, 1656, p. 112. Also in the Rump, i. 313; Loyal Songs, i. 199, and A. Brome's Songs, 1688, p. 69. Title, The Cure of Care.

Page 328. *Now we are met in a knot, &c.*

Probably this likewise is by ALEXANDER BROME, though not included amongst his songs when collected by himself (he probably wrote many others additional). For Tom D'Urfey (to whom we all have a leaning) attributes it to "Old loyal Brome," when beginning his own song (Pills ii. 66), "The Parliament sat as snug as a Cat," which is evidently quoted from verse 14 (p. 331). It is in the Rump i. 315; and Loyal Songs, i. 201.

Page 332. *Have you observed the Wench in the street?*

In Windsor Drollery, 138. With music for three voices, by Thomas Holmes, in John Hilton's "Catch that Catch Can," 52, 1658; and in Walsh's Catch-Club, Pt. ii., p. 25.

Page 333. *Let the trumpet sound, &c.*

This medley is in the Rump, i. 258; Loyal Songs, 1731, i. 149.

Page 337. *Shew a Room, Shew a Room.*

Also in Antidote against Melancholy, 69; Repr. 85. Music by Thomas Holmes, in *Catch that Catch Can*, 1652, p. 44.

Page 339. *He that a happy life would lead.*

By ALEXANDER BROME; written before 1658, at which date it appears in Wit Restored, p. 163; Reprint, 1873, p. 285. In A. B.'s Sgs, 1668, p. 114, entitled "The Advice."

Page

Page 341. *What Fortune had I, poor maid, &c.*

In Antidote against Melancholy, p. 74. Also (if the same as "What ill luck had I, silly maid that I am?") in Choice Drollery, 1656, p. 84. See our next volume loc. cit.

Page 342. *He that intends to take a wife.*

In the Pills, iii. 106, as "The Wife Hater," to same tune (Clark's, on p. 102 of same vol.) as "Now that Love's Holiday is come."

Page 348. *If any so wise is, that Sack he despises.*

This had appeared, with music by Wm. Child, in Hilton's "Catch that Catch can," 82, 1652. We find the music also in Walsh's Catch-Club, ii. 31. Words in Antidote ag. Melancholy, 72; Wit and Mirth, 1684, p. 114; Hive, iii. 143; and Vocal Library, 128.

Page 374, line 13. (For &c. read 5th s. iv. ii.) It is by FRANCIS BACON (? from Posidippus), printed in Farnaby's Florilegium, 1629; *Reliquiæ Wottoniæ*, etc.

FINALE.

FINALE.

THERE are, who, wandering through each trim *parterre*,
Will spy out fungus-growths, neglecting roses;
So Readers, leaving what are choice and rare,
May take exception to these ancient posies.
We grant, some look like weeds; we scarcely dare
Commend them to your bosoms, or your noses!
What then? In *Hortus Siccus* plac'd, with care,
They'll gain historical Metempsychosis.

July, 1875.　　　　　　　　　　　　J. W. E.

ADDITIONAL NOTES
TO THE
WESTMINSTER DROLLERIES.

Our next book will contain fresh Title-pages to the series of Drolleries, completed in three volumes. Meanwhile, let readers accept the following, for CORRECTIONS and ADDITIONS to the Appendix of *Westminster Drollery:*—

Page 10. *Wert thou much fairer than thou art* is by "M. W. M.," before 1651, as it was answered in that year by Thomas Stanley, in a Song beginning "Wert thou by all affections sought."

— 13. *Never perswade me to't.* Also in Playford's Select Ayres, 1652, p. 30, with music by Dr. Colman; where is *O fain would I*, &c., p. 9.

— 17. *Cellamina, of my heart.* By JOHN DRYDEN, same date, 1671, in "An Evening's Love," Act i.

— 20. *Was ever man so vex'd*, &c. Given, with the music, in Wit & Mirth, 1700, ii. 152; Pills, iv. 155.

— 28. Line 30. Note on *Sauncing bell.* See also The Second Maiden's Tragedy, 1611, Act ii. Sc. 2,—"That drowns a *saunce bell.*"

— 30. (Additional.) The two poems *On a Great Heat*, and *On a Mighty Rain*, beginning respectively "*I formerly in Countreys*," &c., and "*Heaven did not Weep*," &c., West. Droll., i. 67, 68, are by WILLIAM CAVENDISH, Duke of Newcastle, in his Comedy of "The Country Captain," 1649.

— 30. *Madam, I cannot Court, &c.* The original poem, of which this is the middle verse (modernized), is attributed to no less a poet than CHRISTOPHER MARLOW (who died, May, 1593), although marked "Ignoto." Alexander Dyce gives it in both editions of that dramatist, and another of our best modern editors, Colonel Francis Cunningham, inserts it in his "Mermaid Edition," p. 271. We transcribe the rare original, printed "At Middleborugh," n.d., about 1597, at end of the earliest edition of "Epigrammes and Elegies. By I. D[avies]. and C. M[arlow]." It begins:— IGNOTO.

IGNOTO.

I Loue thee not for sacred chastitie,
Who loues for that? nor for thy sprightly wit:
I loue thee not for thy sweete modestie,
Which makes thee in perfections throane to sit.

I loue thee not for thy inchaunting eye,
Thy beautie['s] rauishing perfection:
I loue thee not for vnchast luxurie,
Nor for thy bodies faire proportion.

I loue thee not for that my soule doth daunce,
And leap with pleasure when those lips of thine:
Give Musicall and graceful vtterance,
To some (by thee made happie) poet's line.

I loue thee not for voice or slender small,
But wilt thou know wherefore? faire sweet[,] for all.

(Compare Thomas Carew's "O my dearest," in *Westm. Droll.*, i. 91.) *Wit's Interpreter* keeps much closer to the original than our version in W. D., and indeed gives true readings where the "Ignoto" is wrong. *Guilding* my Saint (not Oiling); Buss thy *fist* (not fill), &c. Finally, it reads "*jerk* thee soundly." An obliging correspondent (W. G. Medlicott, of Long Meadow, Massachusetts) drew our attention to this. Third verse reads:—

Sweet wench[,] I loue thee, yet I wil not sue,
Or shew my loue as muskie Courtiers doe,
Ile not carouse a health to honor thee,
In this same bezling drunken curtesie:
and when als quafde, eate vp my bowsing glasse.
In glory that I am thy seruile asse.
Nor wil I weare a rotten burbon locke,
as some sworne pesant to a female smock.
wel featurde lasse, Thou knowest I loue the[e] deare[,]
Yet for thy sake I wil not bore mine eare.   [,]
To hang thy durtie silken shoo[-]tires there.
nor for thy loue wil I once gnash a brick,
Or some pied collours in my bonnet stiche.
    but by the chaps of hell to do thee good,
    Ile freely spend my Thrise decocted bloud.

— 32.

— 32. The Shakespeare Society, in 1846, printed the ballad, "*Come, all you Farmers out of the Country,*" &c. We may include it in our third volume.

— 39. *Beat on, Proud billows.* As far as we are aware, no claim to the authorship of this excellent Song was ever advanced by Colonel RICHARD LOVELACE during his lifetime, or by his friends for him in later time. It neither appears among his Lucasta Poems, 1649, nor among the "Posthume Poems of Richard Lovelace, Esqre ," 1659. David Lloyd, in his "Memoires of those that suffered" in the cause of Charles I., 1668, certainly implies that the author of it was still living, with no other reward than "the conscience of having suffered." Now, unless there were an earlier edition, ten years earlier than 1668, (against the existence of which are good reasons), this assertion by Lloyd disposes of the claim advanced by a learned and genial critic of *Westminster Drolleries* in the *Athenæum* of April 10th, 1875. Nor do we think the internal evidence strongly in favour of Lovelace. The parallelism indicated between his lines,

> *Minds innocent and quiet take*
> *That for an Hermitage;*

and the similar expression in " Beat on, proud billows,"

> *Locks, Bars, and Solitude together met,*
> *Makes me no Pris'ner, but an Anchoret :*

is such (in our humble opinion) as more resembles an imitation, in the latter, of an already famous poem (written certainly before 1649, and then published), than the self-repetition probable from a poet who had already so *fixed his idea.* Tradition assigns "Beat on, proud billows," to Sir Roger L'Estrange; but we confess to doubting the correctness of the supposition. It seems to us, firstly, above his range; secondly, he was appointed to the lucrative office of Licenser (a hangman's duty, too often), so early as 1665. How then can David Lloyd's

Lloyd's assertion of the author being unrewarded, &c., be held to apply to this already pampered official? It still remains in great part a question of dates: Lloyd wrote thus *after* the Restoration.

— 42. *As we went wandering.* This is a variation of "When I do travel in the night," Merry Drollery, Complete, p. 255 (p. 73, edit. 1661); see p. 393.

— 46. Note on WM. HICKS. We find Samuel Pepys recording in his Diary, Sept. 25, 1663, "Pleased to see Captn. Hickes come to me with a list of all the officers of Deptford Yard, wherein he, being a high old Cavalier, do give me an account of every one of them to their reproach in all respects, and discovers many of their knaverys," &c. An important bit, in its way, and not making much in favour of the adventurer.

— 55. Line 29. *Delete* "&," (W. D. being for Westm. Drollery,) and add this:—In J. P. Collier's Extracts, Registers of Stationer's Company, i. 230, we find under date 1569-70, a licence to Wyllm. Greffeth for printing a ballad entitled Taken Napping, as Mosse took his Meare. J. P. C. notes that the proverb is not yet forgotten, and is in the collection by John Heywood.

— 63. Line 33. *Delete* "It appears to be still older, as" and read "It is as early as 1632; and in," &c.

— 68. The Ballad, on a similar theme, entitled "The Devonshire Damsels' Frollick," begins thus:—

"Tom *and* William, *with* Ned *and* Ben,
In all they were about nine or ten," *&c.*

See our next volume, and Rox. Col., iii. 137.

— 72. Bottom line but five, read JOHN CROWNE.
— 74. Line sixth. Read 1618, not 1614.

Introduction to W. D., p. 19, line 11, (note), read 1673: uncertainty about 1672. The *frontispiece* referred to on this page, and on p. 74 of Appendix, is now being engraved for our Readers. It gives a valuable record of a Stage-interior at the exact date of the *Westminster Drolleries*; or, more probably, immediately before the Restoration.   J. W. E.

DROLLERY RE-PRINTS.

Now in the Press, and shortly to be Published,

CHOICE DROLLERY:

Uniform with "*Westminster Drolleries*" and
"*Merry Drollery, Complete.*"

The third and concluding volume of the present series of Drolleries (each complete in itself) contains the whole of the rare CHOICE DROLLERY of 1656, against which the Puritans waged war, destroying every copy that could be obtained. Among the contents are the remarkable verses on *The Time-Poets*, beginning "One night the great Apollo, pleased with Ben," referring to Jonson's companions, the dramatists and songsters. *Jack of Lent's Ballat*, 1625; *The Red Head and the White;* the account of *Aldobrandino*, a fat Cardinal; *The Maid of Tottenham; The Doctor's Touchstone*, with many amatory poems of merit, and merry epigrams, diversify the volume. Several songs are of historical importance, and, like the above-named, are found nowhere but here. Such are the ballads on *Queen Elizabeth*, and on *King James I.*, with another *Upon the Scots being beaten at Musselborough Field;* verses *Upon the Gun Powder Plot*, and *To the King on New Years Day*, 1638. Burlesque Lamentations, Catches, commingle with Sonnets and tender Serenades, in praise of beauty and chaste affection. The *Western Husbandman* sings his complaint against the late wars, and Shepherds lament the loss of their love.

DROLLERY RE-PRINTS.

ADDITIONAL TO THIS, WE GIVE THE 34 SONGS AND POEMS FOUND IN

Merry Drollery, 1661,

But omitted from the later editions.

Nearly two dozen of these are elsewhere unattainable, among them being "A Puritan of late," *The Ladies Delight, The Tyrannical Wife, The Tinker, The Maid a Bathing, A Letany, John and Jone, New England Described, The Insatiate Lover,* and *Love's Dream.*

☞ The above are all now reprinted for the first time.

To further enrich the volume, the whole of the remaining Poems from the

Antidote against Melancholy,
1661

(not already given), are here added, so that four complete works are reproduced in these three volumes.

The whole are carefully annotated in Appendices, with a separate Editorial Introduction to each Collection. Many rare poems from other *Drolleries* and contemporary volumes help to illustrate [the series, which claims to be of a representative character, shewing the Cavalier humours and fancies before and after the Restoration.

☞ *The above, together, will form the Third and concluding volume of the "Drollery Reprints."*

DROLLERY RE-PRINTS.

Now ready. Small 8vo., 10s. 6d. Cloth, uncut.

A RE-PRINT
OF THE
Westminster Drollery,
1671, 1672.

TO those who are already acquainted with the two parts of the *Westminster Drollery*, published in 1671 and 1672, it must have appeared strange that no attempt has hitherto been made to bring these delightful volumes within reach of the students of our early literature. The originals are of extreme rarity, a perfect copy seldom being attainable at any public sale, and then fetching a price that makes a book-hunter almost despair of its acquisition. So great a favourite was it in the Cavalier times, that most copies have been literally worn to pieces in the hands of its many admirers, as they chanted forth a merry stave from the pages. *There is no collection of songs surpassing it in the language*, and as representative of the lyrics of the first twelve years after the Restoration it is unequalled: by far the greater number are elsewhere unattainable.

The WESTMINSTER DROLLERIES are reprinted with the utmost fidelity, page for page, and line for line, not a word being altered, or a single letter departing from the original spelling.

☞ An indifferent copy of the original edition of the *Westminster Drollery* was sold by auction last year for £22 10s. to a bookseller.

OPINIONS OF THE PRESS, &c.

"Strafford Lodge, Oatlands Park,
Surrey, Feb. 4, 1875.

Dear Sir,
    I received the "Westminster Drolleries" yesterday evening. I have spent nearly the whole of this day in reading it. I can but give unqualified praise to the editor, both for his extensive knowledge and for his admirable style. The printing and the paper do great credit to your press. I miss only the old title page to the first part. I enclose a post-office order to pay for my copy.
        Yours truly,
Mr. Robert Roberts.   Wm. Chappell."

From J. O. Halliwell, Esqre.

"No. 11, Tregunter Road, West Brompton,
London, S. W.,

Dear Sir,   25th Feby. 1875.
    I am charmed with the edition of the "Westminster Drollery." One half of the reprints of the present day are rendered nearly useless to exact students either by alterations or omissions, or by attempts to make eclectic texts out of more than one edition. By all means let us have introductions and notes, especially when as good as Mr. Ebsworth's, but it is essential for objects of reference that one edition only of the old text be accurately reproduced. The book is certainly admirably edited.
        Yours truly,
To Mr. R. Roberts.   J. O. Phillipps."

From F. J. Furnivall, Esq.

"3, St. George's Square, Primrose Hill, London, N.W.,
2nd February, 1875.

My Dear Sir,
    I have received the handsome large paper copy of your "Westminster Drolleries." I am very glad to see that the book is really *edited*, and that well, by a man so thoroughly up in the subject as Mr. Ebsworth.
        Truly yours,
           F. J. F."

DROLLERY RE-PRINTS.

From the Editor of the "Fuller's Worthies Library,"
"Wordsworth's Prose Works," &c.

"Park View, Blackburn,
Lancashire, 13th July, 1875.

Dear Sir,
I got the "Westminster Drolleries" *at once*, and I will see after the "Merry Drollery" when published.

Go on and prosper. Mr. Ebsworth is a splendid fellow, evidently. Yours,

A. B. Grosart."

J. P. Collier, Esqre., has also written warmly commending the work, in private letters to the Editor, which he holds in especial honour.

From the "Academy," July 10th, 1875.

"It would be a curious though perhaps an unprofitable speculation, how far the 'Conservative reaction.' has been reflected in our literature. . . . . Reprints are an important part of modern literature, and in them there is a perceptible relaxation of severity. Their interest is no longer mainly philological. Of late, the Restoration has been the favourite period for revival. Its dramatists are marching down upon us from Edinburgh, and the invasion is seconded by a royalist movement in Lincolnshire. A Boston publisher has begun a series of drolleries—intended, not for the general public, but for those students who can afford to pay handsomely for their predilection for the byways of letters.

"The Introduction is delightful reading, with quaint fancies here and there, as in the 'imagined limbo of unfinished books.' . . . . There is truth and pathos in his excuses for the royalist versifiers who 'snatched hastily, recklessly, at such pleasures as came within their reach, heedless of price or consequences.' We may not admit that they were 'outcasts without degradation,' but we can hardly help allowing that 'there is a manhood visible in their failures, a generosity in their profusion and unrest. They are not stainless, but they affect no concealment of faults. Our heart goes to the losing side, even when the loss has been in great part deserved.' . . . . The fact is, that in his contemplation of the follies and vices of 'that very distant time' he loses all apprehension of their grosser elements, and retains only an appreciation of their wit, their elegance, and their vivacity. Without offence be it said, in Lancelot's phrase, 'he does something smack, something grow to; he has a kind of taste,'—and so have we too, as we read him. These trite and ticklish themes he touches with so charming a liberality that his generous allowance is contagious. We feel in thoroughly honest company, and are ready to be heartily charitable along with him. For his is no unworthy tolerance of vice, still less any desire to polish its hardness into such factitious brilliancy as glistens in Grammont. It is a manly pity for human weakness, and an unwillingness to see, much less to pry into, human depravity. 'It would have been a joy for us to know that these songs were wholly unobjectionable; but he who waits to eat of fruit without speck must go hungry through many an orchard, even past the apples of the Hesperides.' . . . . The little book is well worth the attention of any one desirous to have a bird's-eye view of the Restoration 'Society.' Its scope is far wider than its title would indicate. The 'Drolleries' include not only the rollicking rouse of the staggering blades who 'love their humour well, boys,' the burlesque of the Olympian revels in 'Hunting the Hare,' the wild vagary of Tom of Bedlam, and the gibes of the Benedicks of that day against the holy estate, but lays of a delicate and airy beauty, a dirge or two of exquisite pathos, homely ditties awaking patriotic memories of the Armada and the Low Country wars, and 'loyal cantons' sung to the praise and glory of King Charles. The 'late and true story of a furious scold' might have enriched the budget of Autolycus, and Feste would have found here a store of 'love-songs,' and a few 'songs of good life.' The collection is of course highly miscellaneous. After the stately measure may come a jig with homely 'duck and nod,' or even a dissonant strain from the 'riot and ill-managed merriment' of Comus,

'Midnight shout, and revelry,
Tipsy dance, and jollity.'"

DROLLERY RE-PRINTS.

From the "Bookseller," March, 1875.

"If we wish to read the history of public opinion we must read the songs of the times : and those who help us to do this confer a real favour. Mr. Thomas Wright has done enormous service in this way by his collections of political songs. Mr. Chappell has done better by giving us the music with them; but much remains to be done. On examining the volume before us, we are surprised to find so many really beautiful pieces, and so few of the coarse and vulgar. Even the latter will compare favourably with the songs in vogue amongst the fast men in the early part of the present century. The "*Westminster Drolleries*" consist of two collections of poems and songs sung at Court and theatres, the first published in 1671, and the second in 1672. Now for the first time reprinted. The editor, Mr. J. Woodfall Ebsworth, has prefaced the volume with an interesting introduction . . . and, in an appendix of nearly eighty pages at the end, has collected a considerable amount of bibliographical and anecdotical literature. Altogether, *we think this may be pronounced the best edited of all the reprints of old literature,* which are now pretty numerous. A word of commendation must also be given to Mr. Roberts, of Boston, the publisher and printer—the volume is a credit to his press, and could have been produced in its all but perfect condition only by the most careful attention and watchful oversight."

From the "Athenæum," April 10*th,* 1875.

"Mr. Ebsworth has, we think, made out a fair case in his Introduction for reprinting the volume without excision. The book is not intended *virginibus puerisque*, but to convey to grown men a sufficient idea of the manners and ideas which pervaded all classes in society at the time of the reaction from the Puritan domination. . . . . Mr. Ebsworth's Introduction is well written. He speaks with zest of the pleasant aspects of the Restoration period, and has some words of praise to bestow upon the 'Merry Monarch' himself. . . . Let us add that his own "Prelude," "Entr' Acte," and "Finale" are fair specimens of versification."

APOPHTHEGMES OF ERASMUS.

A RE-PRINT

Of the 1564 Edition of this fine old book is now the press, and will shortly be ready.

IT IS BEAUTIFULLY

Printed in the Old Style,

IN DEMY 8VO.,

ON OLD-FASHIONED LAID PAPER

Limited to 250 Copies, at 21s. each to Subscribers

RE-PRINTS of other Rare and Valuable Books are in progress, of which fuller particulars will be given in due time, by *Robert Roberts*, Boston, Lincolnshire

www.ingramcontent.com/pod-product-compliance
Lightning Source LLC
Chambersburg PA
CBHW031954300426
44117CB00008B/754